Frontiers of Consciousness

FRONTIERS OF CONSCIOUSNESS

Interdisciplinary Studies in American Philosophy and Poetry

by

STANLEY J. SCOTT

FORDHAM UNIVERSITY PRESS
NEW YORK
1991

© Copyright 1991 by FORDHAM UNIVERSITY
ALL RIGHTS RESERVED
LC 90–82896
ISBN 0–8232–1302–1

Printed in the United States of America

B
935
.S36
1991

This book is lovingly dedicated
to my mother, Florence M. Luebsen,
and
to my father, Clifford N. Scott

CONTENTS

ACKNOWLEDGMENTS

Like all my work, this book was made possible through the community of my students, colleagues, friends, and the extended family of which I am a part. For their assistance and support at various stages of the thinking process, the writing, and the production of this book, I want to thank the following people: William Hillman and Aileen Hillman, for warmth and light; Bradwell Scott, for humor and a brother's care; Leon Howard and John Espey of the University of California at Los Angeles, for guidance and encouragement; Richard Cohen, Constance Carlson, George Hall, Kenneth Taylor, Guy Gallagher, and other members of the research group at the University of Maine at Presque Isle who read and commented on some of the chapters; James Campbell of the University of Toledo, for supportive criticism of the chapters on American philosophy; Stephen Gottschalk and Christopher Wagstaff, for their friendship and for many discussions of American and contemporary thought; Edward Pols of Bowdoin College, for responding to the chapter on William James at a meeting of the Maine Philosophical Institute; Jeff White, Bill Reed, and other members of the Institute who heard and responded to the same paper; Lee Harding, for compassion and a listening ear; Allison Phinney III of Harvard, and Carl Rapp of the University of Georgia, for reading and constructive criticism of the entire manuscript; Allison Phinney Jr., for help in other ways; Mary Beatrice Schulte, my fine editor at Fordham University Press; Martha Bendegkey, for typing; Pam Codrey, for checking references; Michael Goldstein, for being a wonderful student, for helping me to understand the concept of paradigms more fully, for helping to edit my conclusion, and for talks running well into the night; Lorelei Locke, for work on the Index; Elizabeth Lamb, Todd Snyder, and all my other students at the University of Maine at Presque Isle who have challenged me and stayed with me in the adventure of thinking our way together into a new world; Ryder Scott, my incomparable son and friend; and Gail Scott, my wonderful companion in this work as in everything, for insight and strength to see things through to completion.

PREFACE

"[T]he poet is occupied with frontiers of consciousness beyond which words fail, though meanings still exist."[1] This short line from T. S. Eliot's 1942 essay "The Music of Poetry" raises many fascinating and engaging questions. What is the nature of "consciousness"? What laws, if any, does it obey? How does consciousness organize itself, and how does it work to generate order and meaning in other parts of our experience, including our relations with others? How do we know anything about consciousness, and how can we most effectively describe it? What is meaning? What is involved in moving beyond forms and states of consciousness considered normal by our culture? Can poetry (or the music of poetry) assist the process of growth in the consciousness of its readers? Does critical or reflective thought contradict the kind of understanding derived from the music of poetry, or can they complement each other?

The studies in this book examine the way the problem of consciousness is treated by American philosophers and poets of the late nineteenth and early twentieth centuries. They are creative essays that recognize the presence of philosophical ideas in poetry, and perceive poetic qualities of thought and expression in the work of philosophers. By closely examining selected texts, and by observing instructive parallels between them, these essays seek answers to the questions stated above. The method of these studies does not follow any current fashions in literary theory or criticism which have sources in European philosophy, but makes use of principles derived from the American philosophers under study—for example, James's radical empiricism, Dewey's transactional theory of art as experience, principles of meaning and interpretation in Peirce and Royce—to explore philosophical implications of poetic texts in the context of modern Western cultural and intellectual history.

Ideas contained in the texts of both literature and philosophy are understood here, not as mirroring images of the world outside them, but as leadings from one phase of experience to a more conscious or more significant phase. As William James writes, "*. . . ideas (which themselves are but parts of our experience) become true just in so far as they help us to get into satisfactory relation with other parts of our experience. . . .*"[2] What James means by "satisfactory relation" implies that some ideas have a capability to orient a person's thinking in a significant way to other facts, that, in other words, ideas are powerful tools that have experiential consequences. Understanding an idea is less a matter of perceiving a correspondence between the idea and a fact than an imaginative act of perceiving where the idea leads and constructively following that leading. In this way texts of both philosophy and poetry may become tools for what Dewey called the reconstruction of experience. Ideas such as James's "stream of consciousness," Eliot's "still point," Royce's "unified point of view," or Dewey's "context" and "transaction" do not merely portray pre-existing realities. As we encounter and appropriate their meanings, they may become instruments that enable us to organize experience in specific, potentially new, ways. The texts that contain them are significant, not because of the pictures they give us of a reality presumed to exist outside them, but because they make certain kinds of experience possible. They enable us to orient thought and perception in meaningful ways within the total field of experience. We come to understand the texts most fully, not by treating them as objects of analysis, nor by believing in the images of the world they present, but by seeing them as symbolic modes of experience that invite us to participate in the organized experiential fields embodied in their symbol systems. The texts invite us not so much to learn *about* them (their language games, their narrative or argumentative structures, etc.) as to learn *from* them.[3] In the pragmatic sense implied by James's statement, we acknowledge that they contain modes of experience called ideas that serve as leadings toward other domains of experience that are value-laden.

It might be argued that all thinking occurs within thinking frames. Each thinking frame involves a set of fundamental assumptions, especially regarding such questions as: What is real? What is of value? How do we know what we claim to know? The configuration of answers that a thinker gives (consciously or unconsciously) to these questions makes a thinking frame that implicitly sets an agenda of new significant questions worthy to be asked, and evades others deemed less relevant to her basic assumptions.

The thinking frame of this book is a perspective toward experience, ideas, poetry, and philosophy, based on radical empiricism. As a philosophical perspective, radical empiricism is empiricist in its insistence that no thinking takes place apart from an experiential context, and radical in its insistence on getting to the roots of experience. This entails rejection of the traditional empiricist definition of experience as atomistic deposits placed (either by sensory mechanisms or by education) in an immaterial medium called mind, and a redefinition of experience based on a perception of the continuity and relatedness of facts, including what conventional epistemology has called subjects and objects, in an ongoing natural and historical process. In radical empiricism neither "consciousness" nor "reality" may be understood independently of each other because both are rooted in a sensibly continuous existence-process. For lack of a better name, this contextual–experiential process is called *pure experience*.

Such experience is neither subjective nor objective in the traditional meanings of these words. James explains: "As 'subjective' we say that the experience represents; as 'objective' it is represented." But "what represents and what is represented is here numerically the same." According to James,

> no dualism of being represented and representing resides in . . . experience *per se*. In its pure state, . . . there is no self-splitting of it into consciousness and what the consciousness is "of." Its subjectivity and objectivity are functional attributes solely, realized only when the experience is "taken," *i.e.*, talked-of, twice, considered along with its two differing contexts respectively, by a new retrospective experience. . . . The instant field of the present is at all times what I call the "pure" experience. . . . "every field of experience is so much 'fact.'"[4]

Pure experience to James is "a place of intersection of two processes,"[5] one of which by analytical convention we call subjective, the other, objective. Yet by unwinding our conventional points of view back to their origins, we find the bedrock of our existence as humans, which is both subjective and objective at once; this bedrock is pure experience. The premise that representing (knowing) and represented (the known) are numerically the same does not imply infallibility of an egocentric or sociocentric point of view, but underscores the pragmatic conviction that experience is a continuous whole in which mind is a functional element. We may accept the view expressed in James's version of radical empiricism that all existence is contained within the pluralistic fields of pure experience if (with Charles Hartshorne) we also accept the logic which says that all the forms of existence, the human as well as the nonhuman and inanimate, may be said to "experience" aspects of their environment, at least in the sense of undergoing them.[6] The concept of pure experience as both subjective and objective in James's radical empiricism may also be explained by reference to the concept of the other, whether human or nonhuman, as a "Thou" with whom we enter into dialogue—a concept found, for example, in the philosophies of William Ernest Hocking and Martin Buber, but also expressed in James's essay "The Will to Believe." While various forms of animal life may exhibit signs of inner motivation, the experiential continuum also includes the human form of consciousness that, despite being stripped in radical empiricism of its specious subjectivity, is both self-aware and self-determining. Because experience at the human end of the continuum implies to the radical empiricist an individual power of self-awareness, and because it is a dynamic process rather than a static or mechanical accretion of sense data or intellectual contents, an understanding of radical empiricism may have the effect of empowering the individual to move out of the boundaries of a subjective or egocentric frame of thought.

One implication of radical empiricism for this book is that poetry and philosophy, though representing contrary qualities of thought, are both recognized as modes of pure experience. The texts of philosophy and poetry, though ostensibly written in pursuit of the different ends of intellectual rigor and imagination, are understood within the thinking frame of radical empiricism as differing articulations of one primal actuality: pure experience. As Gregory Bateson argues, intellectual rigor and imagination are the two great contraries of all our mental life. But either one without the other is lethal. "Rigor alone is paralytic death, but imagination alone is insanity."[7] To say that both philosophy and poetry are symbolic modes of pure experience is not to deny that they are contraries, but to argue that there is a meeting between them in the living experience of the individual.

Pure experience may be more or less integrated. The creative struggle of thinking on the part of the student who strives to balance and reconcile the contraries of rigor and imagination is a struggle toward greater actualization of experience. As a thinking frame, radical empiricism enables us to embrace such contrary aspects of our experience as subject and object, self and society, and rigor and imagination, even though traditional systems of logic or cultural prescriptions will deny their mutual validity. Within radical empiricism, thinking in metaphors is just as authentic an aspect of pure experience as linear and calculative thinking. Because it starts from the premise that experience is one thing, not two, radical empiricism presents a vision of potential integration of experience, of movement toward more and more significant orientation of the individual to the social and natural world.

The act of study and interpretation is a creative act, involving surrender to the text, its rhythms and energies as well as its ideas; but it also involves the critical act of choosing whether or not to follow the specific leadings of the text. By our inward initiatives and by the choices we make, we move either toward greater integration of consciousness or away from it. So the ideas we encounter in texts have consequences based on the degree of our creative response to them. One way to understand creative response to a text is in terms of what Hartshorne calls "creative synthesis."

> In every moment each of us accomplishes a remarkable creative act. What do we create? Our own experience at that moment. But, you may say, this experience is not of our own making, since it is produced in us by various causes. But, please note, they are many causes, not one. This is enough to show that the causes alone cannot fully determine the result. For the experience is one, not many. What causal law could prescribe in advance just how the many factors are to fuse together into a new single entity, an experience? There is no psychology textbook which seriously attempts such a thing, or sensibly could attempt it. By no logic can many entities, through law, exhaustively define a single new entity which is to result from them all.[8]

The remarkable creative act of study parallels the creative act of writing. Though guided by them, the act of study is not limited by the sequence of decisions made by the writer in constructing her text. The act of study is itself a new single entity, an emergent synthesis that cannot be accounted for by any series of direct causal elements. The free act of experiencing is the "universal principle of reality," according to Hartshorne. "People have looked for freedom in action, and of course freedom must somehow show up in action. But the first stage of free action is the way in which one interprets or experiences the world."[9] The method of approaching texts in this book sees no fundamental difference between the way one interprets the world and the way one interprets symbols in a text. In either case what one is doing is participating with others or (with a writer) in producing "a unification, an integration, and what is unified is always a many."[10] Out of the many strands of experience, the individual produces in each moment an emergent synthesis, which is the experiential whole of that moment. Such integration of the contrary or disparate elements given as raw material in any experience is actually the achievement of an integrated point of view, standpoint, or orientation.

The studies in this book take their origin from the philosophy of René Descartes (1596–1650) and the principles of consciousness in the culture that developed in the West from his reasoning and ideas. It will be argued in the Introduction that Descartes's philosophy contained a powerful generative idea—an idea that proved to be enormously productive as a thinking frame within which other ideas and whole systems of philosophy were generated for nearly three centuries. That idea is formulated as modern epistemological dualism and the dualistic metaphysics that followed from it; and correlated with it is the radical subjectivism expressed in Descartes's famous line "I think, therefore I am." The principle of dualism, as many writers have argued, is the core idea of a philosophical paradigm that was to dominate the mainstream of modern philosophy until the end of the nineteenth century.

Using the concept of paradigm from Thomas Kuhn's book *The Structure of Scientific Revolutions*, the Introduction goes on to argue that some of the major thinkers in the American philosophic tradition between about 1880 and 1950 struggled to articulate a new generative idea: the idea of emergent unitary experience. This idea, I suggest, based as it is on a process model of existence, is the core of a new paradigm, or frame of thought, from which the experience of twentieth-century man, particularly as expressed in modernist American poetry, can be understood perhaps more fully than it could be without this idea. Chapter 1 describes the experiential orientation of Josiah Royce's constructive idealism and shows how Royce worked, with the assistance of some key ideas from Charles Peirce's theory of signs and meaning, to deconstruct the foundations of epistemological dualism. Chapter 2 is a study of the progression of ideas in T. S Eliot's poetry beyond the subjectivism of the Cartesian paradigm.

Chapter 2 draws specifically on the philosophies of Royce, Hocking, and James for interpreting ideas to clarify Eliot's passage beyond modernity toward a post-Cartesian frame of thought, for which I will also use the word *postmodern* as a descriptive term. Chapter 3 explores the experiential conception of consciousness in James's philosophical psychology, culminating in the idea of pure experience in radical empiricism. This section focuses on James's use of metaphors to articulate post-Cartesian structures of consciousness and shows how James's ideas are pertinent to the interpretation of twentieth-century music, painting, and literature. Chapter 4 examines the poetry and thought of Wallace Stevens in the light of the altered paradigm of consciousness in James's philosophy, and shows similarities between the two writers' efforts toward the decreation of epistemological dualism and their parallel reconstruction of experience on a unitary basis. Chapter 5 addresses the concept of unified experience in the philosophy of John Dewey, particularly with reference to the principle of "transaction" and to the ideas of conscious creativity and of art as experience in Dewey's contextualism. Chapter 6 is an analysis of William Carlos Williams's *Paterson* and other writings as evidence of his progression beyond the Cartesian paradigm, and draws on Dewey's contextualism to illuminate the underlying conceptions of mind and experience in Williams's poetics. Each of the six main chapters of the book is designed as an independent essay, addressed either to undergraduate or graduate students interested in interdisciplinary study of American culture, philosophers and literary scholars interested in the problem of consciousness at the historic moment of passage beyond modernity, or general readers open to the joys and rigors of poetry and philosophy, and the interplay between them. The chapters are arranged so that a reader may either read straight through from beginning to end, or skip around selectively, following the trail of his or her own interests. The Conclusion attempts to put the general thesis of the book in the context of some recent developments in American philosophical and religious thought, including, on the one hand, the epistemological behaviorism of Richard Rorty, and, on the other, the post-Cartesian religious thought of such figures as William Ernest Hocking, Huston Smith, and Dwayne Huebner.

To link American philosophy and poetry as I am doing in this book is in part methodological (using philosophy as a means of interpreting poetic texts) and in part historical (showing connections between the work of philosophers and of poets striving toward common intellectual purposes, with important historical consequences). In pursuing its historical motive, the book seeks neither to present a unified theory of the relations between American philosophy and poetry in this era nor to demonstrate consistent influences of philosophers on poets. Rather, it recognizes that both philosophers and poets were working within a continuous intellectual and

historical environment in which ideas inevitably interact, sometimes regardless of, sometimes because of, the intentions of individual writers or
thinkers. To the extent that direct influences were present, as between
James and Stevens, between Royce and Eliot, and between Dewey and
Williams, these will be examined. But the main purpose of the book is not
to review biographical evidence of the influence of philosophers on poets,
but to explore problems related to the evolution of consciousness in this
historic transition from modernity to postmodernity. The book starts from
the premise that philosophical ideas and poetic insights illuminate each
other, and that they become for readers "mutual sources of understanding
and interpretation."[11] Exploring such mutual sources of interpretation is
different from outlining an explicit intellectual lineage, even when evidence
for this exists. To examine twentieth-century poetry from points of view
given by the classic American philosophers of the preceding generation is
not only to clarify the meaning of both poetic and philosophical texts, but
also to observe and clarify the pattern of this quiet but profound revolution
in thought, the American passage beyond modernity.

The book implicitly shows the educational value of poetry and philosophy as tools that help us develop a critical awareness of one paradigm of
consciousness—the dualism found in the Cartesian tradition—and in revealing the outlines of a new paradigm that can be liberating and empowering. To borrow a Socratic metaphor: it is hoped that these studies will
serve something like the function of a midwife, helping students to bring a
new structure of consciousness to birth from the generative ideas found in
the works of a few of our greatest philosophers and poets.

NOTES

1. T. S. Eliot, "The Music of Poetry," *On Poetry and Poets* (New York: Farrar,
Straus & Giroux/Noonday, 1973), pp. 22–23.

2. "What Pragmatism Means," *Pragmatism*, ed. Fredson Bowers, The Works
of William James 1 (Cambridge: Harvard University Press, 1975), p. 34.

3. Wendell Berry, "The Loss of the University," *Home Economics* (San
Francisco: North Point Press, 1987), p. 77.

4. *Essays in Radical Empiricism*, ed. Fredson Bowers, The Works of William
James 3 (Cambridge: Harvard University Press, 1976), p. 13 and note 12.

5. Ibid., p. 8.

6. Charles Hartshorne, *Creative Synthesis and Philosophic Method* (Lanham,
Md.: University Press of America, 1983), pp. 1–18.

7. *Mind and Nature: A Necessary Unity* (New York: Dutton, 1979), p. 242.

8. *Creative Synthesis and Philosophic Method*, p. 2.

9. Ibid., p. 5.

10. Ibid., p. 3.

11. Art Berman, *From the New Criticism to Deconstruction* (Urbana: University
of Illinois Press, 1988), p. 26. Berman uses this apt phrase to describe the relation
between empiricism and the development of New Criticism.

Frontiers of Consciousness

INTRODUCTION:

The American Passage
Beyond Modernity

A Revolution in Sensibility

THE PHRASE "frontiers of consciousness" implies both a boundary or limit to what is known and a territory beyond that limit. Exploring the frontiers of consciousness may involve critical thought, coming to recognize that the qualities of consciousness in one's own culture and historical epoch constitute a mindset, with limits imposed by the culture to sustain its own purposes, standards, and practices. Or it may involve inner discipline and the surrender of one's natural egoistic point of view to a social context, a principle, or an order of being, larger than the private ego. The limits to an individual's mental horizons take the form of culturally based presuppositions, sometimes so widely and implicitly accepted that they become invisible to those conditioned by them. To become critically aware of the presuppositions that govern one's own thought, and to find a new direction, aside from the inherited beliefs of corporate society, are among the most difficult tasks men and women ever set for themselves.

A poet, a philosopher, or a scientist in one age may invent a generative idea for a revolution in thought that produces a new age. If poets are, in Shelley's famous phrase, the "unacknowledged legislators of the world," it is clear that philosophers—though working more analytically than poets—may also perform similar legislative and constructive functions, altering the cognitive and perceptual paradigms within which men and women experience themselves and their world. In this regard the philosopher Stanley Cavell has written:

> The Spirit of the Age is not easy to place, ontologically or empirically; and it is idle to suggest that creative effort must express its age, either because that cannot fail to happen, or because a new effort can create a new age. . . . But then one is never sure what is possible until it happens; and when it happens it may produce a sense of revolution, of the past escaped and our problems solved—even when we also know that one man's solution is another man's problem.[1]

This book makes a case that just such a new creative effort was undertaken by thinkers in the American philosophic tradition in the period that William Ernest Hocking calls "the period of The Builders" (roughly 1880–1920, dates that I would extend possibly to the death of Dewey in 1952).[2] The culture whose presuppositions the builders (Peirce, Royce, James, and Dewey) attempted to dismantle was not merely that of their own provincial New England. It was the intellectual edifice of modernity itself, as it had descended to their time from the father of modern philosophy, René Descartes (1596–1650). And while the builders in American philosophy were still forging their pioneering views of human nature and experience, probing the boundaries of consciousness established by Descartes and modern cultural tradition, three twentieth-century American poets—T. S. Eliot, Wallace Stevens, and William Carlos Williams— began casting their own searching gaze beyond the frame of modern consciousness.

In *The Use of Poetry and the Use of Criticism* (1933), Eliot concludes that

> Poetry is of course not to be defined by its uses. . . . It may effect revolutions in sensibility such as are periodically needed; may help to break up the conventional modes of perception and valuation which are perpetually forming, and make people see the world afresh, or some new part of it. It may make us from time to time a little more aware of the deeper, unnamed feelings which form the substratum of our being, to which we rarely penetrate; for our lives are mostly a constant evasion of ourselves, and an evasion of the visible and sensible world. But to say all this is only to say what you know already, if you have felt poetry and thought about your feelings.[3]

What is this "substratum of our being" that poetry addresses and unfolds to us? Is it not the primal core of experience—the ground or depth-dimension of our existence—to which we return again and again from the distractions of everyday life, as pain, discipline, thought, action, or grace pushes us to acknowledge it?

Both poetry and philosophy are potential means of that return, for the poet and the philosopher as well as for readers of their texts. And the return to experience in this ultimate sense, which may be fundamentally religious in nature, inevitably has revolutionary consequences. Through their collective attitudes and interpretations, men and women build what has been called a "social construction of reality."[4] Over time, the picture of existence produced in this way remains a "construction," made from "conventional modes of perception and valuation." Philosophy and poetry—ancient enemies, expressing presumably opposed aspects of man's thinking nature called reason and imagination—converge in the American tradition as revolutionary expositors of this deeper substratum of our being. To study them is to participate in a process of returning to experience, thereby radicalizing (discovering the roots of) human (and, by implication, one's own) consciousness. These poets and these philosophers were, of course, not the only participants in the larger revolution of consciousness described in this book. They have been chosen for this study because each of them makes the topic of *mind knowing the world* central to his concerns as a writer, and each shows an interest in challenging the old structures of consciousness inherited from the Cartesian tradition.

In the modern age, the most pervasive metaphysical construction is dualism—the belief that there are two kinds or realms of existence called mind and matter, and that the individual self lives in a private realm of thought and sensation, value-free except for personal preferences, without any universal roots. The modern world since Descartes has lived within the boundaries of an epistemological paradigm that involves the dualism of knowing subject and object known. The paradigm also implies the Cartesian image of the self as private subjective consciousness. Returning to the experiential substratum of our being has the effect of dismantling either unarticulated or rationalized constructions that have been imposed by modern culture on experience. What is left after an act of radical deconstruction of the Cartesian image of self and the dualistic paradigm? That question implicitly underlies the thinking of the builders—those working in poetry, I would argue, as well as those in philosophy. Study of their writings suggests that the builders find only raw experience (not an underlying substance, called matter, mind, or self) as the basic stuff of existence. What is interesting and valuable about their work is the creative aspect of their thought after the paradigm of epistemological dualism and its accompanying image of self and consciousness have been displaced.

CHANGING PARADIGMS OF CONSCIOUSNESS

In *The Structure of Scientific Revolutions* (1970) Thomas Kuhn offers an analysis of how fundamental changes come about in the way scientists understand the universe. A paradigm, according to Kuhn, is the basic set of theories and assumptions that prevails among scientists at a particular time. When the fundamental principles and assumptions acceptable to the scientific community change, the result is a revolution in world view that Kuhn calls a paradigm shift.[5]

Without claiming a too-literal application of the paradigm concept, we may acknowledge (as Kuhn does) that fields outside the natural sciences function according to paradigms of their own. In the nonscientific fields, such as philosophy, the social sciences, and the arts, paradigms are potentially more elastic, and paradigm shifts potentially more volatile, than in the sciences. Because poetry and philosophy depend to a high degree on individual creative thought, and lack the type of community-based standards for evaluating theories and evidence that are used in the sciences, identifying such a thing as an epistemological or metaphysical paradigm (for example) is more difficult than defining a scientific paradigm. Despite these difficulties, the thesis of this book is that the American philosophers and poets under study participated in the deconstruction of the old epistemological paradigm of Cartesian dualism and worked, sometimes consciously, sometimes unconsciously, to implant a new paradigm of consciousness in the thinking of their time. This new paradigm may be described by the concept of unitary or pure experience, as opposed to dualism. Its keynote is the theme of *process* as opposed to the *substance*-based thinking of the Cartesian paradigm. For it defines experience as an organic and historical process rather than a mechanical interaction of substances, some of them called subjects and others objects.

Paradigms are "universally recognized scientific achievements that for a time provide model problems and solutions to a community of practitioners," Kuhn argues.[6] In the sciences, paradigms provide a structural framework for inquiry. A paradigm defines the conventions of research, prescribing which problems are interesting and which are irrelevant, what kinds of questions can be asked and what cannot. A period governed by a specific paradigm is a period of "normal science." Copernicus and Newton were both initiators of paradigm shifts, and the study of physical mechanics after Newton is one example of normal science following from a paradigm shift; exploration in heliocentric astronomy after Copernicus is another. Far from an objective progression toward truth, changes in science, in Kuhn's view, are heavily influenced by nonrational factors. When evidence accumulates to challenge an existing paradigm (as it did in Copernicus's time against the prevailing Ptolemaic model of an earth-centered universe), a crisis is produced among practitioners of normal science until a new model is discovered or invented that accounts more satisfactorily for the evidence. But "the competition between paradigms is not the sort of battle that can be resolved by proofs," says Kuhn. The shift from one paradigm to another "is a conversion experience that cannot be forced." Such a change of view may come about through evidence or arguments that "appeal to the individual's sense of the appropriate or the aesthetic." Logic and empirical evidence are in themselves insufficient grounds for acceptance of a new paradigm that rivals an institutionalized one. "Paradigms are not corrigible by normal science at all," Kuhn argues; "normal science ultimately leads only to the recognition of anomalies and to crises. And these are terminated, not by deliberation and interpretation, but by a relatively sudden and unstructured event like the gestalt switch." He gives the analogy of the line drawing that one moment looks like a duck and the next moment takes on the appearance of a rabbit. The sensory data are the same in both instances, but the mind "sees" the data differently. Scientists who initiate or experience paradigm shifts "often speak of the 'scales falling from the eyes' or of the 'lightning flash' that 'inundates' a previously obscure puzzle, enabling its components to be seen in a new way that for the first time permits its solution.'"[7]

Why is logic inadequate to decide, between rival paradigms, which is "correct"? Because competing paradigms presuppose different, and incommensurable, systems of logic. Though opposing paradigms may seem to use the same words and concepts, in fact their meanings are disparate. In Newtonian physics mass is conserved; in Einsteinian physics mass is convertible to energy. In pre-Copernican astronomy the earth signifies a fixed point.[8]

The concept of *experience* according to the modern Western mindset in philosophy presupposed a dualistic split between subject and object.[9] The influx of sensory data from the object to the subject is the basic definition of experience accepted by Locke, Hume, and Kant. But Western culture entered a period of crisis at the end of the nineteenth century in which the paradigm of duality made less and less sense. At this time, William James reasoned his way to the potentially revolutionary concept of pure experience, in which "experience and reality come to the same thing."[10] As Hartshorne explains, "apart from experience, the idea of reality is empty, as some though not all philosophers admit. . . . Experiences are facts; the only question is, what else is fact? If nothing else, then, and only then, is dualism avoided."[11] Though they all pursued unique, individual paths of development, Peirce, Royce, and Dewey worked along parallel lines. Peirce's concept of experience in his category of Thirdness (see below pp. 27–34) takes on the quality of "meaning" that supersedes the duality of subject and object. Royce worked out a theory of interpretation based to some degree on Peirce's categories that avoids the dualism of percept and concept. According to Dewey, the live creature and the environment are integrally linked in transactional relations as phases of a single experiential fabric. In their redefinitions of the idea of experience, each of these philosophers implicitly attempts a statement of a rival paradigm to the dominant Cartesian dualism.

In the sciences, according to Kuhn,

> Many readers will surely want to say that what changes with a paradigm is only the scientist's interpretation of observations that themselves are fixed once and for all by the nature of the environment and of the perceptual apparatus. On this view, Priestly and Lavoisier both saw oxygen, but they interpreted their observations differently; Aristotle and Galileo both saw pendulums, but they differed in their interpretations of what they both had seen.[12]

The belief that scientific observations are firmly objective, and that only subjective interpretations change, is a product of what Kuhn calls "the traditional epistemological paradigm" that has dominated modern Western thinking since Descartes. That paradigm "has served both science and philosophy well," he argues, but "today research in parts of philosophy, psychology, linguistics, and even art history, all converge to suggest that the traditional paradigm is somehow askew."[13]

Why is the traditional paradigm askew? One answer is that epistemological dualism reinforces a separation of the self from every object, including other humans, and shapes experience into the alienated and potentially pathological framework of "I–It" encounters rather than "I-Thou" relationality.[14] The radical separation of the interpreting consciousness from the world generates what Paul Tillich calls "the anxiety of emptiness and meaninglessness," when the self feels its connectedness to others and to the whole of existence severed or reduced to a minimum.[15] According to the core rival paradigm proposed by Peirce, Royce, James, and Dewey, human consciousness is not defined as centered in a solipsistic ego, necessarily trapped in a state of alienation from others. Each of the American philosophers pursued a decades-long exploration and reconstruction of the idea of "experience." For them all experience is essentially a fabric of relations, with meaning embedded in them. Consciousness as self-enclosed and self-alienated ego disappears, but re-emerges in this philosophical tradition as that which connects the individual to qualitative meanings and to others. The idea of unitary experience in an ongoing developmental process is the core idea of a rival paradigm to dualism, with potential to resolve the crisis of alienation produced by the modern Western mindset. As we near the end of the twentieth century this rival paradigm is still not widely accepted, though it has gained the allegiance of many humanistic philosophers, psychologists, and poets.[16]

MODERNITY AND AMERICAN EXPERIENCE

From Cartesian assumptions about the nature of mind and reality, modernity had evolved two major contrasting philosophic systems, empiricism and idealism. But the fundamental assumptions of metaphysical and epistemological dualism remained common to both. The builders in the American philosophic tradition worked in revolt not so much against either of these historic systems of thought as against the core assumptions of the mainstream. In the seventeenth century Descartes had broken away from the authoritarian rule of ancient philosophy. From the method of authority found in medieval scholastic philosophy, Descartes moved to the method of *a priori* knowing, with the self-conscious ego as his starting point and ultimate frame of reference. In doing so, he released a tide of energy that shaped itself into the dualistic and egocentric structure of modern consciousness. Cartesian culture conceived the human mind as a detached immaterial spectator, confronting an objective universe. Out of this stand-off between perceiving subject and the objects of thought arose the peculiarly modern "problem of knowledge," to which modern epistemology supplied dozens of solutions. Despite its wide acceptance in the Western world, the dualistic paradigm of consciousness and reality, and the epistemology and metaphysics that followed from it, became prime targets of attack by the classic American philosophers.

Each of them saw beyond the spectator paradigm to the way consciousness functions in the field of lived experience. From this perspective, they sought by their individual means to expose the arbitrariness of the paradigm. This book does not systematically address biographical or psychoanalytic reasons why these philosophers felt a powerful call to challenge the authority of the Cartesian paradigm. But it argues that their work implicitly answers the problem of "Cartesian anxiety" by moving conceptually and experientially to a new paradigm involving the functional integration and participation of consciousness in the world.

In her book *The Flight to Objectivity*, Susan Bordo argues that Descartes's famous "method of doubt" in the *Meditations* led in fact not to certainty, as he had hoped, but to "the pervasiveness of Cartesian anxiety."[17] As defined by Bordo, Cartesian anxiety entails the perception that there is no (real) reference point that enables experience to become integrated or to take meaningful shape. Despite Descartes's apparent confidence in the *self* as a center of certainty, a subtext of the *Meditations* takes the anxiety of a centerless experience as its major premise. Cartesian anxiety, it may be argued, pervades twentieth-century culture and is evident in such poems as *The Waste Land*, "Sunday Morning," and *Paterson*, as well as in existentialist philosophy. As if in response to this pervasive tension of Cartesian anxiety, William James asks the question in his *Essays in Radical Empiricism*, "Does 'Consciousness' Exist?" If, as James implies, the private Cartesian self as seat of consciousness proves to be an illusion, what then is left? In their efforts to deconstruct the Cartesian paradigm of consciousness and reality, the American philosophers implicitly wrestle with this question. The poets in some respects perceive the anxiety of meaninglessness more acutely than the philosophers, but like them also display a struggle for orientation. This struggle is the fundamental drama that I see unfolding in the philosophy and poetry of the early decades of the twentieth century in America. Sometimes implicitly and sometimes explicitly, the American poets and philosophers of these two generations confront the problem of Cartesian anxiety. Poetic and philosophic ideas like "the stream of consciousness" and "the still point" are examples of symbolic modes of experience explored in this book that move readers into new and perhaps more satisfactory relation with other parts of experience. Each of them, in other words, has some potential to lead us toward significant orientation, and in this way each presents a means of answering the problem of Cartesian anxiety.

What is the shape of post-Cartesian consciousness, and how did it manifest itself in American poetry? Instead of a private realm of thought, insight, and emotion, separated as if by partition from objective reality, the picture of consciousness evolving in early twentieth-century American poetry is that of a unitary, contextually oriented, participating consciousness.[18] Because of the similarity of their intuitions regarding a new paradigm of consciousness, the American philosophers' reflections provide valuable means of interpreting the ways consciousness is portrayed in the work of the American poets of the following generation.

Passage Beyond Modernity

By seeking not just to overthrow an opposing philosophy, but also to uproot the Cartesian premises embedded in modern thought, the builders were in effect laying foundations ("deep and massive," as Peirce put it) for a fundamental reorientation of modernity's basic understanding of the mind's ways of knowing reality. The notion of a private internal consciousness inherited from the Cartesian tradition is transformed in the writings of the American philosophers into the wooly but powerful idea of *experience*,[19] including mind as an instrumental agent sowing the seeds of the reconstruction of experience.

In modern epistemology, the problem of the relation of subject and object is only a very abstract and technical expression of the larger existential problem of the perceived conflict between the self and the other. From this conflict came two major streams of modern thought: one led to the feelings of isolation and estrangement that produced existentialist literature and philosophy; the other produced modern scientific rationalism based on the principle of objectivity—the ability to look cognitively and analytically at anything and treat it as an object of manipulation or control. When Descartes argued that by the cognitive methods he had discovered men would become "masters and controllers of nature," he articulated the fundamental agenda of scientific rationalism, positivism, and logical empiricism. The rival to the Cartesian paradigm developed by the builders in American philosophy emphasized neither existential estrangement nor rational analysis. Because they rejected the basic paradigm of dualism, they tended to see experience in holistic rather than divided and fragmented frames of reference. And the problem of knowledge tended for all of them to be, not a problem of overcoming estrangement or of analytical control of the object, but a matter of the knower's using his or her powers of mind to get progressively into creative or meaningful relation with the other.

While ancient and medieval cultures showed little of modernity's peculiar obsession with the self-conscious ego, Descartes's "I think, therefore

I am" named for modern philosophy its unshakable first principle, the idea that the cognitive subject, possessing a certain exhilarating but narrow autonomy, is the seat of man's existence. Sustaining the premise of the thinker's functional independence, but rejecting in their turn the idea of subjective privacy as an invalid assumption, the American philosophers disclosed structures of consciousness marking a new epochal frontier between modernity and what I will call the *postmodern* era.[20] Descartes's conviction of the reality of the ego-consciousness (the *cogito* or I-think), dwelling in the certitude only of its own internal cognitions, implanted within the heart of modernity a persistently subjectivist orientation, which is the heritage not only of poets and philosophers but of us all. As I would like to show in these studies, the classic American philosophers and modernist poets articulated a cultural transition that William Ernest Hocking has called the "passage beyond modernity."

Descartes's discovery of the solitary I-think marked a major advance or, as I would argue, a paradigm shift in Western culture. For, according to Hocking, it bred an awareness of the ultimate value of "the free individual, disposed to stand alone against corporate dictation."[21] But like fruit from the tree of knowledge, this discovery also carried within it the germ of a cultural psychosis.[22] The solipsism implicit in Descartes's reasoning "has haunted modernity," Hocking claims. "Stirred by his enlightening certitude, modernity has followed Descartes gladly into his subjective depths, from which it has drawn wondrous harvests."[23] The principle of subjectivity, combined with Descartes's complementary doctrine that the world is constituted of matter and material force, empty of all purpose and value, obeying only mechanical and deterministic laws, led modernity to abandon "man's native rapport with the whole." Hence, Hocking concludes, "the nerve of worth in man's own living and acting silently ceases to function."[24] Within this alienated picture of reality, "the principle of our advance"—the ability to distance oneself conceptually from objective reality—has carried "the germ of our malady,"[25] a loss of qualitative connectedness to a universe "other" than self.[26]

When Descartes lighted upon "the solitary I-exist as his ultimate certitude—meaning for him I-Descartes exist—he published it to the world as the basis for all future philosophy!" Descartes "instinctively sensed what his method could not justify: namely, that his private certitude was every man's certitude in kind." The universality of his implication was irrepressible. "At the extreme depth of his inwardness he joins an infinite outside."[27] In view of this analysis, Hocking finds his "releasing insight" in the idea of *intersubjectivity*, a power of knowing whereby "one self participates, not by imaginative or sympathetic construction, but by actual experience, in the selfhood of another."[28] The self is not extinguished but nevertheless dissolves its egocentric boundaries through participation "by actual experience" in the reality of the other.

Eliot's famous outcry against the "dissociation of sensibility" which "set in" in the seventeenth century, and from which "we have never recovered,"[29] is in effect a protest against the misconstruction of experience implicit in Cartesian dualism. According to Eliot, the English metaphysical poets possessed a vital integration of thought and feeling, an ability to "amalgamate disparate experience"[30] in a manner conforming not to rational standards of clarity but to the mandates of poetic intuition. But after their time, that is, after the advent of the Cartesian frame of mind, "thought" was defined more and more strictly in terms of a positivistic rationality that excluded feeling as mere subjective aberration. Because it operates only in the sphere of qualitative expression, poetry was implicitly deprived of the possibility of making truth claims. Truth lay only in the domain of empirical, quantitative, or rational propositions. "After Descartes," argues one scholar,

> poets were inevitably writing with the sense that their constructions were *not true*, and this feeling robbed their work of essential seriousness. It was felt, as Locke said, that poetry offers "pleasant pictures and agreeable visions," but that these consist in "something that is not perfectly conformable" to truth and reason. All that one could do, then, was either to make one's verse as conformable to truth and reason as possible (e.g., the *Essay on Man*), or to indulge in agreeable visions in the full consciousness that they were fiction. It is the sense that their material is only agreeable fiction which gives the peculiar hollowness to much of the mythological and other "machinery" employed by eighteenth century poets.[31]

The divided or "dissociated" sensibility that was to work miracles in science and technology, by eliminating subjective feeling and superstition from the observation and control of nature, constituted, from Eliot's perspective, the death of the poetic impulse to articulate the truth of being. For the Cartesian frame of mind, along with its picture of an intrinsically meaningless material world-machine, brought a system of valuation in which the qualitative and aesthetic were inevitably judged inferior to whatever could be measured and quantified. In his struggle to articulate an enlarged perspective toward reality, as a means of overcoming the limitations of modern subjectivism, Eliot is united with his contemporaries Stevens and Williams. In the convergence of "imagination" and "reality" in his later poetry, Stevens shows a way that the spell of the Cartesian paradigm can be broken. And Williams's saying "no ideas but in things" typifies his efforts to challenge the culturally conditioned sense of a split between the subject and the object of knowing, and to return to experience. Each of the poets, like the philosophers, wrestles with the problems implicit in the old paradigm by returning in his own way to concrete experience, and by means of the thinking process recorded in his work instructs us in the methods of return. Their common rebelliousness against the Cartesian paradigm comes from a common disposition to explore ranges of sensibility beyond the ordinary limits of modern consciousness.

Words may fail, as Eliot says, in either discipline. When the notion of personal consciousness is stretched beyond its usual limits, the private ego may be either fragmented (as in Eliot's early poetry) or abolished (as in James's later philosophy). But the constructive energies of both writers move them, not to amorphous ethereal or transcendental states, as means of overcoming the subject–object split, but to a new experiential standpoint in which the subjective and objective elements of Cartesian epistemology are embraced in a creative synthesis of conscious experience.[32]

The three poets all begin their journeys of discovery from the premise of a private consciousness, or self, seeking meaning and order. Each in his own way proceeds to refashion his image of the self and to articulate an enlarged frame of perspective reference, or orientation, that no longer assumes the validity of the dualistic paradigm. Their advances in this direction lead to new ideas or principles, like Eliot's "still point of the turning world" in *Four Quartets*; Stevens's ultimate "point of survey," the "axis of everything," in *Credences of Summer*; and Williams's state of "being taut, balanced between eternities," in *Paterson*. Each of these expanded frames of orientation to the world is made more intelligible when seen in the light of the American philosophers' articulation of *the experiential standpoint*. This standpoint represents a point of view no longer tied to the perceptual horizons of ego-subjectivity.

The revolutionary impulse in American philosophy and in American poetic modernism is in one sense a continuation of the Romantic rebellion in philosophy and literature at the beginning of the nineteenth century, against the mechanistic rationalism of Cartesian culture. But it is an impulse allied to Romanticism primarily in its attack on a common enemy. For while the Romantic poet was typically an explorer of the inner world of the ego-subject, and Romantic philosophy typically a form of subjective or transcendental idealism, the revolutionary disposition of American thought involves a more radical approach to the problem of consciousness: a willingness to dislodge the subjective ego itself from the throne of authority upon which Descartes had placed it, and to make an appeal instead to the realities of concrete experience, including the shared experience of social interactions. The builders in American philosophy and poetry, by their fidelity to experience and their developing of ideas that function as pragmatic leadings toward more and more significant modes of orientation, were the architects of a major cultural transition in the early part of this century, a passage beyond modernity, whose value and consequences we are only now beginning to witness.

NOTES

1. "Aesthetic Problems of Modern Philosophy," *Must We Mean What We Say? A Book of Essays* (New York: Scribner's, 1969), p. 73.

2. "Foreword," in Charles Hartshorne's *Reality as a Social Process: Studies in Metaphysics and Religion* (Boston: Beacon, 1953), p. 12.

3. (Cambridge: Harvard University Press, 1933), p. 155.

4. Peter L. Berger and Thomas Luckman, *The Social Construction of Reality: A Treatise in the Sociology of Knowledge* (Garden City, N.Y.: Doubleday, 1966).

5. (Chicago: The University of Chicago Press, 1970); Michael Goldstein, unpublished paper "Paradigm Shifts in Deep Ecology."

6. *Structure of Scientific Revolutions*, p. viii.

7. Ibid., p. 122.

8. Nicholas Wade, "Thomas S. Kuhn: Revolutionary Theorist of Science," *Science*, July 8, 1977, 143–45.

9. Huston Smith, "Beyond the Modern Western Mind-set," *Beyond the Post-Modern Mind* (New York: Crossroad, 1982), pp. 132–61.

10. *Essays in Radical Empiricism*, p. 30.

11. *Creative Synthesis and Philosophic Method*, pp. 6, 9.

12. *Structure of Scientific Revolutions*, pp. 119–20.

13. Ibid., p. 120.

14. Martin Buber, *I and Thou*, trans. Ronald Gregor Smith, 2nd ed. (New York: Macmillan, 1987); see R. D. Laing, *The Divided Self: An Existential Study in Sanity and Madness* (Harmondsworth: Penguin, 1971).

15. *The Courage to Be* (New Haven: Yale University Press, 1952), pp. 46–51.

16. See, for example, *News of the Universe: Poems of Twofold Consciousness*, ed. Robert Bly (San Francisco: Sierra Club, 1980); and the writings of Abraham Maslow and of Carl Rogers.

17. *The Flight to Objectivity: Essays in Cartesianism and Culture* (Albany: SUNY Press, 1987).

18. See Owen Barfield, *Saving the Appearances: A Study in Idolatry* (New York: Harcourt, Brace & World [1965]).

19. See John McDermott, *The Culture of Experience: Philosophical Essays in the American Grain* (New York: New York University Press, 1976).

20. The historical concept of *modernity* is distinguished in these studies from the idea of *modernism*. The latter term names the literary and artistic movements in Europe and America after the turn of the twentieth century—associated with such figures as Joyce, Picasso, Eliot, Pound, and others of their generation. The term *modernity*, synonymous here with *Cartesianism*, suggests the views of Descartes and his immediate followers, but also the disposition of thinkers from the seventeenth century onward to regard consciousness as a "thing" or "realm of being" distinct in ontological status from another realm called "external" or "material." The terms *postmodernity*, *postmodern*, and *post-Cartesian* here designate another epochal category beginning in the West after modernity had in some sense run its course. For further discussion see Richard Palmer, "Post-Modernity and Hermeneutics," *Boundary 2* (1977), 363–93. Huston Smith argues in *Beyond the Post-Modern Mind* that the "Modern Western Mind-set" is made up of a set of rationalistic and mechanistic assumptions about the world that has been pervasive in the West from Descartes's time to the present. His definition of the postmodern mind, like the one I have adopted here, coincides with the period of the twentieth century. Smith believes, however, that postmodernity is simply a grandchild of

modernity. His book is an exploration of ways to escape the equally narrow trap of postmodernity, while my argument in this book claims, along with Whitehead's in *Science and the Modern World* (New York: Macmillan, 1925; repr. New York: Free Press, 1969), that American philosophy at the turn of the century produced the germ of a new ("postmodern") paradigm with the potential to displace its Cartesian ancestor.

21. *The Coming World Civilization* (London: George Allen & Unwin, 1958), p. 21.

22. Ibid.

23. Ibid., p. 22. One of modernity's "harvests" is surely Freudian psychoanalysis. Daniel Yankelovich and William Barrett, in their *Ego and Instinct: The Psychoanalytic View of Human Nature—Revised* (New York: Random House, 1970), document the influence of Cartesianism and the Cartesian–Newtonian world view on psychoanalysis, and through analysis of "a changed background in philosophy," which includes the work of James and Dewey, attempt to show a potential new direction for a post-Cartesian psychology.

24. *Coming World Civilization*, p. 23.

25. Ibid., p. 25.

26. In the phrase "the principle of our advance" Hocking implies that there has been an historical or evolutionary leap from medieval authoritarianism to the modern discovery of subjective consciousness. The modern discovery of the "I" as center of consciousness, symbolized by Descartes, is just one of the later in a series of wakenings of the human spirit to the reality of individual consciousness. One of the earliest of these wakenings occurred in the civilizations of the ancient world during the second millennium B.C., as described and documented by Julian Jaynes in his book *The Origin of Consciousness in the Breakdown of the Bicameral Mind* (Boston: Houghton Mifflin, 1976), when ancient man stopped hearing and responding automatically to hallucinated voices of "the gods" and experienced the beginnings of a reflective consciousness, capable of such autonomous mental acts as narratizing alternate courses of action and consciously choosing the better course.

Another such momentous historical shift occurred in what John Cobb, Jr. (following Karl Jaspers), calls the "axial period"—from about 800 to 200 B.C.—in which "a new type of thinking" appeared in five parts of the Eurasian continent at roughly the same time. "During the sixth century before Christ lived Confucius and Lao-tzu in China, Gautama Buddha in India, and Zoroaster in Persia. In the same century, Thales and Pythagoras were founding Greek philosophy, and the prophetic movement in Israel reached a climax in Second Isaiah. . . . What distinguished axial man was the new role of rationality in the structure of his existence" (*The Structure of Christian Existence* [New York: Seabury, 1979], pp. 52–53).

We might extend this line of argument by acknowledging that modernity represents another axial period in which rationality and subjectivity are confirmed by the modern paradigm of epistemological dualism. Postmodernity as I am defining it in this book represents a paradigm shift potentially leading to a new axial period, in which dualism is abandoned, and the old epistemological subject is reconstructed on the model of intersubjectivity, experiential unity, and dialogical interaction with the other.

27. Hocking, *Coming World Civilization*, p. 22.

28. Ibid., p. 28.

29. "The Metaphysical Poets," *Selected Essays* (New York: Harcourt, Brace & World, 1964), p. 247.

30. Ibid.

31. Basil Willey, *The Seventeenth-Century Background: Studies in the Thought of the Age in Relation to Poetry and Religion* (Garden City, N.Y.: Doubleday, 1953), pp. 93–94.

32. See Hartshorne's "A Philosophy of Shared Creative Experience," in *Creative Synthesis and Philosophic Method*, pp. 1–18.

1
Consciousness and Meaning: Josiah Royce as Empirical Idealist and the Legacy of Charles Peirce

THE PROBLEM OF ORIENTATION

JOSIAH ROYCE WAS BORN IN 1855 in the California mining town of Grass Valley and raised in the rough San Francisco Bay area of the late nineteenth century. A University of California graduate, he taught philosophy at Harvard from 1882 until his death in 1916. Having studied in Germany and at Johns Hopkins before going to Harvard, Royce was an instructor of English at the Berkeley campus.[1] Despite his need, especially in later years, to press his insights into the mold of rigorous logic, he was never to abandon the "interest in literature and literary criticism that had first inspired him as an undergraduate and been his field while teaching at Berkeley."[2]

Like James and Dewey, Royce was concerned with the problem of consciousness. But unlike them, he was interested more in exploring the potentials of consciousness for growth out of its present limitations than in phenomenological description. How does consciousness orient itself to reality? This question, implicit in Royce's books and essays, is answered on the basis of the argument that consciousness possesses inherent powers for growth and self-transcendence. Though human consciousness often remains constrained within a finite point of view, bound by the limits of sense perception, Royce was convinced that nonfinite perspectives are possible within experience, and his philosophy seeks to demonstrate the empirical validity of such perspectives.

To what extent was Royce able to maintain his empirical anchorage, in the attempt to show a way beyond the finitude of ordinary human consciousness? Scholars and critics vary in their answers to this question.[3] But it is clear that Royce achieved something that seems paradoxical, given the limits of traditional idealism and empiricism. He succeeded in showing the possibility of movement—through a process of "mental growth"[4]—from the imprisoned perspective of a finite consciousness, burdened by error, toward what his idealistic instincts led him to call an absolute point of view, yet still within the domain of experience as defined by radical empiricists. Toward the end of his career, Royce found in Charles Peirce's theory of signs a means of sustaining his empirical grounding, while expanding his conception of the higher potentials of consciousness. An understanding of Royce's appropriation of Peirce's ideas clarifies our perception of the empirical backbone of his thinking about higher forms of consciousness, his theory of interpretation, and the relevance of his thought to the study of modernist poetry.

Despite his use of a supernaturalist vocabulary (as in *The Sources of Religious Insight*, 1912) to refer to higher forms of consciousness, Royce was as strongly convinced as James or Dewey of the naturalistic principle that there is only one order of existence—what we call the natural. But within that one order Royce also perceived that it is possible for consciousness to orient itself in radically different ways. If consciousness is oriented primarily to immediate sense impressions, the individual moves through his or her experience feeling sensations in linear sequence and acting only by the light of the individual mind's own "dim candle" (to cite a familiar phrase from Locke). A second possibility is that consciousness may turn inward and obey the call of the rational intellect as the primary guide to truth. If the first option is made clear by British empiricists, the second is essentially the program of Cartesian rationalism. Royce articulates the mind's potential for a third ("higher") orientation within the one order of experience. That third orientation involves not just an American revision of British or continental idealism, but a creative synthesis of empiricism and idealism.

Royce argued that what we call reality is never totally independent of the perspectives brought to bear upon it by the experiencer. Consciousness to Royce is not a passive receiver of information, but a creative agent with the ability to see things from wider or narrower perspectives, depending on the exercise of inner energies. In Royce's later philosophy consciousness is not condemned to remain frozen in a one-dimensional point of view, but possesses the ability to transcend the finiteness of its own states at a given level of development. Consciousness is fundamentally elastic, and may enlarge or contract its standpoint, evolving more organized or less organized forms. Using an archetypal metaphor Royce describes the more organized forms of consciousness with the spatial image of *height*. The potential of consciousness envisioned by Royce is thus to move toward a higher standpoint, or a "higher unity."

VERTICAL THINKING IS MEDITATIVE THINKING

Royce believed that philosophy had a unique mission: to free the thinking process from arbitrary conditioning or self-imposed limitations, and to help channel it into higher and more creative activity. Claiming the authority of experience for his ideas, he rejected the narrowly sensational theory of experience given in British empiricism.[5] "If by empiricist we mean fidelity to experience on its own terms," then, John J. McDermott writes, Royce "was as empirical in outlook and temperament as James or Dewey."[6] But he differed from his explicitly empiricist colleagues by arguing that consciousness is capable of remaining bound to lower (finite) levels or rising (by grace or creative effort) to higher levels of organization and meaning. At the heart of Royce's thinking is an implicit distinction between *vertical* and *horizontal* dimensions of experience. Unlike the empiricists, Royce took the vertical dimension as axiomatic.

What is thinking in a vertical dimension? British empiricism clung tenaciously to sensation as the only foundation of genuine knowledge. This is the way horizontal thinking works. All the data of consciousness are conceived to be at one "level," that of value-free sense impressions, and any knowledge that arises from a source other than sensation (such as the values of love or brotherhood, or the Biblical idea of God) is denied credibility and excluded as irrelevant or invalid. When, on the other hand, a theologian speaks of religion as the "dimension of depth" in human experience, and of depth psychology as a means of contacting this hidden dimension, he is naming a category of existence that is beyond the reach of traditional empirical analysis, though it may be a vital part of experience. He is making deliberate use of a metaphor drawn from the spatial realm to point to an aspect of human experience that cannot be found among sense data.[7]

Metaphors of three-dimensional space appear characteristically in Royce's writings in such phrases as "higher thought," a "higher point of view," or a "higher unity of consciousness." The two-dimensional plane of consciousness is identified metaphorically in Locke's image of mind as a *tabula rasa*, or blank tablet. Because they suggest breaking the surface plane of thought processes tied to sensation, the vertical metaphors of *higher* and *deeper* tend, however paradoxically, to mean the same thing, to inhabit the same zone of meaning. "The way up and the way down are one and the same," wrote Heraclitus in the sixth century B.C. Such imagery of height and depth, of ascent and descent, in philosophy and literature historically suggests the movement of consciousness out of habitual or predetermined patterns. It suggests the lifting of thought from the bondage of social and psychological conditioning, and the acceptance of the mind's potential for such "higher" things as freedom and creativity. But higher being is not necessarily "above" or outside the earthly contexts of live experience. The word *higher* for Royce is a metaphor for a new or altered orientation within the total field of experience. In one respect, it is a name for an inner disposition of mind to unite with the principle of the

Logos, and with the whole universal system of being, a disposition that expands one's way of seeing and knowing (i.e., experiencing) the real.

Spatial metaphors of higher and deeper imply a consciousness that operates by different rules, or follows different patterns of organization, from those in the horizontal plane to which our ordinary sense-based consciousness conforms. When Martin Heidegger distinguishes between two radically different yet complementary kinds of thinking, called *meditative* and *calculative thinking*, he implicitly acknowledges this distinction between vertical and horizontal dimensions of consciousness. Calculative thinking is not just that which computes sums; it is all the thinking that plans and investigates, in ordinary experience as in the sciences, but "never collects itself."[8] It is technological thinking—including the so-called technological imperative to produce more and more advanced and complex technology—apart from matters of ultimate concern, value, and purpose. Nuclear weapons have come into being through the progress of calculative thinking, generating more and more sophisticated means of annihilation, while meditative thinking—which alone is capable of discerning values and distinguishing between higher and lower purposes—goes into eclipse.

To Heidegger, meditative thinking is that which is able to be still, to penetrate into the depth dimension, to contemplate the meanings of things in addition to their bare factuality or their technical usefulness. Heidegger argues, with some alarm, that man in the contemporary world is *in flight from thinking*—i.e., meditative thinking—because he has become mesmerized by his own thought in the horizontal plane, calculation and its technical products. He fears that the neglect of meditative thinking may lead to atrophy of the very power of meditation that alone can make moral and critical judgments about the direction of existence in a technological environment. Meditative thinking alone is capable of moving to that higher (or deeper) standpoint where consciousness takes charge of itself, and begins to govern creatively and compassionately the course of calculative thinking and the technology it produces. Royce stood at an historical crossroads described by Gabriel Marcel as a "transition between absolute idealism and existentialist thought."[9] Though he lived in a time when technology could not have been the kind of pressing concern it was to Heidegger, Royce shared with the German existentialist a recognition that consciousness inhabits a vertical plane, and like him desired to nurture the kind of thinking capable of addressing what both men called the "problem of Being" (BW I 546),[10] without abandoning the existential reality of experience.

IDEAS AND THE PROBLEM OF BEING

To Royce the problem of Being could only be approached by first understanding that we perceive and experience all things by means of ideas. The problem that he posed for himself in his great metaphysical work *The World and the Individual* (1899–1901) was the problem "of knowing how there can be a true relation between the idea and its object."[11] Considered as "pure fact," reality "eludes the mind's embrace."[12] The "idea" has a "representative aspect." It represents something otherwise present in experience through sensation. But to Royce the idea is something more than the mental copy of an external brute fact. The idea is a quantum of energy actively striving to "embrace" its object. Like James and Dewey, Royce was not satisfied with the image of existence given in the modern paradigm of epistemological dualism. His approach to the problem of ideas is in part governed by a desire to overcome the traditional dualism of idea and object maintained historically to varying degrees by both empiricists and idealists. In addition to its representative aspect, the idea for Royce assumes "a volitional or teleological aspect which is no less essential."[13] Ideas "always involve a consciousness of how you propose to act towards the things of which you have ideas." The idea, then, is "any state of consciousness, whether simple or complex, which, when present, is then and there viewed as at least the partial expression or embodiment of a single conscious purpose. . . . An idea appears in consciousness as having the significance of an act of will."[14]

The idea, then, provides a constructive point of view, necessary to an adequate grasp of reality, without which the world would appear to be nothing more than a chaos of atomistic sensations. "If the brute fact itself is a fact, isn't it so as a function of the act by which thought acknowledges it?" asks Marcel.[15] The mind's access to reality is through the idea. Thus "a philosopher should direct his attention to what can be called the ideal face of reality; in that way reality is accessible."[16] The ideas of self and of the world that one carries about are tools that give one experiential access to the realities named by these terms. But if the idea is a way of seeing, it is also a source of energy that springs into action to take hold of the reality of the "other" which it perceives. Experience to Royce is "not purely immediate content," as the empiricist claims; nor is it "whatever happens to come to hand. It is carefully and attentively *selected* experience. It is experience lighted up by ideas" (WI I 285).

The concept of meaning signifies connectedness, or relatedness. A dictionary definition of a word makes us see its connectedness to other words that inhabit the same zone of signification. Reading the definition, we get the "meaning" of the word by sensing its connection to other areas of experience (named by other words called synonyms) that are perhaps more familiar. To say that ideas have meaning implies more than the lexical meaning we get from the dictionary. Though perhaps most ideas can be expressed in words, the idea itself is a fact of experience that has the potential to move us to (or to connect us with) other stages or aspects of experience. Ideas can be more or less meaningful depending on their relative efficacy in connecting us to other parts of experience. The idea of revolution, for example, or spirituality, may be met with a shrug by some people. It will have no effect on their thinking, while to others it may become an awakening factor, enlivening and moving the individuals to action and to relatedness with others, perhaps to a church or to a revolutionary movement.

In Royce's analysis, an idea can have one of two kinds of meaning. It may be one of many contents of consciousness that functions as a statically representative sign, simply referring (i.e., making a connection) to something outside itself, an other or a beyond. The idea of a table in its literal signification would be an example. This is what Royce calls the *external meaning* of an idea, and this essentially is the definition of idea in its "horizontal" or surface aspect. Even germinal religious or philosophical ideas that have been potent forces in the world, like the ideas of God or truth, can remain at this external level in some people's experience. On the other hand, an idea in the vertical dimension is not so much its representative property as "its inner character as relatively fulfilling the purpose . . . which is in the consciousness of the moment wherein the idea takes place" (WI I 24). The idea is one with the intention that not only points beyond itself to the other, but also actively seeks to know the other for what it is in itself. This is Royce's conception of the *internal meaning* of an idea. If I have an idea—an external gestalt—of my neighbor, that idea may remain at the static level of a detached spectator, a calculative and utilitarian device by which I measure and evaluate his usefulness to me or my purposes. This idea is the mere "It" of an "I–It" relation. It refers to something, an other that I regard as an object—not, fundamentally, a subject like myself, with his own inner life and significance. If, however, the idea breaks loose from the horizontal plane, it takes on another characteristic, a dynamic affectional quality that moves it right into contact, so to speak, with the inner content of the other. From this standpoint, which we name the higher or vertical dimension of consciousness, the idea embraces the other. By virtue of this contact, or encounter, the other is transformed in my perception from an "It" to a "Thou," and the "I" of this new "I–Thou" relation becomes a different "I" from that of the "I–It" relation.[17] The subject–object dichotomy of the first relation is dissolved and displaced by a form of affectional and experiential unity. My idea of my neighbor no longer stands detached. I no longer see him merely from the outside but perceive his existence, so to speak, from his own inner perspective, from the inside out. I see from his point of view, and know him creatively. The essential character of the idea, then, is "not its vicarious assumption of the responsibility of standing for a being beyond itself" (WI I 24), but its ability to reveal the inner meaning of the object, taking hold of it by the impulse of a creative purpose. The idea in its internal or vertical dimension is creative in just the sense that the artist's idea is an impulse toward "realization" of a certain quality of experience in the work of art. This purposive aspect of the idea—like that "present in the creative mind of the artist" (WI I 24)—generates a "conscious act," not just a "state" of consciousness, though it may be so interpreted from a static external viewpoint.

In a certain important respect Royce's conception of the internal meaning of ideas resembles Jonathan Edwards' empirical conception of a "new simple idea." Locke's notion of a *simple idea* as a mechanically received atomistic sensation is transformed by Edwards into a source of spiritual potency when consciousness is quickened by "religious affections."[18] Through religious affections—as through the motive power called the internal meaning of ideas—consciousness is wakened by grace, beyond the bounds of sense perception, to realization of the meaning (including the ultimate meaning) of the object, whether the object of perception is a person, a ray of sunlight, or the bark of a tree. While Royce called this animating power of the idea *volition*, Edwards called it *motive*, informed by "spiritual sense," able to grasp the sensory characteristics of experience but also able to penetrate beyond them to its inner (i.e., spiritual) meaning. Both thinkers work from the empirical model of the meaning of ideas, but translate that model into the vertical dimension.

Though experience ordinarily appears fragmentary and incomplete, this to Royce is due to the limitation of the human point of view at one level of development. It is as if one went about with horse blinders on, never taking in the full scope of reality that is actually present. The purpose of philosophy is to strip off the blinders and make the individual see the oneness or completeness of experience as it actually is. The problem of Being for Royce begins as a problem of perception or, rather, a problem of achieving a sufficiently elevated point of view to take in the whole structure and continuum of experience: to "face Being" (BW I 486), instead of turning consciousness away from it, or confining oneself arbitrarily to a narrow corner of it. Our confinement happens as a result of accepting ideas only in their culturally conditioned or external meanings. By taking voluntary initiative, consciousness may orient itself to a higher standpoint of perception. At this higher standpoint we enter a realm "where experience and idea have already fused into one whole"; and this is the realm of "internal meanings" (WI I 289). From this point of view, we begin to build order in experience. The constructive disposition, together with the perceptual act that follows from it, is "at once an experience of fact, and an idea" (WI I 289)—the conjunction of purpose with empirical observation.

While "lower" perspectives give us a fragmented "picture of Being" rather than a direct meeting with Being, the very desire for wholeness, for completion of the knowing process, is prophetic of the possibility of overcoming the fragmentary quality of finite experience. The external meaning of the idea, its ability to represent something (i.e., finite beings) outside itself, "is only apparently external, and, in very truth, is but an aspect of the completely developed internal meaning" (WI I 36). The sense of a split between idea and fact, as in epistemological realism, is only a matter of the incomplete perspective (toward Being) of the consciousness holding the idea. Each of the three historic conceptions of Being outlined by Royce—Realism, Mysticism, and Critical Rationalism—represents just such a faulty orientation to reality, and an incomplete experience of Being. If the realist errs by maintaining a too rigid independence of idea from object, mysticism involves a too uncritical surrender to the presence of the other, and so too easily falls prey to the pitfalls of subjectivism. The critical rationalist shapes his conception of Being in terms of the principle of validity, whereby "ideas express with more or less precision, and in their own way, precisely that truth which is to be valid beyond them" (WI I 350). What is lacking in each of the three historic conceptions of Being is the spiritual element that Royce calls volition, in the point of view of the knowing consciousness. These three conceptions are brought into a unique synthesis in Royce's own Fourth Conception of Being. "What is [i.e., Being itself], is authoritative over against finite ideas, as Realism asserted, is one with the true meaning of the idea, as Mysticism insisted, and is valid as critical Rationalism demanded" (WI I 358).

The distinctive aspect of Royce's Fourth Conception of Being is his insistence on the purposive character of the ideas that know (i.e., relate us to) Being. "What is, presents the fulfilment of the whole purpose of the very idea that now seeks this Being" (WI I 358). For Royce, Being as such is a name for the conjunction of mind and reality in a "higher" point of view. The split between mind and reality is a result of a weak and unnecessarily circumscribed point of view that relies too heavily on the external meaning or representational aspect of ideas. In Royce's Fourth Conception of Being, also called constructive idealism, the purposive internal meaning of ideas drives the individual consciousness toward experiential contact with the other, and so finds the true meaning of Being itself.

The "whole problem of the nature of Being" (WI I 32) for Royce reduces to the question: "How is the internal meaning of ideas consistent with their apparently external meaning?" (WI I 32). He is led to the "idealistic thesis" that "the idea itself, as idea, as a fragment of life, as a conscious thrill, so to speak, of inner meaning . . . learns so to develop its internal meaning as to assign to itself just the specific purpose" (WI I 33). He finds either that "the external meaning is genuinely continuous with the internal meaning, and is inwardly involved in the latter, or else that the idea has no external meaning at all'' (WI I 33). If an idea merely represents something external to itself, it is incomplete, and finds completion only when it becomes united to the sources of affectional energy within consciousness and moves to actualize its inner intent.

Though Royce believes that Being itself is grasped only as "the genuine and final unity of internal and external meaning" (WI I 34) of ideas, he also holds that the "abstract sundering" of the two aspects of ideas is a necessary dialectical step toward that significant unity. Why? Because the separation of internal from external planes of experience is a fundamental step in the vertical direction, whereby consciousness becomes self-aware of its identity as consciousness. Development of an individual conscious point of view is necessary to the experiential process of moving to the higher point of view that alone brings us close to Being.

In the course of his definition of Being and the possible avenues to it, Royce presses his appeal to experience. To "face Being" is first of all to face the immediate data of experience. There is "no truth that is not an empirical truth, whatever further character it also possesses" (WI I 362). In the fulfillment of the intent embodied in the idea, the true nature of Being is realized. But this fulfillment of an idea "could not possibly take any form that was not also empirical. Neither God nor man faces any fact that has not about it something of the immediacy of a sense datum. That is for my conception [of Being] a logical necessity. For what finite ideas seek is expression, embodiment, life, presence. Experience then is real. Ay, but what experience" (WI I 362)?

The reality of experience is the only reality, yes, but what is the individual's orientation to experience? If the sense datum is the philosopher's paradigm of immediacy, it is also fraught with error and subjective delusion. Is there such a thing as a "higher" orientation that retains the characteristics of immediate experience? Probably the most creative aspect of Royce's philosophy is his answer to this question.

Toward a Solution

In his controversial lecture *The Conception of God* (1895), Royce presents an ingenious argument, not for the existence of a traditional God, conceived as a transcendent Person, but for an "absolute experience" or "divine point of view," correlated with the total context of reality. The consciousness of the moment, our actual empirical consciousness, appears to itself to be limited to the moment, and therefore fragmentary and incoherent. For limited as it is, it still perceives that there is a wider whole of possible experience beyond the limits of its finite sense perception and attention span. Consciousness continually senses its own ignorance as a frontier beyond which is a wider world than can at present be known. Finite experience is carried on largely within the parameters of physical sensation, and consciousness appears to itself as confined to the cognitive domain of the senses. Without making a spurious leap of faith, Royce undercuts what he believes to be the illusory bondage of consciousness to the physical senses, by an appeal to science. Our human experience is "determined by our peculiar organization," he argues.

> [T]he specific energies of our sensory nerves determine our whole experience of the physical world. . . . The physical fact beyond us never gets directly represented in our mental state; for between the physical fact and our experience of its presence lie the complex conditions that give our sensations their whole specific character. And what is true of our sensations is true of the rest of our experience. . . . this experience is our specific and mental way of responding to the stimulations which reality gives us. This whole specific way therefore represents, not the true nature of outer reality, so much as the current states of our own organisations [BW I 364].

At a given moment the individual may perceive his consciousness to be bound by the sensory stimulation that forms his immediate experience. But by the empirical sciences that "we men have wrought together upon the data of our senses, we have gradually woven a vast web of what we call relatively connected, united, or organised knowledge" (BW I 368). Despite the limitation or fragmentariness of the organization of individual consciousness, the achievements of modern science are a sign of the power of consciousness to transcend the limits it ordinarily places on itself.

Like Kant before him, Royce alludes to the Copernican reversal of astronomical perspectives as an example of the potential of consciousness to expand beyond the limits of the given.

> The sun seems to rise and set; but in reality the earth turns on its axis. Here the apparent movement of the sun is somewhat indirectly presented to a narrow sort of human experience. A wider experience, say an experience defined from an extra-terrestrial point of view, would have presented to it the earth's rotation as immediately as we now can get the sunrise presented to us [BW I 373].

The shift in perspectives that we call the Copernican revolution was, of course, initially accomplished on imaginative and theoretical grounds, without benefit of the technology (telescope) that would eventually help to confirm its empirical validity. Royce uses this example to suggest that in order to be known for what it is in itself, reality must be experienced from a perspective *wider* or, as he also says, *higher*, than that of the senses. Absolute reality, the ideal object of knowledge in modern science, implies a perspective unconditioned by cultural or subjectivistic biases. Just as false belief points by inversion to truth, so the boundaries of finite perspectives point us by constructive logic to an unbounded point of view.

"To conceive any human belief as false—say, the belief of a lunatic, a fanatic, a philosopher, or a theologian—is to conceive this opinion as either possibly or actually corrected from some higher point of view, to which a larger whole of experience is considered as present" (BW I 373). The very intuition of one's own ignorance and fallibility is then, according to Royce, a sign of the possibility of an expanded consciousness in which there is no gap between idea and fact, in which our conceptions find themselves actualized in experience.

Royce's method prescribes that the existence of this higher point of view be proved logically. But his logic is founded on the ability to conceive intuitively and in imagination what the actual experience of a higher point of view may be. Critics who lack that intuitive power, or who feel that the imaginative enterprise to which Royce invites us is impractical or merely speculative, are cut off from the experience at the outset. To say that a world of reality exists is to say that it is experienced. "All knowledge is of something experienced. . . . nothing actually exists save what is somewhere experienced" (BW I 382). Reality and experience, then, are "correlative conceptions." We never get outside reality; and so we never get outside experience. But within experience, consciousness can be oriented in different ways. If oriented solely to sense data, our consciousness is fragmentary and incomplete. But the very feeling of fragmentariness brings with it the intuition of a contrast with an experience that is unified and complete. The inward intuition of "an ideal organized experience" corresponds to the outward intuition of reality as a whole, a total organized system of facts as conceived theoretically by the scientist or by the layman, whose wholeness lies beyond the grasp of the finite senses and the consciousness that rests with sense data. That whole, or totality of facts, Royce calls *absolute reality*. If there is such an absolute reality, then, it must be "that which is present to an absolutely organised experience" (BW I 373). If we are to accept that a real world ultimately exists, in Royce's terms we must also accept the principle of "an absolute point of view" (BW I 383) capable of experiencing the full dimensions of reality.

The intuitive act of conceiving of such a higher perspective implies also the possibility of uniting the human consciousness with it. The mental growth that Royce projects as possible involves just such a uniting, not with an anthropomorphic God, but with an omniscient mind or Logos defined as an experiential perspective, necessary to the very existence of a real world. "To assert that there is any absolutely real fact indicated by our experience, is to regard this reality as presented to an absolutely organised experience, in which every fragment finds its place" (BW I 380). For a "final reality" to exist, there must be a "final experience" (BW I 380) corresponding to it. This universal perspective is the "divine point of view" (BW I 383) that Royce's philosophy attempts to make accessible experientially to the reader.

INTERPRETATION AS KNOWING

The empirical basis of Royce's vision of organized experience is clarified partly by the fact that he attributes such organization to "a social origin" (BW I 374). Royce saw in the institution of modern science, with its strict criterion of public verifiability, a model for his idea of the social origin of organized experience. This idea, which appears in embryo in *The Conception of God*, is more fully developed in *The Problem of Christianity* (1913), a work completed toward the end of Royce's life which many regard as his crowning achievement. In this work, Royce is still seeking the experiential meaning of higher consciousness or a higher point of view. But here his study of the social dimension of consciousness brings him to an innovative conception of the cognitive process, a conception that evolved under the influence of Charles Peirce's theory of signs.

The history of philosophy, in Royce's reading of it, is dominated by a contrast between two kinds of cognitive processes, called respectively perception and conception.[19] These terms are names for the primary functions of consciousness as defined in the modern Western philosophic tradition. Perception is classically the field of empiricism; conception, the field of rationalism. Reaching beyond the limits of both traditions, Royce believed he had discovered a third type of cognitive process, one that is so pervasive a part of our conscious life, including the consciousness we share with others in every kind of social intercourse, that we barely notice its presence. That process he called *interpretation*.

Consciousness may be occupied with external perceptions originating from the five senses, with reflection on those perceptions, or with abstract concepts as in mathematics or in the type of reasoning represented by Descartes's meditation on his ball of wax. Descartes claimed he had conceptual access to the essential properties of the ball of wax, regardless of its sensory characteristics. The empiricists who followed him reasoned that the only cognitive access to objects in the world was through the senses. But Royce was impelled not just toward cognition, but more importantly to understand the *meaning* of cognitions. This impulse led him to intuit the limitation of the dualistic paradigm of consciousness in both the empiricist and the rationalist positions. Interpretation is a name for that drive toward meaning. In *The Problem of Christianity* the idea of interpretation, which has an inevitable social aspect, is presented as a ground-breaking discovery that would penetrate beyond the static subject–object schema held by both rationalists and empiricists. His third form of cognitive process is neither perception nor conception, and cannot be described as a synthesis of the two. It can best be understood as the power of consciousness to go to higher ground, where the dichotomy no longer exists and the data of consciousness, whether perceptual or conceptual, are understood in terms of the category of meaning. The functions called perception and conception represent consciousness in a horizontal plane. Their products are mere data. But when consciousness exercises its ability to move into the vertical dimension, the data are lit up; they become means of passage from one stage or level of experience to another. "In our inner life it not infrequently happens that we have—like the traveller, or like Hamlet in the ghost-scene, or like Macbeth when there comes the knocking on the gate—to pass a boundary, to cross into some new realm, not merely of experience, but of desire, of hope, or of resolve" (PC 285). The process of passing a boundary of consciousness is essential to Royce's conception of meaning, which involves the awareness of order and continuity between different phases of experience. Meaning does not demand more data, but involves a "dramatic transformation" of the data already present in consciousness. Royce seeks to define the conditions in which consciousness passes the "great boundaries of the spiritual world" (PC 284), the moments of experience in which truth is disclosed, or in which consciousness is wakened to new energies and moves creatively beyond its normative or habitual states. A philosophy that counsels us to seek the solution of problems in terms of either perception or conception alone is simply inadequate, for it remains chained to an image of a noninteractive self—a structure of belief that may bear little resemblance to the dynamic contexts of our social experience. In his idea of interpretation, generated under the inspiration of Charles Peirce, Royce believed he had found a long-eclipsed key to the social implications of meaning and to the nature of consciousness.

PEIRCE'S CATEGORIES AND THE THEORY OF SIGNS

Peirce too had early shown dissatisfaction with the Cartesian dualism of subject and object, as well as with the Cartesian teaching that "the ultimate test of certainty is to be found in the individual consciousness."[20] This dissatisfaction led him to his idea of a community of knowledge, based on the premise that consciousness always works by signs. From the axiom that all phenomena of experience are signs he concluded that all things possess and communicate meaning. Seeking his own way out of the subjectivism of the Cartesian position, Peirce developed a phenomenology of experience culminating in the theory of signs and meaning that Royce took as a starting point for his theory of interpretation. It is the business of phenomenology, wrote Peirce, "to unravel the tangled skein [of] all that in any sense appears . . . ; or in other words, to make the ultimate analysis of all experiences the first task to which philosophy has to apply itself" (CP 1.280).

For Kant, the categories of the understanding provide the structure needed for consciousness to perceive, conceive, and make order out of what is given to it in sensory experience. Because, for example, the mind possesses the categories of unity, plurality, and causality, it is able to perceive oneness, diversity, and causation in the things of experience. In making his own ultimate analysis of experience, Peirce sought to go behind the conceptual and subjectivistic bias of the Kantian categories. "What I undertook to do was to go back to experience, in the sense of whatever we have forced upon our minds" (CP 1.337). While Kant maintained that the categories of understanding were internal properties of consciousness, existing prior to sense experience, Peirce's effort to return to the ground of experience—especially as expressed in his essay "On a New List of Categories" (1867)—involved a revolutionary redefinition of experience itself, in nonsubjective terms. Though Kant had distinguished twelve categories of understanding, Peirce identified but three universal categories that would in his view account for all the phenomena of experience. He called these categories Firstness, Secondness, and Thirdness, the very conceptual neutrality of the names stressing his desire to articulate the primal qualities of experience, without the imposition of a secondary conceptualization process on them.

Peirce's categories represent a radical attempt (as Wallace Stevens put it in another context) to name that which "never could be named."[21] That something is neither the substantive objects of rational analysis nor a self treated as an object of such analysis, but the "raw diffuse matrix"[22] of experience. To Peirce experience was not a matter of subjective perception within an internal center of consciousness. "We perceive objects brought before us; but that which we especially experience—the kind of thing to which the word 'experience' is more particularly applied—is an event. We cannot accurately be said to perceive events . . ." (CP 1.336).

The category of Firstness implies the bare qualitative immediacy of experience, apart from any conceptualization, and prior to the aesthetic or cognitive "distancing" of a world of objects that characterizes reflective consciousness. Firstness is the undifferentiated awareness of a "realm," or sensory field—the form of consciousness often attributed to primitive man—before reflective consciousness distinguishes a self from a world of facts. Firstness implies human awareness, but may also suggest the type of awareness that an animal experiences in its environment. The animal, we presume, knows no totality of facts, has no "world view" or cosmic perspective. The relation between consciousness and environment implied by Firstness is like the immediate relation between a fruit and its skin. "The origin of things, considered not as leading to anything, but in itself, contains the idea of First . . ." (CP 6.32). "*Originality* is being such as that being is, regardless of aught else" (CP 2.89). Of course the phenomenological description of Firstness is necessarily a conceptual act, standing apart from the primitive matrix of experience. But this act, for Peirce,

nevertheless voluntarily subordinates itself to the experiential phenomenon. "The idea of First is predominant in the ideas of freshness, life,
freedom" (CP 1.302). Firstness is something that

> cannot be articulately thought: assert it, and it has already lost its character-
> istic innocence; for assertion always implies a denial of something else. Stop
> to think of it, and it has flown! What the world was to Adam on the day he
> opened his eyes to it, before he had drawn any distinctions, or had become
> conscious of his own existence—that is first, present, immediate, fresh, new,
> initiative, original, spontaneous, free, vivid, conscious, and evanescent. Only,
> remember that every description of it must be false to it [CP 1.357].

Peirce's need to get back to experience is initially a matter of breaking
free from the magnetic influence of conceptualization, and of recontacting
that raw quality of Firstness. In apprehending Firstness we are not
concerned with the interaction either between things or between consciousness and world. We are not concerned with reflective thought at all,
but with the simple qualitative experience of things in themselves. Through
the apprehension of Firstness, Peirce made the claim that his philosophy
was "instantly fatal" (CP 8.13)[23] to the Kantian idea of a thing in itself
independent of all knowing and all experience. There is nothing absolutely
unknowable. The notion of an unknowable noumenon, forever divorced
from phenomenal experience, is a product of abstract conceptual analysis
that has lost touch with the actuality of Firstness—the actuality of the
primal matrix of experience.

While conceptual analysis may have a tendency to forfeit the apprehension of qualitative immediacy, the sensibility of the poet often involves a
gift of responsiveness to the qualities of Firstness. Wallace Stevens is one
such poet who not only is responsive to the bare experiential quality of
Firstness, but has an extraordinary ability to articulate his phenomenological awareness. For the Stevens of *Notes Toward a Supreme Fiction* "the
celestial ennui of apartments . . . sends us back to the first idea."[24]
Stevens's "first idea" bears a generic resemblance to Peirce's category of
Firstness. The "first idea" is a matter of "the ravishments of truth" to
Stevens. The "first idea becomes / The hermit in a poet's metaphors."[25]
Firstness in Peirce's phenomenology is pure consciousness, like that of
the hermit, unencumbered by cultural constructs. Only *after* the experience of Firstness are we able to consider the meaning or use of objects in
our experience.

The concept of "reality" or the domain of fact involves the category of
Secondness. "The reality of things consists in their persistent forcing
themselves upon our recognition" (CP 1.175). Secondness implies what
Martin Buber calls "the primal setting at a distance."[26] It is the condition
in which consciousness finds itself set over against things and other minds

in its environment, and feels the sense of external relation and conflict. The quality of Secondness is captured eloquently in Stevens's lines

> Soldier, there is a war between the mind
> And sky, between thought and day and night.[27]

Confrontation between consciousness and the other, between self and not-self, is the predicament of modernity, the legacy of Cartesian culture and its dualistic epistemological paradigm. It is the predicament of a self-aware mind that has acknowledged its own reality principle. "In the idea of reality," Peirce writes, "Secondness is predominant; for the real is that which insists upon forcing its way to recognition as something *other* than the mind's creation" (CP 1.325). The real, in one scholar's words, "is what demands our attention, and on more than one occasion Peirce interpreted the human phenomenon of *willing* as our response to the insistence of what stands over against us."[28] Secondness involves "*Reaction* as an element of the Phenomenon" (CP 5.66). Another scholar writes "Firstness is absolutely simple, whereas secondness exhibits a degree of complication. This complication consists in the opposition of a second subject to the quality of a first subject."[29] If experience were only made up of Secondness, we should be submerged in conflict, or at best in mechanical interaction with an alien and always potentially hostile world of fact. Within the dimension of Secondness alone, the only possibility for meaning is by artificially or imaginatively importing a sense of transcendence—as by a *deus ex machina*—into the raw interactions of the experiential field.

With the category of Thirdness, Peirce's phenomenology enters the vertical dimension, but without abandoning the qualities of immediacy and stubborn empirical reality of the first two categories. Under the category of Thirdness we find continuity, the operation of signs, not mere fact but "laws of fact" (CP 1.483), and meaning. "Continuity represents Thirdness almost to perfection" (CP 1.337), writes Peirce. If the meaning of one phase of experience is its continuity or relatedness to other phases of experience, Thirdness is exemplified by the appearance of meaning to consciousness, and the actualization of meaning necessarily involves a social context in which one individual is interpreting signs to another or others, generating a community of knowing. The perception of relationships between things is Thirdness. Thirdness brings Firstness and Secondness into unity, and endows "the sensuous, reactant world man encounters in experience with meaning and intelligibility" (CP 1.344). To acknowledge the reality of Thirdness as a universal category implies the underlying principle that all the phenomena of experience are signs. Since the existence of a sign designates a meaning, the reality of Thirdness establishes the actuality of meaning for Peirce. "If the sceptics think that any account can be given of the phenomena of the universe while they leave Meaning out of account, by all means let them go ahead and try to do it" (CP

1.344). In Peirce's view meaning is inherent in the structures of experience, not artificially brought into experience from supernatural, conceptual, or subjective sources. Thirdness is a primal quality of thought that involves the empirical apprehension of transcendent meanings.

The three categories describe the way experience happens. Firstness represent bare qualitative immediacy of awareness, and Secondness is concerned with the way things (and individual minds) impinge upon one another in the natural and social environments. These categories are incomplete without Thirdness, which like Dewey's idea of "transaction" accounts for the way the experiential interaction is brought to completeness, acknowledging the dimension of meaning and the reality of completed relations between individuals in a community of experience.

Beyond the Dichotomy of Percept and Concept

In his search for the "creative insight" (PC 307) that would elevate consciousness to a level of understanding above mere perception or conception, Royce incorporated a version of Peirce's doctrine of signs—one aspect of the category of Thirdness—into his theory of interpretation. "[W]henever we think," wrote Peirce in one of the essays cited by Royce as a source for *The Problem of Christianity*, "we have present to the consciousness some feeling, image, conception, or other representation, which serves as a sign" (CP 5.283). Moreover, "everything which is present to us is a phenomenal manifestation of ourselves. This does not prevent its being a phenomenon of something without us, just as a rainbow is at once a manifestation both of the sun and of the rain. When we think, then, we ourselves, as we are at that moment, appear as a sign" (CP 5.283). Hence all thought, as well as all experience—"everything which is present to us"—has the characteristics of a sign. The person herself is a sign, pointing to a meaning beyond the self.

From Peirce's complex semiotic theory Royce distilled a generic conception of signs, which he put to his own purpose of defining the principles of interpretation, particularly as they pertain to the social context of human relations. Both Royce and Peirce attempted to articulate the process of coming into the presence of the inner life of others in a community. While Firstness and Secondness failed to attain this end, Peirce claimed that "Sympathy, flesh and blood, that by which I feel my neighbor's feelings, is third" (CP 1.337). Similarly, for Royce, while perception and conception were both inadequate to gain knowledge of the "inner life of our fellow men," he found one cognitive process able to accomplish this end, and that was interpretation.

The sign-situation or the meaning situation, according to Peirce, has a triadic structure. As reconstructed by Royce, it involves an object that serves as sign-function (such as the words of a text), an interpreter (or interpretant), and one to whom the interpretation is addressed. The vehicle by which meaning is carried is a sign (or symbol). In an alternate way of stating the issue, "For a symbol to function as such there must always be three factors present, the symbol itself, its object (i.e., what it denotes or signifies), and an interpretant. Where these obtain, the symbol possesses a meaning. It appears, then, that this form of Thirdness is irreducibly triadic."[30] From either way of looking at the problem of signification, Royce drew the conclusion that the fundamental structure of all experience is triadic. The elements of the triad may exist within a single human consciousness, as in the act of interpreting my own idea to myself. More typically, according to Royce, consciousness is engaged in social encounters between individuals in a community of interpretation, and between persons and objective facts. The sign-character of experience suggests that life is a matter of a perpetual conversation, in which consciousness strives to articulate the meaning of objects and events either to itself or to others. The pervasive human disposition to interpret things as having meanings is an indication of the fact—apparent to both Royce and Peirce—that all the objects and events of experience have sign-values. They may be treated merely from a standpoint of Secondness, or inert conceptualization, a standpoint that remains inwardly blind to the dimension of meaning in things. Yet the "higher" dimension of meaning is invariably present in any situation. In human society the sign-function is found chiefly in the use of language, though every human being, every thing, and every thought, can be considered a sign, pointing beyond itself to something else, called its meaning. From a strictly naturalistic or behavioral viewpoint, the sign may be regarded only as a stimulus—under Peirce's category of Secondness—provoking a mechanical or chemical response in the perceiver. Yet the sign characteristic of experience when understood from the standpoint of Thirdness always entails something that transcends naturalism. "Five minutes of our waking life will hardly pass," writes Peirce, "without our making some kind of prediction; and in the majority of cases these predictions are fulfilled in the event" (CP 1.26). No phenomenon of our conscious life is totally isolated or merely in mechanical interaction with other facts. Everything is connected by patterns of prediction or presentiment and fulfillment (i.e., meaning). Future events—a conception which transcends both the monadic sensuous immediacy of Firstness and the dyadic interactions of Secondness—"are in a measure really governed by a law" (CP 1.26). That law, which Peirce names "continuity," gives meaning to events. It is the heart of Thirdness, the law of interconnectedness of all things, bound up intimately with the sign-process of experience.

In *The Thought of C. S. Peirce* Thomas Goudge argues that Peirce's temperament "harbored a conflict which exhibits itself philosophically in the espousal of two incompatible sets of premises for his thought. One of these is his naturalism [which took the form of his scientific logic]; the other is his transcendentalism"[31] (which found expression in his appeal to sentiment and meaning). What Goudge perceives as a conflict is likely to turn out on further analysis to be a creative struggle toward a postmodern outlook that overcomes the traditional dichotomy between the transcendental and the empirical (or naturalistic) perspectives. Peirce's doctrine of signs, which starts from empirical observation of objects, and insists on the necessity of meaning, beyond bare perceptual data, is evidence of at least partial success in the quest for the actuality of the transcendent. Because of the reality of Thirdness, empirical data are always translatable into something beyond themselves, and so inherently partake of a transcendent character.

In a similar vein, Royce claims that the interpretive process "transcends both perception and conception" (PC 295) yet "touches the heart of reality" (PC 295). Interpretation is a "new act" of consciousness, which "consists in the invention or discovery of some third idea, distinct from both the ideas which are to be compared." This third idea takes "one of the ideas which are the objects of the comparison, and interprets it to the other, or in the light of the other" (PC 304). The reader may relate dyadically to a literary text and so—implicitly "comparing" his own ideas to those revealed in the text—take the latter in as mere information or data. But the discovery of a third interpreting idea (drawn perhaps from philosophy), or the invention of such an idea directly out of the encounter with the text, changes the character of the meaning situation from one of passivity to one of active engagement and potential growth for the reader. The third idea not only allows us to interpret its object—whether a text or our neighbor's mind—but also gives us a new self-awareness. It "shows us, as far as it goes, ourselves, and also creates in us a new grade of clearness regarding what we are and what we mean. . . . it also enriches our world of self-consciousness. It at once broadens our outlook and gives our mental realm definiteness and self-control. It teaches one of our ideas what another of our ideas means" (PC 305). The insight given by such a third idea, manifested only in what we have called the vertical dimension of consciousness, "looks down upon ideas as from above, . . . thereby uniting what was formerly estranged" (PC 307).

Interpreting the symbols constituting a literary text in the way given in Royce's theory is an act of participating in the experience of its meaning— entering the dimension of Thirdness. Participation, in this sense, has existential consequences. An experience of the text that takes on the intensity and reality of participation—entering into transactional relation with its symbols—generates a meaning event that transcends the reader's ordinary perceptual horizons and so has potential to transform his consciousness.[32]

Interpreting poetic texts on the basis of philosophic ideas illustrates the triadic structure of all interpretation as outlined by Royce. The individual is always confronted with a choice between a dyadic and a triadic orientation to any fact, whether it is a text, a molecule, or a neighbor. But triadic interpretation, as in the discovery or invention of a philosophical idea to interpret a text, has a peculiar power to extend consciousness. The idea of consciousness itself as explored in this book is an example of what Royce calls a third idea. Such an idea gives the reader a perspective that enables him not just to respond interactively to the text, but also to perceive the symbols, structure, and point of view in the text from a constructive standpoint, to interpret by entering into the meaning of the text, and in effect to become that meaning.

NOTES

1. John Clendenning, *The Life and Thought of Josiah Royce* (Madison: University of Wisconsin Press, 1985).

2. Bruce Kuklick, *The Rise of American Philosophy: Cambridge, Massachusetts, 1860–1930* (New Haven: Yale University Press, 1977), p. 142. See also chap. 8, "Royce and the Argument for the Absolute, 1875–1892," pp. 140–58, and chaps. 14–16, pp. 259–314.

3. Kulick, in ibid., pp. 140–58, 275–90, 370–411, tends to minimize Royce's empiricism, while Hocking stresses it in his "On Royce's Empiricism," *The Journal of Philosophy*, 53 (1956), 57–63. Royce is of course most frequently treated as an idealist in the classic mold, with little or no reference to his empirical instincts. For an excellent critical appraisal of Royce's roots in German idealism, see Peter Fuss, "Royce on the Concept of the Self: An Historical and Critical Perspective," in *American Philosophy from Edwards to Quine*, edd. Robert W. Shahan and Kenneth R. Merrill (Norman: University of Oklahoma Press, 1977), pp. 111–47.

4. *The Basic Writings of Josiah Royce*, ed. John J. McDermott, 2 vols. (Chicago: The University of Chicago Press, 1969), I 375; hereafter cited as BW.

5. John E. Smith, *Themes in American Philosophy: Purpose, Experience, and Community* (New York: Harper & Row, 1970), p. 4.

6. Introduction to BW I, p. 11.

7. Paul Tillich, "Religion as a Dimension in Man's Spiritual Life," in *Man's Right to Knowledge*, ed. Herbert Muschel (New York: Columbia University Press, 1954), p. 184.

8. *Discourse on Thinking*, trans. John Anderson and E. Hans Freund (New York: Harper & Row, 1966), p. 45.

9. *Royce's Metaphysics*, trans. Virginia Ringer and Gordon Ringer (Chicago: Regnery, 1956), p. xii.

10. See also Heidegger's "What is Metaphysics?" *Basic Writings from* BEING AND TIME *(1927) to* THE TASK OF THINKING *(1964)*, ed. David Farrell Krell (New York: Harper & Row, 1977), pp. 91–112.

11. Marcel, *Royce's Metaphysics*, p. 3.

12. Ibid.

13. Ibid., p. 4.

14. Royce, *The World and the Individual* (New York: Dover, 1959), p. 16 (hereafter cited as WI).

15. *Royce's Metaphysics*, p. 3.

16. Ibid.

17. See Buber's *I and Thou*.

18. *Treatise on Religious Affections*, ed. John E. Smith, The Works of Jonathan Edwards 2 (New Haven: Yale University Press, 1959), p. 205.

19. *The Problem of Christianity* (Chicago: The University of Chicago Press, 1968), p. 277; hereafter cited as PC.

20. *Collected Papers of Charles Sanders Peirce*, edd. Charles Hartshorne, Paul Weiss, and Arthur Burks, 8 vols. (Cambridge: The Belknap Press of Harvard University Press, 1931–1958), 5.264; hereafter cited as CP, with references to volume and paragraph. On Royce's relationship to Peirce, see James Harry Cotton, *Royce on the Human Self* (New York: Greenwood, 1968), chap. 6, "Royce, James, and Peirce," pp. 190–237; John E. Smith, *Royce's Social Infinite* (New York: Liberal Arts Press, 1950), chap. 2, "The Background: Peirce's Thought and the Philosophy of Loyalty," pp. 11–63; and Kuklick, *Rise of American Philosophy*, pp. 388–93.

21. *The Collected Poems of Wallace Stevens* (New York: Knopf, 1967), p. 381.

22. Anton Ehrenzweig, "The Hidden Order of Art," *British Journal of Aesthetics*, 1 (1961), 1323.

23. See Kuklick, *Rise of American Philosophy*, p. 112.

24. *Collected Poems*, p. 381.

25. Ibid.

26. "Distance and Relation," *The Knowledge of Man: A Philosophy of the Interhuman*, trans. Maurice Friedman and Ronald Gregor Smith (New York: Harper & Row, 1965), pp. 59–71.

27. *Collected Poems*, p. 407

28. John E. Smith, "Community and Reality," in *Perspectives on Peirce*, ed. Richard J. Bernstein (New Haven: Yale University Press, 1965), p. 96.

29. James K. Feibleman, *An Introduction to the Philosophy of Charles S. Peirce* (Cambridge: The MIT Press, 1969), p. 164.

30. Thomas A. Goudge, *The Thought of C. S. Peirce* (New York: Dover, 1969), p. 92.

31. Ibid., p. 5.

32. See Robert S. Corrington, *The Community of Interpreters: On the Hermeneutics of Nature and the Bible in the American Philosophical Tradition* (Macon, Ga.: Mercer University Press, 1987), esp. chap. 1, "The Origins of American Hermeneutics: C. S. Peirce and Josiah Royce," pp. 1–29.

2

Beyond Modern Subjectivism: T. S. Eliot and American Philosophy

EGO-SUBJECTIVITY AND BEYOND

THOUGH SCHOLARS HAVE INTERPRETED the thought and art of T. S. Eliot through critical lenses borrowed from European and Eastern philosophies—including those of Bradley, Bergson, Plato, the Bhagavad Gita, etc.—many significant links between Eliot and the American philosophic tradition have been left relatively unexplored.[1] Yet Eliot's poetry and the development of his ideas can be studied profitably in relation to the expositions of consciousness and experience found in American philosophy. The basic conceptions of man implicit in Eliot's poetry underwent a process of evolution between about 1915 and 1943. Many of Eliot's early poems portray man as locked inside a private and finite psyche. But looking at his development as a whole, we see that Eliot moved steadily toward a new image of man as able to think and act from an enlarged standpoint, outside the cramped arena of finite subjectivity. "The Love Song of J. Alfred Prufrock" (1915), his first major poem, is an ironic and humorous expression of the idea that consciousness may be trapped within the limits of a personal ego. The image of self-consciousness in the poem is a literary descendant of Descartes's solitary "I-think." At the end of his poetic journey, in *Four Quartets* (1943), Eliot arrived at a redefinition of the self, superseding the traditional Cartesian image of an autonomous but finite personal consciousness. In this late masterpiece he defined an enlarged perceptual standpoint in accord with the Christian/Greek concept of Logos, a principle that lends order and meaning to ordinary human experience. This pattern of growth—a move beyond the subjectivism typical of modernity—shows some striking parallels to the work of the American philosophers Josiah Royce, William James, and William Ernest Hocking.

Eliot's years as a student at Harvard, from 1906 to 1914, were in fact concurrent with the germination of revolutionary new ideas about the nature of consciousness and experience in American philosophy in that same Harvard environment. Two of the major figures active in the extraordinary Harvard philosophy department of this period were James and Royce. However diverse their methods, these thinkers were united in a struggle to win freedom from the premises of Cartesian subjectivism, which had been the glory, but also what Royce called the "scandal," of modernity.[2] As a graduate student in philosophy Eliot may well have imbibed intellectual and spiritual seeds that would germinate later in his poetry, from participating in this creative climate of thought, including his year-long seminar with Royce.[3] This hypothesis, I would argue, could make stronger claims on the imagination of scholars and students of Eliot's work. For despite obvious differences in temperament and outlook between Eliot and the philosophers, as a Harvard graduate student he did have a significant bond with some of them, and their works present interpreting ideas that enable us to explore more precisely the structures of Eliot's poetry and the evolution of his conception of consciousness. These ideas can incidentally help us to experience and enjoy Eliot's difficult poetry more fully than if we remained unacquainted with the philosophers.

Grounded as they were in the principle of experience, James, Royce, and Hocking all made claims that consciousness cannot be circumscribed within the bounds set for it by modern philosophic tradition since Descartes, a tradition that characteristically views man as an immaterial perceiving subject, trapped in a world of extension. Each of them in his own way pushes the definition of consciousness outside the framework of the closed cognitive and perceiving subject that they had inherited from Descartes, and into the open field of experience. This post-Cartesian disposition of their thought indicates a basic affinity with Eliot's. James's denial that "consciousness" exists signals the anti-subjectivist tendency of his later philosophy. For he sees consciousness as a form of action and relation, rather than an entity—as a zone of experience where "fact comes to light," not a Cartesian "soul substance" set over against physical substance.[4] Hocking discovers an empirical solution to the problem of solipsism in the idea of intersubjective awareness. And Royce finds that at higher levels of mental development experience becomes "absolute experience," and so expands beyond the limits of its apparent subjective finitude.

THE COMIC SOLIPSIST AND THE POETRY OF EXPERIENCE

In his self-imposed exile cross the Atlantic, Eliot, like the American philosophers, was moved by a parallel desire to disclose the actual struc-

tures of experience, in his poetry. To use an exact term invented by Robert
Langbaum, Eliot's work exemplifies the idea of the "poetry of experience."[5] But Eliot seeks in his poetry to move beyond the boundaries
placed on experience by long-standing conventions. Hence the definitions
of experience implicit in his work change over the years, along with his
expanding conception of consciousness and its possibilities.

The distinctive mark of Eliot's poetry is its experimentalism. One
implication of experiment in art—as in the action painting of Jackson
Pollock, for instance—is that the artwork is a reflection of the immediate
rhythms and unfoldings of experience. It is not an expression of pre-
established ideas. The term poetry of experience as used by Langbaum
and as we may apply it to Eliot's poetry suggests something about the
empirical—or more accurately, experiential—attitudes embodied in it. The
poet strives to express what can be and is experienced, whatever can be
sensed as immediate data of consciousness. Since Eliot perceived experience as a fluid evolving process, the conception of experience implicit in
his poetry was also subject to evolution. And his poetry became, in the
words borrowed from him for the title of this book, an exercise that probes
the "frontiers of consciousness."[6] The content of his dramatic mono-
logues—"The Love Song," "The Journey of the Magi," "Portrait of a
Lady"—is precisely a speaker's intensely conscious response to a problematic situation that he is actually living through (or has recently passed
through) at the moment of speaking. Such poems document a live thinking
process and a unique point of view that we as readers are invited, for the
duration of the poem, to share. By its exclusion of either authorial
commentary or the competing perspectives found in dialogue, the poetry
of experience has an extraordinary power. As suggested by Langbaum, it
is a power to unite the reader's perspective with that of the speaker of the
poem. So the poem becomes an experience for us, in the specific sense
that we are made to share the immediate experiential perspective of the
speaker.

Though any literary text has some such power to involve the mind of
the reader at levels deeper than a simple rational assimilation of subject
matter, the poetry of experience guides the reader in a peculiarly forceful
way to reorganize his perceptions, in conformity with the poem's single
dominant point of view. We are moved, as Conrad once said, by "the
power of the written word" in the poem to hear, to feel, and to see
differently than if we had never encountered the poem.[7] We are placed not
as observers but within the speaker's very experiential standpoint. The
poem then becomes something more than an object to be taken in intellectually. It becomes an encounter with the mind of the poet, and with the
creative process symbolized indirectly by the text. By this encounter,
through the alchemy of art, our consciousness is changed in the direction

of growth beyond the finitude of our own patterns of awareness. When Prufrock describes the London evening as "spread out against the sky / Like a patient etherized upon a table,"[8] the text, partly by its pure adherence to a single perspective, demands our participation in that specific way of seeing. The nonlinear form in *The Waste Land* works on us to break down the less creative linear habits of thinking that we have inherited from modern rationalistic culture. And when the "speaker" of the *Quartets* announces his vision of the "still point of the turning world," his metaphor in its context invites us too into the possibility of experiencing his discovery of a new form of spiritual consciousness.

The unique standpoint presented in "The Love Song" is that of the self-enclosed psyche. The character of Alfred Prufrock is both charming and comic, when we come to know him. But the poem displays the nightmarish irony of being trapped inside one's own head, sensing only one's own feelings, limitations, doubts, embarrassments, etc., and having little intuition of the genuine presence—or, as Royce would say, the inner meaning—of the other. Through reading the poem we come to sense, and not just to understand abstractly, what it feels like to be a solipsist. The poem gives concrete life to the concept of the "finite centre," discussed by Eliot in his doctoral dissertation on F. H. Bradley and in other philosophical essays written between 1911 and 1916. The term "finite centre," which he borrowed from Bradley, is Eliot's name for the "problem" of solipsism, one of the logical consequences of the subjectivist orientation bequeathed to the modern era by Descartes. In his essay on Bradley and Leibniz, for example, Eliot explains that "a finite centre is a universe in itself."[9] This statement helps us to grasp the thinking that lies behind Alfred's question:

> Do I dare
> Disturb the universe?

How indeed can the self-imprisoned ego "disturb" or otherwise genuinely touch a "universe" of fact, or others, outside itself? The subjectivist premise, pushed to its extremity, renders such an act impossible. Having entered an artificial realm where the psychic fact is the only fact, Alfred struggles in vain to consummate some real relation with others in his environment. Yet at every stage he is thwarted by the intrusion of a hyper–self-consciousness:

> And should I then presume?
> And how should I begin?

The mind of the comic solipsist, who grows old and wears the bottoms of his trousers rolled, is a closed system, capable of taking in sense data from the external world, but only after it has been filtered and translated into the presuppositions of an excessively private psyche. And as the final lines of the poem suggest, the inevitable outcome of an experience oriented

to such radical subjectivity is a kind of "drowning," a deeper immersion
in the dream of a world composed entirely of private sensation. From such
a world there is little hope of escape, even when "human voices" (the call
of actuality, as opposed to the fantasy of the mermaids' song) threaten to
"wake" the dreamer.

THROUGH *The Waste Land*—PASSING BEYOND MODERNITY

The pivotal and perhaps most stunning experimental work of Eliot's career
is *The Waste Land* (1922). In this great, misunderstood classic of modernist
poetry, Eliot was still preoccupied to a degree by the problem of the
imprisoned psyche. The poem represents a moment of deep personal crisis
for Eliot, as well as his perception of a momentous crisis of values in
Western culture, following the spiritual upheaval of the First World War.[10]
The poem is dark, yet comic. Like "The Love Song," it is a cry for
awareness of the alienation of the self from others and the consequent
sense of meaninglessness characteristic of the modern era. Yet it also
displays a poet's intuition that the finite center, presumed to be the basic
condition of experience in this era, is itself an illusion. From this basic
intuition, the destruction or disappearance of the self in its alienated
modern incarnation, he can begin building a new sense of man's experiential standpoint, on a broader basis. If it is true, as suggested by Langbaum,
that *The Waste Land* embodies the principles of the poetry of experience,
but extends its structural possibilities far beyond their traditional limits,[11]
we ought to ask: What is the underlying conception of the structure of
experience implicit in the poem? If there is a central consciousness in the
poem, like a speaker in a dramatic monologue, what is the nature and form
of that consciousness?

The question as to the protagonist's identity has rarely been confronted
in a way that accounts adequately for the poem's structural complexity. It
has often been suggested that the protagonist is identical to the Fisher
King borrowed from ancient North European myth. A first-person narrator
who once speaks of "fishing in the dull canal" (CPP 67) says later:

> I sat upon the shore
> Fishing, with the arid plain behind me
> Shall I at least set my lands in order [CPP 74]?

Our natural disposition (bolstered by Eliot's notes) to regard this speaker
as a modern Fisher King, and indeed to conceive of him as a single
personality, is disrupted in this context: first by Prince Ferdinand's lament
for his father's death (borrowed directly from Shakespeare's *The Tempest*),
then by interwoven allusions to poems by Marvell, Day, Verlaine, and
others. And soon after the scene of the speaker's fishing in the dull canal,
we meet the enigmatic figure of Tiresias:

I Tiresias, though blind, throbbing between two lives,
Old man with wrinkled female breasts, can see
At the violet hour, the evening hour that strives
Homeward, and brings the sailor home from sea,
The typist home at teatime, clears her breakfast, lights
Her stove, and lays out food in tins [CPP 68].

Both Ferdinand and the Fisher King, like Tiresias in this passage, speak in the first person, so that their distinct identities seem unmistakable. Yet their disparate voices and angles of vision are juxtaposed sharply, as in a collage, without the expected narrative transitions. This structural method, familiar to all readers of *The Waste Land*, typifies the organization of the poem as a whole. The number of "I's" and other first person references proliferates in such a way that the sense of exact distinction between one "I" and another eventually breaks down. In one of his notes to the poem, Eliot calls Tiresias the "most important personage in the poem." He then claims, paradoxically, that although Tiresias is "not indeed a 'character,' " he "unites" all the other characters in the work. The one-eyed merchant "melts into" the Phoenician Sailor, who in turn is "not wholly distinct from" Ferdinand, Prince of Naples. Moreover "all women are one woman, and the two sexes meet in Tiresias" (CPP 78).

What are we to make of this explanatory note? The notion of the "melting" of one character (or perspective) into another will at first seem highly contradictory to the expectations of literary realism established in other portions of the poem. But the idea of intersubjective awareness—the interrelating of two or more centers of consciousness—helps to resolve the enigma of Eliot's notes, as well as the problem of the dramatic point of view in the poem. This idea, as expressed by Hocking, helps us to understand the phenomenon of the coalescence of individual perspectives, from experiential premises that do not violate the principles of literary realism.

Finding the " 'blind gate of sensation' " to be an inadequate way of accounting for the transference of meaning from one individual to another, Hocking claims that " 'something like a direct participation of mind in mind is a primary datum of experience.' "[12] Tiresias is the one "personage" in *The Waste Land* equipped for the "participation of mind in mind" that must characterize the speaker of such a multi-dimensional "monologue." If the poem indeed dramatizes an individual's experience, the experiential standpoint at its center is a radically intersubjective one. It is the standpoint of one who grasps the inner perspectives of others as a "primary datum" of his own experience. Just such an explicit meshing of points of view occurs early in the poem. When the typist is waiting alone in her flat for "the young man carbuncular," the speaker exclaims:

> I Tiresias, old man with wrinkled dugs
> Perceived the scene, and foretold the rest—
> I too awaited the expected guest [CPP 68].

Clearly, the "I" here is not a conventional subjective ego, but the self-identification of an enlarged frame of perspective reference, incorporating both male and female principles.

According to the myth upon which Eliot relies, Tiresias embodies more than a simple one-dimensional psyche. Not only is he both male and female, but though physically blind he possesses the divine gift of "second sight"—prophecy, or vision beyond the finite senses. "What Tiresias *sees* is the substance of the poem" (CPP 78), Eliot tells us further in his notes. Tiresias's multi-perspectival seeing, captured in the intricate network of signs, allusions, and points of view in the poem, exemplifies in literary form that blending of diverse perspectives the philosopher calls intersubjectivity.

After the scene of loveless sexual encounter between the typist and her insensitive young friend, Tiresias again reveals his presence in the scene:

> (And I Tiresias have foresuffered all
> Enacted on this same divan or bed;
> I who have sat by Thebes below the wall
> And walked among the lowest of the dead) [CPP 69].

The love-making scene illustrates the failure of love between the psychically alienated inhabitants of the modern waste land, just as the scene in Part II depicting the elegant woman and her husband portrays modern man's characteristic inability to break down barriers to genuinely shared feeling.

> 'What are you thinking of? What thinking? What
> I never know what you are thinking. Think' [CPP 65]

the woman protests, displaying the nervous and fragile condition of an alienated ego. The husband's reply (unspoken as indicated by the absence of quotation marks) suggests the mental inertia of one unable to leave the bondage of listless self-absorption:

> I think we are in rats' alley
> Where the dead men lost their bones [CPP 65].

Yet the all-conscious Tiresias not only observes but "foresuffers" "all" such events in the poem, from the internal perspectives of the participants. Tiresias is the all-experiencer; he represents, in one critic's phrase, the poet's effort "to focus an inclusive human consciousness."[13] What he "sees" is the "substance of the poem," as noted above, precisely because his consciousness is wide and elastic enough to encompass the historical and existential conditions of all other characters. Tiresias is both the

Theban prophet whom we also find in the ancient world of Ovid's *Meta-morphoses* and *The Odyssey* and a modern man who walks the streets of London, exercising his powers of vision to enter intersubjectively into the highly personal circumstances of modern lovers, but also to relive in present time such past events as the dalliance of Leicester and Queen Elizabeth I. Eliot may not entirely succeed in his implied effort to give dramatic definition to a universal center of consciousness. But in his experimental portrait of Tiresias, without resorting to the extra-experiential resource of an omniscient narrator, he evidently was working toward portrayal of a new principle of identity,[14] based no longer on the premise of a closed private ego, but on the perception of human potential for intersubjective awareness.

The three Hindu admonitions at the end of the poem, which the protagonist hears in the form of thunder claps—translated as give, sympathize, control—show in highly concentrated form what is needed to move beyond the nightmare of psychic alienation that philosophers call solipsism. For the words suggest the ingredients of a discipline that could enable one to make authentic contact with the other. But following the second thunder clap—"*Dayadhvam*," sympathize—in a passage echoing a section from Dante's *Inferno*, the protagonist tell us:

> I have heard the key
> Turn in the door once and turn once only
> We think of the key, each in his prison
> Thinking of the key, each confirms a prison [CPP 74].

Eliot's note to these lines, an unannotated quotation from the writings of F. H. Bradley, states the case for solipsism in the starkest terms: "My external sensations are no less private to myself than are my thoughts and feelings. In either case my experience falls within my own circle, a circle closed on the outside. . . . In brief, regarded as an existence which appears in a soul, the whole world for each is peculiar and private to that soul" (CPP 80). The note reinforces our sense of the "problem" of unmitigated subjectivity in the world of *The Waste Land*. Yet as a whole the poem is built on a *tension* between this sense of the impenetrability of the private point of view and the poet's impulse to step beyond the subjectivist framework.[15]

While attempting to retain both "the treasure of subjective depth" and the "universal validity in our experience," Hocking asks "could there be such a thing as a veritable consubjectivity whereby one self participates, not by imaginative or sympathetic construction, but by actual experience, in the selfhood of another?" He concludes that "within 'experience' . . . is an intersubjective Thou-art, inseparable from each subjective I-am, serving to bind their several experiences together." Striving to sustain his sense of empirical soundness, he argues:

> What we can now verify is that private experiencing . . . is a certain participation of each I-think in the experience of an intersubjective Thou-art. Through this participation my experience acquires the substantial "objectivity" of being no private dream of my own. . . . My aims cease to be mere psychological distillates of private passions, they have "an anchorage in reality." Therewith a way of hope opens for the individual, groping for significance.

Hocking believes that the "paradoxical immediacy of otherness" is the philosophical insight that can unpack the dilemma of solipsism. To "pass beyond modernity"[16] means to reject the Cartesian paradigm that binds our thinking and feeling in such hopeless dilemmas.

Hints are at best dim in *The Waste Land* of something like Hocking's ever-present "Thou-art," a disposition inherent in human experience that guides each one to unite with the universe of the other. There is, however, the "hooded" figure who, like Tiresias, may be either "a man or a woman," whom Eliot identifies in another note with the risen Christ of the journey to Emmaus recorded in Luke's Gospel. "Who is the third who walks always beside you?" (CPP 73) the speaker asks. This "third," we infer, is neither the "I" (personal self) nor the "you" who enter into conventional (dyadic) human relationships, but the principle of relatedness (which Peirce would call Thirdness, and Hocking calls the *Thou-art*) inseparable from each personal I-am, binding otherwise finite perspectives experientially into a larger and inclusive whole.

From the vantage point of Hocking's analysis (a Roycean third idea) we can see that Eliot too was engaged in his own "passage beyond modernity." For while Prufrock represents what Hocking calls "an unsharable center of feeling and perspective reference,"[17] Tiresias, though blind and in some respects spiritually paralyzed by the horrors and indifference he "sees," represents that enlarged perspective which participates by actual experience in the selfhood of others, and hence signals the poet's ability to leave an outmoded subjectivism behind.

TIME AND EXPERIENCE IN *Four Quartets*

In *Four Quartets* Eliot discovered and sought to define an experiential standpoint that includes a new conception of the mind as incorporating a universal point of view. The heart of *Four Quartets* is a philosophic exploration of the experience of *time* at advanced levels of mental development. Through this exploration of higher orders of consciousness, Eliot defines an order of experience beyond subjectivity, which he terms "the still point of the turning world."

Far from a retreat into either orthodox Christian doctrine or a misty transcendentalism, Eliot's still point is a conjunction of the empirical sensibility seen in the poetry of experience with a radical spirituality. This conjunction of the spiritual with concrete experience in the *Quartets* confronts the reader with the complex notion of spiritual empiricism. Such embracing of contraries in the poem shows us a way to expand mental and spiritual capacities beyond their normal limits, without taking leave of experience but by adhering more fully to the reality of it. Our understanding of Eliot's unique integration of these traditionally disparate attitudes may be enhanced by examining the *Quartets* alongside the penetrating analyses of time and consciousness in the writings of James and Royce.

Time is a way of accounting for the succession of nows that make up immediate experience. It is also "history" in a broad sense. Schematic time is a symbolic reduction in the form of clock or calendar measurements, in which each hour or day has exactly the same quantitative measurement as any other. But in the *Quartets* Eliot examines the qualitative aspects of the experience of time. He distinguishes between schematic time as a meaningless sequence of events and the "timeless moment" at which consciousness touches the deeper patterns of order and meaning embedded in the tissues of experience. The concept of time in the *Quartets* thus takes on the symbolic value of empty or fragmentary experience, while timelessness signifies radically organized experience. The two concepts come to represent what radical empiricists might call differing *experiential densities*.

"A people without history / Is not redeemed from time," Eliot writes in "Little Gidding," "for history is a pattern / Of timeless moments" (CPP 197). Pointing the way beyond the disarray of the historical process as men ordinarily perceive it, the poet states the conditions that would make possible a redemptive transformation of both self and society. To be "without history" implies a lack of significant development. A true sense of "history" is the basic structure of meaning in events ("a pattern / Of timeless moments"). Hence the "timeless moment" is not a mere abstraction; nor does it stand for some obscure metaphysical realm of essence. It is the genuine reality of existential meaning, known by means of "right action," which Eliot defines as "freedom / From past and future also" (CPP 190). The moment of right action, or the timeless moment, is a convergence and concentration of meaning. "And approach to the meaning restores the experience / In a different form beyond any meaning / We can assign to happiness" (CPP 186). The word "timeless" thus signifies a state of experience at higher levels of density or "meaning," though not necessarily of complexity. The timeless moment is "A condition of complete simplicity / (Costing not less than everything)" (CPP 198). Man's redemption is not a matter of somehow moving outside history (as through death or dreams). It is a conscious emergence out of the dream of a deterministic time-construct, and discovery of the organizing principle immanent in the historical process.

True consciousness is found in moments of "sudden illumination" (CPP 186), when submerged patterns of meaning in experience come to light. Such a moment is not a mere speck of time, but has actual breadth. It may perhaps measure only a few seconds according to the calculations of schematic time, an instant "in the stillness / Between two waves of the sea" (CPP 198), or "sudden in a shaft of sunlight" (CPP 196). But by virtue of its high density of content—involving "concentration / Without elimination" (CPP 173)—this moment has "durational spread."[18] Hence, for Eliot

> Time past and time future
> Allow but a little consciousness.
> To be conscious is not to be in time
> But only in time can the moment in the rose-garden,
> The moment in the arbour where the rain beat,
> The moment in the draughty church at smokefall
> Be remembered, involved with past and future.
> Only through time time is conquered [CPP 173].

The limited conceptions of past and future "allow but a little consciousness," for they permit an awareness of time only as a succession of isolated (and for that reason meaningless) moments. Moving out of a time-oriented experience suggests living in terms of a universal rather than a limited and personal standpoint. It does not suggest taking flight into an abstract realm apart from concrete existence, for it is only "through time" (the actuality of experience) that we enter the higher ground where time as limitation is "conquered."

With a wonderfully clear use of metaphors in his study of "The Perception of Time," William James describes the structure of experience in psychological terms analogous to Eliot's notions of the temporal and the timeless. James shows that experience is never in fact a mere "string of bead-like sensations and images, all separate." If it were so, "our consciousness would be like a glow-worm spark, illuminating the point it immediately covered, but leaving all beyond in total darkness." When we see our "real nature" as it is, we find that "our feelings are not thus contracted, and our consciousness never shrinks to the dimensions of a glow-worm spark." On the contrary,

> the practically cognized present is no knife-edge, but a saddle-back, with a certain breadth of its own on which we sit perched, and from which we look in two directions into time. The unit of composition of our perception of time is a *duration*, with a bow and a stern, as it were—a rearward- and a forward-looking end. It is only as parts of this *duration-block* that the relation of *succession* of one end and the other is perceived. We do not first feel one end and then feel the other after it, and from the perception of the succession infer an interval of time between, but we seem to feel the interval of time as a whole with its two ends embedded in it.[19]

James's "practically cognized present" is not necessarily a special illuminated moment. But like Eliot, James is attempting to disclose the reality of consciousness as an actual event, not just as it may be intellectually reconstructed. The idea of "the specious present" (or "durational time") offers us an interpretation of the way consciousness works in the kind of heightened spiritual awareness recorded in Eliot's poem. In James's analysis the perception of time involves a "fusion" of what ordinary usage calls past, present, and future into the unexpected patterns called contextual wholes. James makes greater use of metaphors to describe this peak experience than Eliot does. Yet clearly they are talking about the same kind of experience. To James the content of a duration

> is in a constant flux, events dawning into its forward end as fast as they fade out of its rearward one, and each of them changing its time-coefficient from "not yet," or "not quite yet," to "just gone," or "gone," as it passes by. Meanwhile, the specious present, the intuited duration, stands permanent, like the rainbow on the waterfall, with its own quality unchanged by the events that stream through it.[20]

Although Eliot's notion of timelessness has distinctly religious implications absent from James's phenomenological analysis, James's image for the two aspects of time—his "rainbow on the waterfall"—is a metaphor that opens up the meaning of Eliot's "intersection of the timeless / With time" (CPP 189). The rainbow, or "duration" intuited from a perspective free from the human construction called *time*, though still firmly rooted in experience, "stands permanent," like Eliot's timeless consciousness, calmly viewing the events that flow through it.

> Men's curiosity searches past and future
> And clings to that dimension. But to apprehend
> The point of intersection of the timeless
> With time, is an occupation for the saint—
> No occupation either, but something given
> And taken, in a lifetime's death in love,
> Ardour and selflessness and self-surrender [CPP 189–90].

The experience of knowing the permanent structures of being (the timeless) requires us not to reject but to apprehend more fully the very circumstances of immediate existence (time). Eliot shows that such an apprehension is predicated on a new principle of identity, beyond the subjective, that is actualized by "selflessness and self-surrender." The move beyond a private self is necessary to the attainment of the expanded consciousness that Eliot envisions. We never move outside experience as such, for experience is a fact beyond which analysis (or any other human construction) cannot go. But within experience, we may progress from one orientation (that which is time-bound and self-centered) to another (which is timeless and universal), and so find in the texture of experience the "intersection" point "where time stops and time is never ending" (CPP 185).

> See, now they vanish,
> The faces and places, with the self which, as it could, loved them,
> To become renewed, transfigured, in another pattern [CPP 195].

In lines like these Eliot points a way beyond the subjectivism of modern thought. This way is a process of growth, not of self-annihilation, as suggested in his description of the phenomenon of mystical union with absolute reality.

> At the still point of the turning world. Neither flesh nor fleshless;
> Neither from nor towards; at the still point, there the dance is,
> But neither arrest nor movement. And do not call it fixity,
> Where past and future are gathered. Neither movement from nor towards,
> Neither ascent nor decline. Except for the point, the still point,
> There would be no dance, and there is only the dance [CPP 173].

Since it involves freedom from the normal human vibration between dreading the future and regretting the past, the still point involves neither "ascent nor decline." The still point cannot be called an avenue of escape from experience into a realm of immutable Platonic forms ("And do not call it fixity, / Where past and future are gathered"). Rather, it refers to a revised conception of the experiential standpoint, at which consciousness is distilled and heightened to include apprehension of the original patterns of being, represented in these and other lines by the image of the dance.

The Still Point as Absolute Experience

If the graceful ordered movement of the dance is Eliot's symbol for the one order of reality, or call it absolute reality ("there is only the dance"), "the still point" is his equivalent for what " 'that extraordinary philosopher' "[21] Josiah Royce terms "Absolute Experience." By "absolute reality," Royce argues—in *The Conception of God* (1897)—"we can only mean . . . that which is present to *an absolutely organized experience*."[22] Yet from the very fragmentariness of ordinary experience we can infer the possibility of higher levels of organization or unity, and can act on the basis of that inference to bring such unity to light.

Perhaps the clearest account of this higher form of experiential organization emerges from Royce's analysis of time. Royce carries forward James's argument about "the specious present" in a significant way in his essay on "Immortality" (1906) by examining the way we experience time when listening to music. "Whoever aimlessly half listens to the musical accompaniments of a dance . . ." he writes, may . . . be so absorbed in the passing instant's sound that he gets no sense of the whole. True listening to music grasps, in a certain sense as a *totum simul*, entire sequences—measures, phrases, movements, symphonies. But such wiser listening and appreciation is not timeless. It does not ignore sequence. It is time-inclusive. . . . In this grasping of the whole of a time process one gets a consciousness of a present which is no longer merely a vanishing present, but a time-including, a relatively eternal present.[23]

From this premise of the simultaneous apprehension of a total musical idea by the experienced music listener, Royce arrives at the more general conception of an "absolute point of view" that "sees at a glance all time, past, present, future" in the wider field of experience "just as the true appreciator of music knows the entirety of the sequence as a sort of higher or inclusive present."[24]

Similarly, Eliot employs musical analogies in the *Quartets* to articulate the special quality of the "stillness," which finds an exact counterpart in Royce's "absolute point of view."

> Words move, music moves,
> Only in time; but that which is only living
> Can only die. Words, after speech, reach
> Into the silence. Only by the form, the pattern,
> Can words or music reach
> The stillness, as a Chinese jar still
> Moves perpetually in its stillness.
> Not the stillness of the violin, while the note lasts,
> Not that only, but the co-existence,
> Or say that the end precedes the beginning,
> And the end and the beginning were always there
> Before the beginning and after the end.
> And all is always now [CPP 175].

This "co-existence" of musical notes in the mind of the attentive listener is the poet's way of naming the "higher or inclusive present" described by Royce. When Royce suggests that true listening is "not timeless" but "time-inclusive," his distinction implicitly supports Eliot's idea that the timeless moment is not something outside time (a pure fantasy or an abstract ideal) but rather a matter of the "intersection" of the timeless with time. "And all is always now" for the person attuned to "time-inclusive" moments of qualitative stillness, when attention becomes organized to the point of assimilating an extended musical work—or indeed any extended phase of experience—all at once.

"At the still point there the dance is." Eliot's still point is neither a mathematical instant of time, nor a point in physical space, but a state of high experiential density or attentiveness. Submitting to the discipline of selflessness, we open ourselves to the "eternal present," a universal or "absolute experience," in Royce's terminology.[25] The key to such an expanded experience, for both Eliot and Royce, is not moving to another sphere of being, but more simply, the quality of attention that we bring to our present experience. The still point of Eliot's poem may be regarded as a spiritual awakening from a state of inattention. Similarly, for Royce "the world of the facts that we ought to acknowledge is . . . present . . . as the object of possible attention in every act of finite insight. Finitude means inattention to the wealth and organization of the world's detail."[26] We move beyond the prison of finite subjectivity by the mental and spiritual discipline that expands our attentiveness to the real. A parallel direction of Eliot's thought is evident in the following lines from "The Dry Salvages":

> For most of us, there is only the unattended
> Moment, the moment in and out of time,
> The distraction fit, lost in a shaft of sunlight
> The wild thyme unseen, or the winter lightning
> Or the waterfall, or music heard so deeply
> That it is not heard at all, but you are the music
> While the music lasts. These are only hints and guesses,
> Hints followed by guesses; and the rest
> Is prayer, observance, discipline, thought and action [CPP 190].

Like the writer of these lines, Royce attempts to widen the scope of experience while adhering to empirical premises—in other words, to work out the visionary possibilities of a universal or eternal standpoint from within the domain of experienced actuality.

The brief span of our consciousness, the small range of succession, that we grasp at once [he maintains], constitutes a perfectly arbitrary limitation of our own special type of consciousness. But in principle a time-sequence, however brief, is already viewed in a way that is not merely temporal, when, despite its sequence, it is grasped at once, and is thus grasped not through mere memory, but by virtue of actual experience. . . . The only thing needed to complete our idea of what an actually eternal consciousness is, is the conceived removal of that arbitrary limitation.[27]

To remove arbitrary mental boundaries from himself, and implicitly from us as readers—in order to move (and to help us to move) into an enlarged field of consciousness "by virtue of actual experience"—is the aim of Royce's whole philosophic enterprise. The term "absolute" is used most significantly by Royce as an adjective to modify "experience." And Royce's insistence on the concrete actuality of his "absolute point of view" is a sign of affinity between his philosophy and Eliot's ultimate experiential standpoint, a timeless consciousness that is also the ground of all experience.

The Logos as Forming Principle in Experience

The publication of "Ash Wednesday" in 1930 marked Eliot's turning to a source of spiritual renewal that might heal the fragmented or dissociated sensibility portrayed in *The Waste Land,* "The Love Song," and other poems. That spiritual principle, articulated eloquently in the opening lines of section V, is called "the Word"—implicitly identified with the Logos (word, speech) of ancient Greek philosophy, and with the Christ of the first chapter of the Gospel of St. John.

> If the lost word is lost, if the spent word is spent
> If the unheard, unspoken
> Word is unspoken, unheard;
> Still is the unspoken word, the Word unheard,
> The Word without a word, the Word within
> The world and for the world;
> And the light shone in darkness and
> Against the Word the unstilled world still whirled
> About the centre of the silent Word [CPP 96].

In Eliot's career "Ash Wednesday" records a major turning point, his conversion to Anglican Christianity. The "silent Word" represents his perception of the clarity of truth in the face of the world's chaos and error. Even though receiving no expression in the modern world—though the Word remains "unspoken, unheard"—the Word, as both controlling principle in the universe and spirit of Christ, still lives "within" and "for" the world. Poetry may be only a dim reflection of the Word. But if it articulates the primal ordering principle called Logos, poetry is of inestimable value, for it can move us into a form of experience based on this universal principle. The "silent Word" remains a still "centre" about which the "unstilled world still whirled." The "whirling" of our world on its axis, like the orbit it describes around the sun, and like the Hindu image of the wheel of life, is a metaphor for the unstilled, disquieted, whirl of unredeemed human consciousness. The axis itself, like the sun, symbolizes the center of being, which though it may be forgotten still persists, engendering order and life. Despite all the world's disquiet and disorientation, Eliot implies, the Word remains, a "centre," or Archimedian point, by which human consciousness may become aligned with the true nature of reality and so also become authentically self-actualized.

As in "Ash Wednesday," Eliot is concerned in *Four Quartets* with the ancient idea of the Logos. "Burnt Norton," the first of the *Quartets,* begins with a "cosmic fragment" from the Presocratic philosopher Heraclitus (sixth to fifth century B.C.), which puts in capsule form the essential pattern of Eliot's development as a poet: "[A]lthough the Logos is common, the many live as though they had a private understanding."[28] The Greek word ξυνός here translated "common" may also be rendered "universal." Thus a line that suggests the possibility of movement from private to universal understanding stands at the head of Eliot's last major poetic work. One critic translates the epigraph in a way that gives it further significance in terms of the pattern of the poet's growth that we have seen: "Although there is but one Center, most men live in centers of their own."[29] The same critic explains that the epigraph is related to "an empirically psychological point of view. . . . We each think that time passes, but in the logos it is eternal. We each think that the past endures in our memory, but in the logos it endures in immediate actuality."[30] For Heraclitus, Logos is a name for the central regulating principle in the universe, as well as the principle in man by which the basic order of things is perceived. In other words, it is neither subjective nor objective in the modern sense, but both at once.

In the context of Eliot's art, the epigraph articulates the poet's understanding of a fundamental organizing principle within consciousness and experience. Logos is a name for the principle that makes individual consciousness possible in the first place, but also organizes perception in such a way as to generate intersubjective awareness of the thoughts, feelings, and motives of others. In "Ash Wednesday" as in the *Quartets*, Logos is the creative Word underlying all the particular words of poetry. To borrow a term from modern anthropology and linguistics, it is a name for the "deep structure" of poetry.[31] It is the universal Mind, or Center of consciousness, of which each man's personal center or "private understanding" remains but a semi-adequate counterfeit, as long as each clings to that finite boundary of mental development. But finally Logos is a fact experienced directly as the "intersection of the timeless with time," when man uncovers the dimension of depth in his own consciousness, "at the still point of the turning world."

NOTES

1. This study is a revision of my article of the same title that appeared in *Thought*, 51, No. 203 (December 1976), 409–27.

2. See *Basic Writings*, II 756. For a detailed account of the development of the Harvard philosophy department in the relevant period, see Kuklick, *Rise of American Philosophy*, esp. Parts 2 and 3 on "The Golden Age at Harvard."

3. See *Josiah Royce's Seminar, 1913–1914*, ed. Grover Smith (New Brunswick, N.J.: Rutgers University Press, 1963), for the secretarial notebooks kept by one of Royce's students, Harry T. Costello, who records in some detail Eliot's participation in the seminar. The following is a selective list of books that take brief note of ties between Eliot and Royce: Staffan Bergsten, *Time and Eternity: A Study in the Structure and Symbolism of T. S. Eliot's* FOUR QUARTETS (Stockholm: Svenska, 1960), pp. 12, 30; Kristian Smidt, *Poetry and Belief in the Work of T. S. Eliot* (London: Routledge & Kegan Paul, 1961), pp. 15–18, 162; Eric Thompson, *T. S. Eliot: The Metaphysical Perspective* (Carbondale and Edwardsville: Southern Illi-

nois University Press, 1963), pp. xiii, 5–6, 14–16, 62, 66–67, 77, 125, 130, 151. In *T. S. Eliot's Intellectual and Poetic Development, 1909–1922* (Atlantic Highlands, N.J.: Humanities, 1982), pp. 95–106, Piers Gray offers a slightly more extended treatment of the Eliot–Royce relation, based to a large extent on Eliot's dissertation and the Costello notebooks. In *T. S. Eliot's Impersonal Theory of Poetry* (Lewisburg, Pa.: Bucknell University Press, 1974), pp. 37–38, 155–156, Mowbray Allan makes use of Dewey as a means of criticizing Bradley's Absolute. And in *T. S. Eliot: Aesthetics and History* (LaSalle, Ill.: Open Court, 1962) Lewis Freed gives an account of some aspects of Eliot's criticism in terms of James's psychology. But no one to my knowledge has observed the broad pattern of affinities between Eliot's poetry and the ideas of James, Royce, and Hocking explored in this study.

4. *Essays in Radical Empiricism*, pp. 3–44.

5. *The Poetry of Experience: The Dramatic Monologue in Modern Literary Tradition* (New York: Norton, 1963).

6. "Music of Poetry," p. 23.

7. "Preface," *The Nigger of the Narcissus* (New York: Doubleday, Doran, 1930), p. xiv.

8. *The Complete Poems and Plays* (London: Faber & Faber, 1969), p. 13; hereafter cited as CPP. Lines quoted from "Prufrock" below appear between pages 13 and 17 in CPP.

9. Eliot, *Knowledge and Experience in the Philosophy of F. H. Bradley* (New York: Farrar, Straus, 1964), p. 205.

10. For an insightful clinical account by a physician of the period just prior to and during the writing of *The Waste Land* when Eliot experienced a crisis that "eventuated in exhaustion and depression and a brief period of psychotherapy" in Switzerland, see Harry Trosman, M.D., "T. S. Eliot and *The Waste Land*: Psychopathological Antecedents and Transformations," *Archives of General Psychiatry*, 30 (1974), 709–17.

11. *Poetry of Experience*, p. 77.

12. Quoted in Daniel S. Robinson, *Royce and Hocking: American Idealists* (Boston: Christopher, 1968), p. 74.

13. F. R. Leavis, *"The Waste Land"* in *T. S. Eliot: A Collection of Critical Essays*, ed. Hugh Kenner (Englewood Cliffs, N.J.: Prentice-Hall, 1962), p. 92.

14. See Robert Langbaum, *The Mysteries of Identity: A Theme in Modern Literature* (Chicago: The University of Chicago Press/Phoenix, 1982), Part II, "Loss of Self," including Chap. 3, "Eliot: The Walking Dead," pp. 83–119, esp. 94–98, on *The Waste Land*.

15. Eliot completed his doctoral dissertation on Bradley in 1916, under the guidance of Royce (published in 1964 as *Knowledge and Experience in the Philosophy of F. H. Bradley*). But he never returned to Harvard to take his degree. Reasons for his turning away from the promising possibility of an academic career in philosophy are matters of speculation. Clearly he felt his gifts were in the area of poetry rather than philosophy. But it may also be that he found in Bradley's skepticism—especially concerning the possibility of genuinely intersubjective experience—the very culmination of philosophic reasoning, and so followed his own instincts as a poet instead. Though he apparently had great respect for Bradley, and was influenced to a degree by George Santayana while at Harvard, his own

poetic intuitions, on the other hand, led him to believe implicitly, even during the writing of *The Waste Land*, that experience as understood through the medium of poetry was broader than the reasoning of these admired philosophers could comprehend. Though he probably was not consciously aware of the fact, other philosophers at Harvard—James, Royce, and, later, Hocking—who were in effect pursuing intuitions foreign to both Bradley and Santayana, were all working in a direction similar to the way Eliot was searching out, even at this early date, as a poet. That direction, as this book shows, was a way beyond the Cartesian paradigm that was responsible for problems like solipsism.

16. Hocking, "Passage Beyond Modernity," *Coming World Civilization*, pp. 28–32.

17. Ibid., p. 33.

18. See Stephen C. Pepper, "Contextualism," *World Hypotheses: A Study in Evidence* (Berkeley: University of California Press, 1942), pp. 239–42.

19. *The Principles of Psychology*, ed. Fredson Bowers, 3 vols., The Works of William James 8 (Cambridge: Harvard University Press, 1981), I 570–71, 574.

20. Ibid., 593.

21. Eliot's phrase for Royce, quoted in Smidt, *Poetry and Belief*, p. 15.

22. Royce, *Basic Works*, I 373; emphasis added.

23. Ibid., 394.

24. Ibid., 395.

25. Ibid., 378.

26. Ibid., 611.

27. Ibid., 631.

28. *Heraclitus: The Cosmic Fragments*, ed. G. S. Kirk (Cambridge: Cambridge University Press, 1962), p. 57.

29. Grover Smith, *T. S. Eliot's Poetry and Plays: A Study in Sources and Meaning* (Chicago: The University of Chicago Press, 1956), p. 255.

30. Ibid., p. 256.

31. See Noam Chomsky, *Language and Mind* (New York: Harcourt, Brace & World, 1968), pp. 21–88; see also Jack Burnham, *The Structure of Art* (New York: Braziller, 1971), esp. chap. 1, "Search for a Structure."

3

Metaphors for Consciousness: William James and the Arts of the Twentieth Century

METAPHOR AS METHOD

TO ADDRESS THE PROBLEM of consciousness William James often worked in metaphors.[1] Why metaphors? As Alfred North Whitehead eloquently argued in *Science and the Modern World* (1925), James was the architect of a new set of fundamental assumptions about the mind that contradicted the assumptions cherished by the modern age since Descartes.[2] As poets and students of metaphorical thinking have often observed, metaphors are means of breaking through the bounds of an existing system of logic in order to enable other principles of thought and perception to be born. In the Introduction I described such changes of outlook as examples of what Thomas Kuhn calls paradigm shifts. I would like to argue here that James participated in a process of shifting paradigms for the study of mind, and that in that process he found metaphor to be an indispensable part of his thinking method. While the old model held mind to be a kind of substantial entity, located in a "space" of its own with certain definite limits, and perceiving an equally static external reality, the new paradigm that emerges gradually in James's thought over a period of three or four decades understands mind essentially as a process. This shift from the definition of mind as an entity to a process model yields a type of understanding that cannot express itself effectively in analytical argument, but (like poetry) requires the fluid multivalent method of metaphor.[3]

According to the model that James helped to fashion, to understand is to form a mental image of an unknown or little-known phenomenon by the discovery of an analogue with something known. In trying to understand consciousness, contemporary psychologist Julian Jaynes argues:

we are like children trying to understand nonsense objects, . . . in trying to understand a thing we are trying to find a metaphor for that thing. Not just any metaphor, but one with something more familiar and easy to our attention. . . . And the feeling of familiarity is the feeling of understanding. . . . If understanding a thing is arriving at a familiarizing metaphor for it, then we can see that there always will be a difficulty in understanding consciousness. For it should be immediately apparent that there is not and cannot be anything in our immediate experience that is like immediate experience itself. There is therefore a sense in which we shall never be able to understand consciousness in the same way that we can understand things that we are conscious of.[4]

This argument specifies the terms under which James worked, from the 1880s to the end of his life in 1910, in wrestling with the problem of consciousness. He appears to have accepted the premise that to understand is to generate metaphors of understanding. Like the methods of poets working to articulate the nature of consciousness, James's method involves a subordination of reason to intuition. And James's own intuitive process of thinking, or noninferential grasp of his subject, seen in his persistent use of metaphors, brings him into a phenomenological understanding of consciousness that to a degree bypasses traditional methods of philosophical or scientific reasoning.

Metaphor is a way of understanding a phenomenon by means of indirection. The more familiar philosophic drive to find truth by means of linear calculative logic has often led thinkers to the complete rejection of metaphor. Both logical positivism and the analytic philosophy of the Anglo-American tradition are examples of this tendency. Yet metaphors persist, not only in poetry, but sometimes at the very heart of philosophic discourse, partly because some topics, especially one as fluid and nonobjective as consciousness, do not yield readily to conceptual analysis alone.[5] "Consciousness" as a topic in philosophy has seemed to many to demand the indirection of the intuitive methods expressed in metaphor.

Henri Bergson claims that the mode of expression most natural to *reason* is the concept (the purest examples of which are the concepts of mathematics), while the mode of expression appropriate to *intuition* is the metaphor.[6] Metaphors belong not to philosophy, one might say, but to poetry. They are the tools of the poetic sensibility. Plato expelled the poets from his ideal Republic because of the mesmerizing powers of the poetic performance in the prephilosophical Homeric era.[7] Clearly that metaphorical power—for instance, "explaining" the thunderstorm by putting anthropomorphic gods in the clouds—was a captivating force able to control the emotions and volitions of living men. Because of this power to captivate, poetry became a threat to the new mode of reflective consciousness known as Reason, celebrated in Plato's dialogues as the only authentic path to Truth. But Plato himself was an instinctive myth-maker. And partly because of his metaphorical gifts, Plato's mode of thought was in turn rejected by his own pupil Aristotle, the philosopher who perhaps epitomizes cognitive rationalism supremely. Unlike Plato, who freely generated characters, imagery, and myths (like those of the sun, the charioteer, and the cave) to convey both his metaphysics and his theories about the soul, Aristotle strove deliberately to exclude metaphors, which he regarded as sources of error and deceit, from his naturalistic philosophy. Both Descartes and Newton strove for similar reasons to escape from the highly metaphorical systems of alchemy, astrology, and traditional Christian typology, in developing the rudiments of a new scientific rationalism.[8]

James used metaphors because they captured the essence of scientific evidence about the mind available in his time, but also because they most naturally expressed his iconoclastic views concerning the structure of consciousness. Metaphors not only describe consciousness, but, as Julian Jaynes argues, they generate consciousness.[9] Studying James's account of "the stream of consciousness" makes us subjects of a combination of intuitive and reflective processes. We sense the appropriateness of the metaphor because we "feel" consciousness as if it were a continuously flowing current of ideas, images, sensations, rationalizations, etc., all pushed along toward various goals by the energies of emotion and volition. The metaphor has a power—which could hardly be explained rationally— to attract and hold our attention. It is something like the power of a real stream that we come upon in the woods to attract us and in its way speak to us. We "see" in our mind's eye the image of water, held within certain bounds by banks and the stream bed, flowing perhaps toward the sea or a lake. And we make the leap from this image to another kind of "seeing," connecting the imagistic picture of the stream (the *vehicle* of the metaphor) with the object described by the image (its *tenor*), consciousness itself. The vehicle has a way of proliferating meanings, all of which adhere to the tenor. Jaynes suggests that a close link exists between metaphor and the operations of consciousness because metaphorical processes are at the very root of all consciousness.[10]

By means of metaphor and phenomenological description, James moved from an early acceptance of a dualistic–subjectivistic model of consciousness to an experiential model in his later writings. The imagery he uses is often designed to challenge errors or deficiencies in prevailing philosophic conceptions of mind that he perceived to be (in Julian Jaynes's phrase) "errors of attempted metaphors."[11] Within the old paradigm, the mind had been depicted as a *container*, with ideas for contents, like marbles in a box, or water in a barrel. It was often likened to a *mirror*, or a photographic plate, receiving sensory impressions from the external world and reflecting them mechanically (or chemically) as psychical "copies" of parts of that world. The mind of the Cartesian paradigm was known as a *spectator*, aloof and coolly observing the objects in its environment. In all these cases the cognitive subject is portrayed as existing at a distance from an objective world made of an alien stuff called matter. To overthrow the assumptions of the dualistic paradigm required not just the analytical and conceptual skills that had been so far perfected by the Cartesian tradition, but also the intuitive and imaginative methods of metaphor.

In his monumental *Principles of Psychology* (1890), James began his reconstruction of the idea of consciousness, and completed his argument in a series of published articles collected in 1912, two years after the author's death, as *Essays in Radical Empiricism*. Rooted in a passionate commitment to the actuality of living experience, James's rebelliousness from traditional authority was indigenous to his character. This commitment expressed itself as a need to expel from his philosophy the artificial constructions of rational analysis, however time-honored, whenever such constructions missed the target of experience. His metaphors for the mind express his struggle to rescue consciousness from the mechanistic categories of the Cartesian paradigm and to understand the dynamics of consciousness within the processes of lived experience.

Though an unruly and unpredictable agent in an unfinished universe of experience, consciousness is nevertheless characterized by a kind of primal unity. The *Principles* moves toward the central idea of radical empiricism: *the unity of experience*. To James consciousness "does not appear to itself chopped up in bits,"[12] but "remains sensibly continuous and one," its elements "inwardly connected" as "parts of a common whole" (p. 232). Attacking classic empiricist images for consciousness, James writes: "Such words as 'chain' or 'train' do not describe it fitly as it presents itself in the first instance. It is nothing jointed; it flows. A 'river' or a 'stream' are the metaphors by which it is most naturally described" (p. 233). In an especially witty passage, James exposes the absurdity of the mechanistic psychologist's images of mind as a container:

> The traditional psychology talks like one who should say a river consists of nothing but pailsful, spoonsful, quartpotsful, barrelsful, and other moulded forms of water. Even were the pails and the pots all actually standing in the stream, still between them the free water would continue to flow. It is just this free water of consciousness that [mechanistic] psychologists resolutely overlook. Every definite image in the mind is steeped and dyed in the free water that flows round it [p. 246].

By clinging to the "actual constitution" (p. 266) of the thought process as it occurs, James strives to bring the "free water of consciousness" to light.

If classic empiricists such as Locke, Hume, and their successors, Alexander Bain and James Mill, erred by too great a passion to impose an atomistic formula on the mind, idealists tended to commit what James called "the psychologist's fallacy" in an opposite direction, by defending too zealously a conception of mental structure based on the notion of a Cartesian self, variously termed soul, ego, or Kant's "transcendental unity of apperception." Like the atomism of empiricists, the postulate of a substantial ego, existing somehow "behind the passing state of consciousness," involves a formulaic rather than experiential approach to consciousness—an unwarranted leap outside of experience, into a dislocated realm of abstraction.

In an early paper James had written: "I, for my part, cannot escape the consideration, forced upon me at every turn, that the knower is not simply a mirror floating with no foot-hold anywhere, and passively reflecting an order that he comes upon and finds simply existing."[13] This "mirror floating with no foot-hold anywhere" describes the disembodied intellect of the rationalist tradition. In Descartes's philosophy, as in centuries of the Christian and Greek traditions, the mind (or soul) of the individual was conceived as detachable from the body and the empirical world, and so, as James perceived, found itself ultimately rootless and homeless. What remedy, then, for modern man, when he confronts his existential condition of disrelation from the world? The answer found in James's philosophy is twofold: (a) to recognize that metaphors of detachment and distancing represent only half-truths; and (b) to understand that consciousness is not a thing but a form of energy—a potency to move into action and dispel its own illusions, however backed up by the authority of traditions—and that this energy has an ethical dimension, moving the individual into more and more significant relation to the world. Dismissing the image of mind as a mirror, he offers an alternate metaphor, hinting at the principles of mental energy and creativity that would become axioms of the study of mind in his later writings: "The knower is an actor, and co-efficient of the truth on one side, whilst on the other he registers the truth which he helps to create. Mental interests, hypotheses, postulates, so far as they are bases for human action—which to a great extent transforms the world—help to *make* the truth which they declare." And denouncing the static image of mind as a spectator, he continues: ". . . there belongs to mind, from its birth upward, a spontaneity, a vote. It is in the game, and not a mere looker-on."[14]

The image of mind as an actor, "in the game," implies the principle of *participation*. The metaphor of the "game" is correlated with the image, presented in the *Essays in Radical Empiricism*, of consciousness as a "field." To the later James, consciousness as a subjective entity is displaced by a more primal reality, called "pure experience."[15] Consciousness and its object, thoughts and things, are not ultimately separable, but are names for different aspects of one fluid and unfractured material of which everything in the world is made—the open-ended yet organized "field" of experience itself. The ego-consciousness of Cartesian tradition disappears, replaced by its "equivalent in realities of experience."[16]

THE DILEMMA OF DUALISM

In the *Principles* James attempted to place the study of mind firmly on scientific foundations, to establish laws of causal relation between physical states of the nervous system and states of consciousness. Yet the effect of this inquiry into the phenomena and conditions of mental life is to undermine the conventional nineteenth-century mechanistic view of man as a "conscious automaton" (p. 137). Gradually from James's study emerges a new image of consciousness as a restless vital "stream of thought," characterized by creative volition and possessing creative potentials beyond the sphere of scientific investigation.

Early in the book James writes: "The psychologist's attitude towards cognition . . . *is a thoroughgoing dualism*. It supposes two elements, mind knowing and thing known, and treats them as irreducible" (p. 214). The knower and the known are "two mutually external entities." "The world first exists, and then the states of mind; and these gain a cognizance of the world which gets more and more complete."[17] The knowing mind and the object of knowledge seem without doubt "external" to each other; so far as empirical observation can tell us neither enters into the internal existence of the other. Yet this cannot be the whole story. James admits that he cannot hold to these rigid categories: ". . . it is hard to carry through this simple dualism, for idealistic reflections will intrude."[18]

What were James's "idealistic reflections," and why do they "intrude" almost involuntarily into his inquiry? James later describes his radical empiricism as a modified "identity-philosophy," a form of the idealist doctrine of the identity of subject and object. But unlike the classic idealists of the modern tradition, he rejected the postulate of an "Absolute Mind" knowing a "block universe" as a condition for this identity. In radical empiricism the experiential field itself comprises a seamless unity of mind–body–nature, while the notion of a split between subject and object is seen as a product of conceptual analysis at a high level of abstraction.

But during the writing of the *Principles* he seems to have realized that the paradigm of dualism represented an imposition of a rational construction on experience, a construction that would not necessarily bear up under careful scrutiny of the phenomena themselves.[19] His method for seeing through the construct, for recognizing it as a philosophic preconception, not the intrinsic structure of our mental life, is basically the method of metaphorical thinking.

Perhaps the most compelling aspect of Descartes's *Meditations* involves his effort to overcome the intellectual and cultural biases that inevitably worked to condition, distort, and control the thinking in his age. Descartes set out "to begin afresh from the foundations" by "the general destruction of all [his] former opinions."[20] Those opinions, he implies, are the cumulative product of intellectual conventions, based less on experience than on venerated philosophic and religious authorities of the past. James was motivated by a similar impulse to penetrate through the mirage of conventional beliefs, to uncover the naked facts of our mental life. But while the path of deductive reasoning led Descartes to the picture of an ego-consciousness standing opposite to an objective material world, James elected the very different path of phenomenological observation. This, coupled with his method of metaphorical description of our minds "as they actually live," led *him* to repudiate the very epistemological dualism which Descartes had discovered and which the Cartesian tradition held to be the only secure foundation for scientific analysis of either the material world or the mind.

VOLITION AS CREATIVITY

Is there a factor in experience that gives unity to the stream of consciousness? Seeking to avoid the reifying tendency that would make a concept into a substantial "faculty" or "entity," James in various contexts gave to this unifying factor the names of "attention" and "will," making use of metaphors of the mind as artist to clarify its characteristics. Though he left little room in his psychology for the ego, James identified the principle of volition as the organizing factor in the stream of consciousness.

This commitment grew out of an experience of personal crisis in his early life. While still in his twenties, as a result of his medical and scientific studies, he found himself forced to accept the conclusion that man is nothing but a physical object among other objects doomed to purposeless conditioned action and reaction within a closed mechanistic universe. Suicide or madness seemed the only possible response to this bleak world view. Other fears, experiences of horror and dread, like those of the "French correspondent" (who is really James himself) described in *The Varieties of Religious Experience*, plagued him relentlessly.[21] Finally, in the year 1870, he made the following remarkable entry in his diary, which indicates a healing process begun in his life by his new commitment to creative volition: " 'I think that yesterday was a crisis in my life. I finished the first part of Renouvier's second "Essais" and see no reason why his definition of Free Will—"the sustaining of a thought *because I choose to* when I might have other thoughts"—need be the definition of an illusion. . . . My first act of free will shall be to believe in free will.' "[22]

He describes his intention to " 'abstain from mere speculation' " and to " 'voluntarily cultivate the feeling of moral freedom, by reading books favorable to it, as well as by acting.' " He exhorts himself to " 'recollect that only when habits of order are formed can we advance to really interesting fields of action—and consequently accumulate grain on grain of willful choice like a very miser.' " He speaks of the " 'exceptionally passionate initiative' " necessary to the acquisition of productive habits, and goes on to exclaim:

"I will go a step further with my will, not only act with it, but believe as well; believe in my individual reality and creative power. My belief, to be sure, *can't* be optimistic—but I will posit life (the real, the good) in the self-governing *resistance* of the ego to the world. Life shall [be built in] doing and suffering and creating."[23]

Strains of both Emersonian self-reliance and the voluntarism of American pragmatism are apparent in this passage. Emerson—a close friend of William's father, the elder Henry James, and a frequent visitor in the James household during William's childhood—had proclaimed in "Self-Reliance" (1841) the moral and religious impulse of self-trust as the "law of consciousness," and maintained that "with the exercise of self-trust, new powers shall appear."[24] There is little doubt that the formative stages of James's thought were influenced by the spiritual disposition represented by Emerson and the American tradition of Romantic individualism. The moment of decision recorded in his diary marked a major turning point in James's life, the beginning of his prolific career as a writer, teacher, renowned psychologist, and philosopher. One can also see in the diary entry germs of the pragmatism that James, following Peirce, developed some thirty years later: the principle that men participate in making truth actual, by the degree of passion and commitment that they pour into their volitions; and that the truth of an idea is *demonstrated* in the real conditions of existence by its consequences in action, not simply by its internal or theoretical coherence.

In the *Principles* James focused on the phenomenology of volition. The desire to attend to certain elements of the perceptual continuum, and to ignore others, gives shape not only to perception but to the whole experience of the objective world: "Out of what is in itself an undistinguishable, swarming *continuum*, devoid of distinction or emphasis, our senses make for us, by attending to this motion and ignoring that, a world full of contrasts, of sharp accents, of abrupt changes, of picturesque light and shade" (p. 274). In sensory experience as well as in higher levels of moral and intellectual awareness, "volition is nothing but attention" (p. 424), for attention implies "reactive spontaneity" able to "break through the circle of pure receptivity which [to the British empiricist] constitutes 'experience' " (p. 380). The knowing and perceiving subject is not a kind of "passive clay" upon which " 'experience' rains down" (p. 381. "*My experience is what I agree to attend to.* Only those items which I *notice* shape my mind—without selective interest, experience is an utter chaos. Interest alone gives accent and emphasis, light and shade, background and foreground—intelligible perspective, in a word" (pp. 380–81).

In such treatment of the issue of attention one can see traces of the author who, once a student of painting, has matured into a gifted descriptive psychologist. "The artist notoriously selects his items, rejecting all tones, colors, shapes, which do not harmonize with each other and with the main purpose of his work," he writes. Like the artist in the creative act, consciousness shapes its materials into significant form: "[T]he mind is at every stage a theatre of simultaneous possibilities. Consciousness consists in the comparison of these with each other, the selection of some, the suppression of the rest by the reinforcing and inhibiting agency of attention" (p. 277).

The mind works on its raw perceptual data in the same way a sculptor works on his shapeless block of stone. The statue may have "stood there from eternity," in a sense.

> But there were a thousand different ones beside it, and the sculptor alone is to thank for having extricated this one from the rest. Just so the world of each of us, howsoever different our several views of it may be, all lay embedded in the primordial chaos of sensations, which gave the mere *matter* to the thought of all of us indifferently [p. 277].

By our secondary reasonings we may unwind things back to "that black and jointless continuity of space and moving clouds of swarming atoms" which science calls the "real world" (p. 277). But "the world *we* feel and live in" will be, in James's words, "that which our ancestors and we, by slowly cumulative strokes of choice, have extricated out of this, like sculptors, by simply rejecting certain portions of the given stuff" (p. 277). Through disciplined acts of attention, consciousness becomes creative, its "ethical energies" directed outward to the ceaseless process of constructing a world, like that of the artist, possessing form and qualitative meaning. The mind does not merely *receive* sensory data, or merely *correspond* to the external world; it "works" as the artist does.

TRANSITIVE STATES OF CONSCIOUSNESS AND THE ARTS

As we observe the "wonderful stream of our consciousness," James writes, "Like a bird's life, it seems to be made of an alternation of flights and perchings" (p. 236). The "resting-places" are points of focused "sensorial imaginations," which "can be held before the mind for an indefinite time, and contemplated without changing . . ." (p. 236). These "perchings" stand for "substantive parts" of the stream. His analysis of the other, more fluid portions of consciousness, the "transitive parts"— like the bird's periods of flight—bears a significant relation to the experimental tendencies in American poetry written after the turn of the century, and to similar tendencies in the music and painting of the same period.

If traditional Western art is predominantly concerned with what has been called "form properties of simplicity, compactness, [and] coherence, which add up to an aesthetic 'good' gestalt,"[25] the experimentation in the arts in the early decades of our century produced a very different phenomenon: the presentation of forms that at first appeared—by traditional aesthetic standards—chaotic, disorienting, and difficult to grasp. In poetry, works like the first three of Ezra Pound's *Cantos* (originally published in *Poetry* magazine in 1917) and Eliot's *The Waste Land* (1922), followed by Book I of William Carlos Williams's *Paterson* (1946), all displayed disjunctive semantic and syntactical patterns and extreme metrical irregularities. Each of them juxtaposed the poet's own words with passages "quoted" from seemingly anomalous literary and cultural sources. Readers of these poems typically found themselves strangely attracted yet repelled by the apparent absence of standard structural devices such as plot, character, and a dominant point of view. In music, the harmonic system in which musical ideas were organized around the central tone of a key signature gave way to the seemingly chaotic structures of atonality—in the Second String Quartet (1907–1908) of Arnold Schoenberg, written prior to his discovery of the twelve-tone row, and in works like the Second Orchestral Set (1909–1915) of Charles Ives.[26] In painting, the principle of Renaissance perspective—creating a precise illusion of depth in three-dimensional space, with all the areas of the two-dimensional picture plane organized around a central vanishing point— was displaced by a diffuse structural ambiguity in the early Cubist works of Picasso and Braque produced around the year 1907.[27]

Were these revolutionary developments in the arts of poetry, music, and painting merely signs of the disorientation of Western thought and values in the new century? Or were they independent efforts of individual artists to push beyond the mental frontiers of their time? James's psychology helps us to answer these questions by providing in his study of transitive states of consciousness a model for this revolutionary experimentation in the arts.

In the ordinary flow of the stream of consciousness transitive states are "inarticulate form experiences"[28] constituting the transitions between relatively stable and articulate substantive contents of consciousness. The formulation of a well-defined idea, James suggests, is preceded by a state of inarticulate transitive anticipation. James asks the reader to consider "what kind of mental fact is his *intention of saying a thing* before he has said it?" The answer to this question touches the heart of the creative process in the arts as well as in everyday life. "It is an entirely definite intention," he writes, "distinct from all other intentions, an absolutely distinct state of consciousness." Yet very little of it consists of "definite sensorial images, either of words or of things." If we linger,

> the words and things come into the mind; the anticipatory intention, the divination is there no more. But as the words that replace it arrive, it welcomes them successively and calls them right if they agree with it, it rejects them and calls them wrong if they do not. It has therefore a nature of its own of the

most positive sort, and yet what can we say about it without using words that belong to the later mental facts that replace it? The intention *to-say-so-and-so* is the only name it can receive [p. 245].

James cannot accept this substantive "name" as appropriate to the phenomenon of the "anticipatory intention." To accept it would be to commit the psychologist's fallacy, imposing a later articulate formulation on the original inarticulate thought. What is the nature of that original thought form, apart from the name of the substantive mental content toward which it is driving? The phenomenological method involves the attempt "to see the transitive parts [of the stream] for what they really are" in themselves (p. 236).

Let anyone try to cut a thought across in the middle and get a look at its section, and he will see how difficult the introspective observation of the transitive tracts is. The rush of the thought is so headlong that it almost always brings us up to the conclusion before we can arrest it. Or if our purpose is nimble enough and we do arrest it, it ceases forthwith to be itself [p. 236–37].

Premodernist literature typically leads the reader to expect relatively articulate gestalt structures with well-defined "substantive" imagery, characters, settings, and points of view. Experimental works like Eliot's *The Waste Land*, Pound's *Cantos*, and Williams's *Paterson*—as well as many novels in the new "stream of consciousness" mode—represent the literary attempt to "cut" the thought process "across in the middle" and "get a look," through the language of poetry, "at its section." The result, as in atonal music, was to expose the "dissonant" substructures of consciousness, which failed to fulfill the traditional artistic criteria of harmony, coherence, and aesthetically good gestalt, yet were profoundly revealing about the way consciousness works. The "difficulty" that James encounters initially in his approach to the problem is due to the fact that philosophy and psychology historically had "only fully articulate static *gestalt* structures" as tools for their task of "grasping the utterly mobile and fluid structures" that James calls transitive tracts.[29] The artist subjects these transitive tracts to a kind of discipline, and gives them expression in metaphors, new poetic forms, musical structures, and the forms of plastic art.

To render the transitive tract (the "headlong rush") of experience and "arrest it" in language has always been a preoccupation of poets and fiction writers. It is the province of metaphor to accomplish this record of living experience.[30] And like the poet, James found himself impelled to the use of metaphors in order to lay hold of the dynamic parts of the stream. The transitive aspect of consciousness is represented as a "snowflake crystal," threatened by dissolution if caught in the warm analytical hand of the too-intellectual observer. James also argues that attempting discursive analysis of its fluid process is "like seizing a spinning top to catch its motion, or trying to turn up the gas quickly enough to see how the darkness looks" (p. 237). Discursive language, apart from the tools of the creative artist, cannot adequately express the living quality of the mobile and potentially creative states of thought called transitive tracts.

English and American literature prior to the turn of the twentieth century ordinarily emphasized stable imagistic gestalt forms, which hold the reader's interest in substantive objects of focused attention. The early poetry of Eliot, Pound, and Williams, on the other hand, had an effect like that of "freeing the dissonance" in music. This poetry exposed the subconscious aspects of the creative process, bringing these relatively unstructured dynamic energies of the poet's thought directly into the foreground of the reader's attention. Though he called these deeper levels *transitive parts* of our mental life, and distinguished them verbally from the *substantive parts*, James viewed consciousness as in fact an energy-continuum, a "sensibly continuous" (p. 231) stream, not literally divisible into "conscious" and "unconscious" elements, as in Freudian psychology.[31]

According to his "field view of consciousness," James's image of the "horizon" parallels Eliot's image of the frontiers of consciousness: "When very fresh, our minds carry an immense horizon with them," James writes. "The present image shoots its perspective far before it, irradiating in advance the regions in which lie the thoughts as yet unborn" (p. 247). Vague and diffuse as it may be, the transitive state may perform a definite creative function in guiding the thought toward a destination initially unknown to it. The "inarticulate feeling" of intention, like the creative impulse of the poet, becomes "an affection of consciousness" indicating "*signs of direction* in thought, of which direction we nevertheless have an acutely discriminative sense, though no definite sensorial image plays any part in it whatsoever" (p. 244). These are "psychic transitions, always on the wing, so to speak, and not to be glimpsed except in flight" (p. 244). How does one get "in flight" in order to glimpse the truth of this deep structure of the mind's activity? Certainly one way is by experiencing the magic energy of art, manifested in the formal properties of music, painting, and literature, including the power of intuitive thinking in metaphor.

The inarticulate "feeling of tendency" is a "gap" in the stream, "beckoning us in a given direction" (p. 243), says James. In our voluntary or creative thinking, there is inevitably "a problem, a gap we cannot yet fill with a definite picture, word, or phrase, but which . . . influences us in an intensely active and determinate psychic way. Whatever may be the images and phrases that pass before us, we feel their relation to this aching gap. To fill it up is our thought's destiny" (p. 250). The activity of the poet in the creative process consists largely in attending to the pregnant and "aching gap" at the horizon of consciousness, and capturing its living quality in poetic language. Modernist poetry attempts to articulate, through the deliberate use of "dissonant" structural elements the literal and unaesthetic character of the "gap" itself, thereby giving us explicit knowledge of frontiers of consciousness that otherwise remain unknown.

RADICAL EMPIRICISM CHALLENGES THE CARTESIAN PARADIGM

For Descartes, the world is essentially a system of interacting chunks of matter or things, extended substances, governed by mechanical laws. Discovered by Newton in the eighteenth century, the "laws" of gravitation, thermodynamics, etc., fit well into the world theory already established by Descartes.[32] Consciousness is the nonmaterial (non-extended) counterpart of material substance. But consciousness is described by Descartes in materialist metaphors of *thinghood*. The mind is *une chose qui pense*, "a thing which thinks."[33] It is a substance, like matter, that happens to have the attribute of "thinking," but is believed to obey mechanistic laws analogous to those governing material substances. Though Descartes intended the word *think* to bear connotations of feeling and volition as well as rational deduction, the predilection of his philosophic method, and of the Age of Reason to which he gave a voice, was to elevate the rational, calculative, side of the human mental apparatus above the affective and aesthetic side. "[E]ach substance has one principal property. . . . Thus extension in length, breadth and depth constitutes the nature of corporeal substance; and thought constitutes the nature of thinking substance."[34] "By *substance* we can understand nothing other than a thing which exists in such a way as to depend on no other thing for its existence."[35] "I see clearly that I am a thinking substance," Descartes tells us, "and that [a] stone, on the contrary is an extended non-thinking thing." Yet there is an abiding similarity between the "I" and the "stone," for "they both represent substances."[36] Immaterial by definition, the ego-consciousness is symbolically reduced to properties corresponding to physical substance. If "man's body [is] a machine," the mind is a mechanistic instrument designed to "pilot" the machine.[37]

While Descartes's *Meditations* had established the ego-centered consciousness for future generations as the first principle of philosophic analysis, James began his *Essays in Radical Empiricism* with a simple question, "Does 'consciousness' exist?" By asking this question, he displayed a quiet but potent revolutionary impulse, an impulse to overthrow the previously unchallenged authority of the tradition of Cartesian subjectivity.

Suzanne Langer has argued that it is "the forms of his questions" rather than his explicit propositions that reveal the true significance of a philosopher's thinking. While the answers a philosophy gives establish an edifice of facts, "its questions make the frame in which its picture of facts is plotted. . . . In our questions lie our *principles of analysis*, and our answers may express whatever those principles are able to yield."[38] From a new basic question a new "generative idea" may emerge. A new idea, of this momentous kind, "is a light that illuminates presences which simply had no form for us before the light fell on them. We turn the light here, there, and everywhere the limits of thought recede before it. A new science, a new art, or a young and vigorous system of philosophy is generated by such a basic innovation."[39] The Cartesian picture of mind as an inner realm, counterpart to an outer world, was one such generative idea, Langer argues.[40]

James's question is a sign that he is starting his essay from a new principle of analysis. Based on a new generative idea, the idea of unitary experience, James's radical empiricism translates the conception of consciousness out of the Cartesian framework of dualism and subjectivism into a new framework of understanding. As applied to consciousness, the word "entity"—like the words "thing" and "substance"—belongs to the vocabulary of mechanistic materialism. In the essay "Does 'Consciousness' Exist?" James supplants the conceptual vocabulary of substantial materialism with a new terminology of *process* and *function*. To deny that "consciousness" exists seems absurd, he admits, "for undeniably 'thoughts' do exist. . . . Let me then immediately explain that I mean only to deny that the word stands for an entity, but to insist most emphatically that it does stand for a function."[41]

James's answer to his own question may seem less significant than the question itself. Denying that "consciousness" exists, he hastens to explain that he rejects its definition as an "entity," though to him the word does define a "function" of our experience. His denial is a momentous one, however, for to discount the existence of consciousness *as an entity* is to reject the application of the Cartesian category of *substance* to mind. It is, in effect, to step outside the Cartesian paradigm, or to make a gesture toward a paradigm shift.

Having crossed the boundary of the old paradigm, and moving into a new territory, James posed the precise question that enabled him to plant his feet, so to speak, on new metaphysical ground. It gave him a new principle of analysis from which to approach the broader issue of the nature of reality.

> There is . . . no aboriginal stuff or quality of being, contrasted with that of which material objects are made, out of which our thoughts of them are made; but there is a function in experience which thoughts perform, and for the performance of which this quality of being is invoked. That function is

knowing. "Consciousness" is supposed necessary to explain the fact that
things not only are, but get reported, are known. Whoever blots out the notion
of consciousness from his list of first principles must still provide in some way
for that function's being carried on.[42]

Behavioral psychology has amply shown in the past several decades the
results of blotting out the notion of consciousness to achieve goals of
manipulation and conditioned response in human beings. The behavioral
psychologist who purports to follow James by extinguishing the idea of
consciousness from his vocabulary and substituting for it brain physiology,
and "behavior" in a mechanistic context of stimulus and response, misses
the generative thrust of James's view of the place of consciousness in
experience. By holding on to the physicalist component of Cartesian
dualism, and merely discounting its mentalist aspect, the behaviorist stays
within the boundaries of the Cartesian system.

Radical empiricism makes its contribution to the process of deconstruct-
ing the Cartesian paradigm by acknowledging that experience is the primal
reality beyond which analysis cannot go. "The instant field of the present
is always experience in its 'pure' state, plain unqualified actuality [or
existence], a simple *that*, as yet undifferentiated into thing and thought,
and only virtually classifiable as objective fact or as someone's opinion
about fact."[43] The innovativeness of much modernist art and literature—
including the work of abstract expressionists like Jackson Pollock, the
Cubists, the modernist fiction of Proust and Joyce, and the poetry of Eliot,
Pound, and Williams—consists in its ability to render just such "undifferentiated" states of thought. This historical development is prefigured in
James's conception of undifferentiated pure experience, in which the
Cartesian substantial ego disappears.[44] Within James's conception of the
experiential field, "consciousness" is denied existence as a substantive
"entity," but is reborn as "a particular sort of *relation* towards one
another into which portions of pure experience may enter."[45] The move
beyond Cartesian subjectivism witnessed in James's later philosophy
involves the discovery that consciousness loses its character as a private
realm of thought and sensation, and is redefined as the aspect of our
experience that connects us to others and so gives meaning to life.
Consciousness, in and of the field of experience, is understood in radical
empiricism no longer as the inner space of a Romantic self, nor as an arena
of private psychosis, but as a means of action, and the principal form of
relatedness between the individual and all other facts, human as well as
nonhuman. Because the radical empiricist expels the dogma of epistemological dualism from his first principles, he enables himself to make an
existential commitment to one order of experience to which all men and
women, as well as all things of nature and spirit, belong. Pure experience
is "the one primal stuff or material in the world, a stuff of which everything

is composed.''[46] This conception of pure experience as the basic reality of all things, including human consciousness, breaks down the widely accepted mechanistic images of consciousness and reality that we have inherited from the Cartesian paradigm. If artists and poets are working within the parameters of a similarly changed paradigm of consciousness, James's idea of pure experience provides a key to new understanding of their art.

NOTES

1. This study of William James's philosophical psychology is a revised version of a paper given at a meeting of the Maine Philosophical Institute in the Spring of 1983.

2. See chap. 9, "Science and Philosophy," pp. 139–56. Speaking of Descartes and James, Whitehead writes: "They each of them open an epoch by their clear formulation of terms in which thought could profitably express itself at particular stages of knowledge, one for the seventeenth century, the other for the twentieth century" (p. 147).

3. A number of useful books and articles have appeared which relate James's work to the aesthetics of modern art. See, for example, John J. McDermott's "To Be Human Is to Humanize: A Radically Empirical Aesthetic," in *Culture of Experience,* pp. 21–62; and William J. Gavin, "Modern Art and William James," *Science, Technology and Human Values,* 1 (1978), 45–54. Two earlier pieces of work to which I am indebted are Jacques Barzun, "William James and the Clue to Art," in *The Energies of Art: Studies of Authors Classic and Modern* (New York: Harper & Row, 1956), pp. 325–55; and Anton Ehrenzweig, *The Psycho-Analysis of Artistic Vision and Hearing* (New York: Braziller, 1965), chap. 1, "The 'Psychologist's Fallacy' in the Observation of Inarticulate Perceptions," pp. 3–21.

4. *Origin of Consciousness,* pp. 52–53.

5. Stephen Pepper's outline of the fundamental world hypotheses that have appeared in Western civilization, and their accompanying definitions of mind and evidence, is based on the idea of "root metaphors." Examples include organicism and mechanism. The idea of root metaphor is itself a metaphor implying that each of the major cosmological theories stems not from reasoning alone, but from an original (i.e., root) insight into the world's structure and the nature of reality. Such insight has historically originated and found expression in the language of metaphor. See his *World Hypotheses,* chap. 5, "Root Metaphors," pp. 84–114.

6. *Introduction to Metaphysics,* trans. Mabelle L. Andison (Totowa, N.J.: Littlefield, Adams, 1975).

7. Eric A. Havelock, *Preface to Plato* (Cambridge: Harvard University Press, 1963), pp. 3–35, 145–64.

8. For an analysis of Newton's relation to the alchemical tradition, see Morris Berman, *The Reenchantment of the World* (Ithaca: Cornell University Press, 1980), pp. 121–25.

9. *Origins of Consciousness,* p. 56.

10. Jaynes's suggestion that all consciousness is metaphorical finds an analogue in the section on "Language" in Emerson's *Nature* (1836). There is a "radical

correspondence," says Emerson, "between visible things and human thoughts." Because of this root correspondence "savages, who have only what is necessary, converse in figures. As we go back in history, language becomes more picturesque, until its infancy, when it is all poetry; or all spiritual facts [i.e., the facts of consciousness] are represented by natural symbols. . . . We are thus assisted by natural objects in the expression of particular meanings" (in *Ralph Waldo Emerson: Essays and Lectures*, ed. Joel Porte, The Library of America 15 [New York: Viking, 1983], pp. 22, 23). Probably both William James and Julian Jaynes would have agreed with Emerson's suggestion of a radical correspondence between visible things and thoughts, though neither would go so far as to express it as a statement of metaphysical truth, as Emerson does in the following three sentences: "Have mountains, and waves, and skies, no significance but what we consciously give them, when we employ them as emblems of our thoughts? The world is emblematic. Parts of speech are metaphors, because the whole of nature is a metaphor of the human mind" (ibid., p. 24). Extreme as it is, though, Emerson's view of metaphor as a deep correspondence between things and thoughts provides another significant context for understanding James's metaphorical impulses. In his metaphors for the structure of consciousness, James was really working toward an understanding of the basic structure of reality.

11. *Origin of Consciousness*, p. 53.

12. *Principles of Psychology*, I 233; this volume cited hereafter by page number only.

13. "Remarks on Spencer's Definition of Mind as Correspondence," *Essays in Philosophy*, ed. Fredson Bowers, The Works of William James 5 (Cambridge: Harvard University Press, 1978), p. 21.

14. Ibid. In what is surely one of the most important philosophical works of recent decades, Richard Rorty argues in *Philosophy and the Mirror of Nature* (Princeton: Princeton University Press, 1979) that the classic epistemological notion of the mind as mirror of an external world no longer has any authority, and that instead of exploring the puzzles as to how the subject and object of epistemology interact, philosophers would do better to spend their energy on the pragmatic and hermeneutical task of making dialogue possible between different contexts of discourse.

15. *Essays in Radical Empiricism*, pp. 21–44.

16. Ibid., p. 4.

17. *Psychology: Briefer Course*, ed. Fredson Bowers, The Works of William James 12 (Cambridge: Harvard University Press, 1984), p. 398.

18. Ibid.

19. Bruce Wilshire, *William James and Phenomenology* (Bloomington: Indiana University Press, 1968), p. 14. Wilshire's book is one of several important studies that stress the phenomenological aspects of James's thought. Others include Hans Linschoten, *On the Way Toward a Phenomenological Psychology: The Psychology of William James*, trans. Amedeo Giorgi (Pittsburgh: Duquesne University Press, 1968); John Wild, *The Radical Empiricism of William James* (Garden City, N.Y.: Doubleday/Anchor, 1970); H. Spiegelberg, *The Phenomenological Movement: An Introduction* I (The Hague: Nijhoff, 1976), pp. 66–69, 111–17; and Alfred Schuetz, "William James' Concept of the Stream of Thought Phenomenologically Inter-

preted," *Philosophy and Phenomenological Research*, 1 (1941), 442–52. See also James Edie, "William James and Phenomenology," *The Review of Metaphysics*, 23 (1970), 481–526.

20. *Meditations*, in *Discourse on Method and Other Writings*, trans. J. Wollastrom (Harmondsworth: Penguin, 1970), p. 95.

21. Ed. Fredson Bowers, The Works of William James 13 (Cambridge: Harvard University Press, 1985), p. 125. See also H. S. Thayer, *Meaning and Action: A Critical History of Pragmatism* (Indianapolis: Bobbs-Merrill, 1968), pp. 133–35.

22. Quoted in *The Letters of William James*, ed. Henry James, 2 vols. (Boston: Atlantic Monthly Press, 1920), I 147.

23. Ibid., 147–48.

24. In *The Essays of Ralph Waldo Emerson* (Cambridge: The Belknap Press of Harvard University Press, 1987), pp. 42, 43.

25. Ehrenzweig, *Psycho-Analysis of Artistic Vision and Hearing*, p. 3.

26. George Perle, *Serial Composition and Atonality: An Introduction to the Music of Schoenberg, Berg, and Webern* (Berkeley: University of California Press, 1963), pp. 1–37.

27. See Douglas Cooper, *The Cubist Epoch* (London: Phaidon, 1970), esp. chap. 1, "True Cubism, 1906–1912," pp. 17–64; and Herbert Read, *A Concise History of Modern Painting* (New York: Praeger, 1959), esp. chap. 3, "Cubism," pp. 67–104.

28. Enrenzweig, *Psycho-Analysis of Artistic Vision and Hearing*, p. 11.

29. Ibid.

30. See Philip Wheelwright, *Metaphor and Reality* (Bloomington: Indiana University Press, 1967).

31. For an extensive treatment of Freudian ego-psychology as bound within the presuppositions of the Cartesian tradition, see Yankelovich and Barrett, *Ego and Instinct*, pp. 3–166. Yankelovich and Barrett also see James as part of a "changed background in philosophy" that has the potential to alter the deeply engrained dualistic assumptions of psychoanalysis (pp. 232–35).

32. Ibid., pp. 47–57.

33. *Meditations*, p. 19.

34. *Principles of Philosophy I*, trans. John Cottingham, *The Philosophical Writings of Descartes* I, trans. John Cottingham, Robert Stoothoff, and Dugald Murdoch (Cambridge: Cambridge University Press, 1985), art. 53, p. 210.

35. Ibid., art. 51, p. 210.

36. *Meditations*, p. 123.

37. Ibid., 163, 159.

38. *Philosophy in a New Key: A Study in the Symbolism of Reason, Rite, and Art*, 3rd ed. (Cambridge: Harvard University Press, 1980), p. 4.

39. Ibid.

40. Langer does not go so far as to suggest that James—with the question "Does 'consciousness' exist?"—brought forth a new generative idea, with potential to supersede its powerful Cartesian ancestor. But my analysis in this study is indebted in part to Whitehead's argument precisely to this effect in *Science and the Modern World*; see esp. chap. 9, "Science and Philosophy," pp. 139–56.

41. *Essays in Radical Empiricism*, p. 4.

42. Ibid.

43. Ibid., pp. 36–37.

44. Wylie Sypher called this phenomenon the "loss of the self in modern literature and art." See his *The Loss of the Self in Modern Literature and Art* (New York: Random House, 1962).

45. James, *Essays in Radical Empiricism*, p. 4.

46. Ibid.

4

Pure Experience as Revelation: Wallace Stevens and William James

Stevens and James as Explorers of Unified Experience

IN MANY ESSAYS AND POEMS Wallace Stevens makes the point that poetry originates in the interplay (sometimes the clash) of opposites which he names *imagination* and *reality*. Like the words "subject" and "object" in Cartesian epistemology, these terms in Stevens's essays imply an intractable dualism. Yet, as a perceptive critic has argued, Stevens's later poetry springs from a mind that is beyond the limits of such dualism. "At first, after the dissolution of the gods," it seemed that Stevens was left "in a world riven in two, split irreparably into subject and object, imagination and reality." All Stevens's earlier poetry seems, even by his own account, based on this dualism.

> Any attempt to escape it by affirming the priority of one or the other power leads to falsehood. But as his work progresses, Stevens comes more and more to discover that there is only one realm, always and everywhere the realm of some new conjunction of imagination and reality. . . . The later Stevens is beyond metaphysical dualism, and beyond representational thinking.[1]

This statement raises many questions not only about Stevens's poetry but also about the practical potential of our minds to pass beyond the dualistic form of experience presupposed by our culture. Passage beyond epistemological or metaphysical dualism implies a radical reorientation of thought—a shift of thinking frames from a culturally established picture of reality as split between mind and matter toward what Stevens evidently regarded in key passages of his later writings as reality itself. How can we account psychologically and philosophically for this mental turning process? What does it mean pragmatically "to discover that there is only one realm"? Without falling into the snares of the "block universe" of either the idealist or the materialist, Stevens implicitly offers answers to these questions in his essays and later poetry. His writings present evidence that he experienced such a basic reorientation of consciousness.

Though a solitary explorer of unknown dimensions of consciousness, Stevens was not entirely alone in his pioneering enterprise. The turning away from epistemological dualism to an alternative conception of consciousness, based on an intuited sense of the unity of experience, represents a pattern of intellectual development observable in the work of other thinkers of Stevens's period and before, including William James. A common spirit of struggle to shed the metaphysical straitjacket of dualism, and to move toward a nondualistic frame of mind—which we might call, following Owen Barfield, "participating consciousness"[2]—unites Stevens and James in a kinship of which Stevens himself was perhaps never fully aware. Yet in a series of letters regarding his late work *Notes Toward a Supreme Fiction* (1942),[3] Stevens leaves hints of a vital link between key ideas in the *Notes* and certain elements in James's thought. In these letters Stevens implies that James's concept of "the will to believe" had a germinal influence on his own thinking and writing. But this may be only a hint of a deeper affinity between them, an affinity that may have practical implications for a more complete understanding of Stevens's work. Understanding the relationship between Stevens and James may in fact have important consequences for the reader's own potential to enter the new region of consciousness that they mapped out. James's nondualistic portrait of consciousness in his radical empiricism provides a valuable but neglected critical approach to Stevens's later art and thought. Radical empiricism may indeed serve the reader of Stevens's poetry as a guide to a pragmatic understanding of the unified experience that Stevens strove to articulate.[4]

Stevens struggled for many years to resolve the problem of belief in a world "riven in two." Many of the poems in *Harmonium* (1923), built on the premise of an egoistic hedonism, depend on the principle of metaphysical opposites—"mind" and "reality"—in conflict and interaction as a source of the intensity of the aesthetic experience. The works included in *Ideas of Order* (1935), especially the great though obscure "Idea of Order at Key West," represent the beginnings of a kind of mental equilibrium between the warring elements of human reality (described later as a "war between the mind and sky") and point toward the attainment of a higher standpoint of consciousness presented to us in the *Notes* and in *Credences of Summer* (1946). This higher standpoint involves an expanded form of perception, counterpart to what theologians call *revelation*.[5] My contention is that this revelational form of perception in Stevens's late work can be fully understood only by the reader who grapples with the poet's move beyond dualistic structures of thought in his poetics. James's essay "The Will to Believe" (1897) and the later *Essays in Radical Empiricism* (1912)

can shed new light on our understanding of the philosophical dimensions
of this progression in Stevens's thought.

POETIC TRUTH IS BEYOND DUALISM

The pattern of James's thinking suggests a significant parallel between his
philosophy and Stevens's poetry. While Stevens's early preoccupation
with the interaction of imagination and reality gives way to an expanded
perceptual experience akin to the core religious experience of revelation,
the subjectivism of James's early psychology is superseded by the radical-
ized principles of pure experience. Both James and Stevens exemplify
development beyond the dualism of subject and object.[6] By poetic modes
of thinking, and through the theological language of revelation, Stevens
expresses his discovery of expanded forms of perception. James uses his
own secular terminology of radical empiricism and pure experience to
describe kindred discoveries.[7] But the kinds of experience denoted by
their respective terms are generically similar.

In one essay Stevens offers an analysis of a paradox involved in
traditional theories of perception shaped by dualistic categories.

> According to the traditional views of sensory perception, we do not see the
> world immediately but only as the result of a process of seeing and after the
> completion of that process, that is to say, we never see the world except the
> moment after. Thus we are constantly observing the past. . . . The material
> world, for all the assurances of the eye, has become immaterial. It has become
> an image in the mind. The solid earth disappears and the whole atmosphere is
> subtilized not by the arrival of some venerable beam of light from an almost
> hypothetical star but by a breach of reality. What we see is not an external
> world but an image of it and hence an internal world.[8]

Implicit in the passage is a longing for greater immediacy of awareness and
a dissatisfaction not only with traditional philosophical theories, but also
with the experience of ordinary sense perception itself. The split between
mind and external reality, even in what is called immediate sense perception, as Hume and Berkeley had argued, leads paradoxically to the
dissolution of perceived objects into insubstantial mental "images." The
psychic tension issuing from this "breach of reality" impels the poet to
seek a more penetrating and effectual mode of perception, capable of
grasping directly and holding on to the "solid earth" as fact, without a
mediatory "process of seeing." This deeper level of perception involves a
perceptual capacity whereby such dissolution of objects into immaterial
thoughts and "images" is no longer possible. And the effort to define his
"supreme fiction," the ultimate act of imagination, is motivated by this
need to pass beyond the limitations of dualistic psychology.

Though Stevens finds ordinary sense perception to be frozen into a dualistic mold, he does not reject the "physical" and attempt to seize a "mental" or ideal realm as his domain.[9] He does not seek to transcend sense data, or that which is experientially "given," but, through poetic and revelational means, to penetrate more completely into the given, and thus to find in fact the true nature of being in its wholeness—a unity of experience that the Cartesian tradition had split apart into a reified material realm and a hazy (but also reified) subjective realm of spirit and ego. In *The Necessary Angel* (1951), he argues that "poetic truth is a factual truth, seen, it may be, by those whose range in the perception of fact—that is, whose sensibility—is greater than our own" (NA 59). The peculiar meaning that Stevens assigns to the terms "fact" and "factual" in his essays throws much light on the higher level of perception articulated in the *Notes*. He distinguishes between absolute fact—the raw perceptual datum, "destitute of any imaginative aspect whatever" (NA 60)—and fact as perceived by means of the agency of poetic imagination.

> [T]he truth that we experience when we are in agreement with reality is the truth of fact. In consequence, when men, baffled by philosophic truth, turn to poetic truth, they return to their starting-point, they return to fact, not, it ought to be clear, to bare fact (or call it absolute fact), but to fact possibly beyond their perception in the first instance and outside the normal range of their sensibility [NA 59–60].

Notice that "fact" is defined here not as external reality, but as "agreement with reality." It is not, in other words, simply the objective side of a subject–object schema, but the intersection, the "precise equilibrium" (NA 9) of an experiential complex. The word "agreement" is Stevens's way of naming the primacy of experience as a complete transaction that cannot be arbitrarily partitioned. Hence agreement with reality is an achievement, which still does not presume either an external world or an internal world regarded as independent ontological realms.[10]

Stevens's emphasis on the need to "return to fact" indicates his basic method of dispelling the psychosis of dualism, a method central to the poetics of *Notes Toward a Supreme Fiction*. For Stevens, entry into the world of fact means breaking through the artificial images that the mind, in a dualistic framework, devises as mediation between itself and the real. His return to fact finds a counterpart in James's expression of the need for psychology to leave intellectual presuppositions about the structures of consciousness behind, and return to the actual phenomena of consciousness.[11] This effort to describe the phenomena just as they happen indicates James's fundamental agreement with the method at the heart of Stevens's poetics and practice as a poet. In both cases, the method results in a return that is a new realization of the truth of concrete experience.

Through his great care for the integrity of the phenomena themselves, James uncovers in his *Essays in Radical Empiricism* the irreducible facts of "pure experience,"[12] the phenomena of the "instant field of the present,"[13] as it comes to our awareness apart from any conceptual analysis of it. Like Stevens's "agreement with reality," where the so-called objective and subjective are grasped in their essential integration as life-activity, the Jamesian pure experience is the "one primal stuff" of which everything in the world is made. It is "experience in its 'pure' state, plain unqualified actuality, . . . as yet undifferentiated into thing and thought. . . ."[14] It is thus the one fact, final in itself, behind which we cannot go; and "we have every right to speak of it as subjective and objective both at once."[15]

The notion of pure experience offers us as readers a psychological (phenomenological) tool that clarifies Stevens's move beyond dualism. What distinguishes Stevens's approach from James's is the poet's more insistent interest in the "imagination" which manifests itself in poetry and art as the power that cuts through the fabric of mental presuppositions, the mind forg'd manacles, that bind perception within the limits prescribed by one's culture. Like James's "pure experience," the imagination to Stevens is a "pure power" (CP 382) which makes possible the "revelation of reality" (OP 214) that is the main concern of poetry. But while James simply attempts to describe the way experience happens, Stevens is more interested in the "power" that makes experience happen the way it does, that gives experience its structure, and that moves men and women to higher levels of perceptual development. Because the imagination at the level of its greatest vitality is at one with reality, and not confined to a subjective realm, it can bring about illuminated "moments of awakening . . . in which / We more than awaken" (CP 386). The imagination is the agent of a kind of revelation that is possible within a wholly naturalistic context. It is a revelation not of a supernatural or otherworldly reality, but of the "exquisite environment of fact" (OP 164).

SUPREME FICTION AS PURE EXPERIENCE

The event of a revelatory awakening to new powers of perception is the central experience recorded in the *Notes*. In the opening stanza of the poem Stevens announces the first principles of his own phenomenology of perception.

> Begin, ephebe, by perceiving the idea
> Of this invention, this invented world,
> The inconceivable idea of the sun [CP 380].

Here the "invented world" is the symbolic reduction of experience, the image of a "world" built up historically through the accretion of common sense and rational thought. But the "idea" he mentions is the creative idea, and is another name for "fact" as imaginatively discerned. It is that which can be "perceived" directly. Hence the reader, along with the ephebe, or student, to whom the poem is addressed, is invited to "perceive the idea," the basic reality, sometimes obscured by human "invention," but nonetheless present to the imaginative awareness. The "idea of the sun" symbolizes ultimate fact, paradoxically "inconceivable," but only because it is not reducible either to poetic symbols or to the forms of rational conception.

That sense of paradox is partially clarified in the following stanzas.

> You must become an ignorant man again
> And see the sun again with an ignorant eye
> And see it clearly in the idea of it.
>
> Never suppose an inventing mind as source
> Of this idea nor for that mind compose
> A voluminous master folded in his fire [CP 380–81].

To become "an ignorant man again" means to "return to fact" as actually experienced by abandoning the learned or fabricated opinions which put unnecessary shackles on perception. When the sun, Stevens's symbol for reality, is seen with an "ignorant eye," that is, without being filtered through the lenses of culturally induced beliefs and prejudices, it is seen "clearly." Yet this ultimate reality must be understood in terms of its "idea," for that is the way fact comes to light in experience. For Stevens the idea of the sun is not an internal reproduction of an external thing; it is the actual sun as men are capable of experiencing it in the immediacy of pure experience. Though he does not name the "source" of this idea directly, Stevens takes care to explain that it is neither an "inventing mind" nor some extra-experiential deity, a "voluminous master," which might exist only as a thing "composed" by that mind.

The student is asked to penetrate through such anthropomorphic or mythical conceptions. And in the next stanzas Stevens examines the myth-making tendency even more critically.

> How clean the sun when seen in its idea,
> Washed in the remotest cleanliness of a heaven
> That has expelled us and our images. . . .
>
> The death of one god is the death of all. . . .
>
> Phoebus is dead, ephebe. But Phoebus was
> A name for something that never could be named [CP 381].

When seen "in its idea," that is, from the standpoint of the creative idea, the sun (reality) is perceived directly as fact. It is "clean," like James's pure experience, without the sediment of human dogma or any of the superstitions endorsed by culture. The "heaven / That has expelled us and our images" is not the heaven of traditional religion, which for Stevens is precisely one of man's projected "images," a hereafter conceived apart from actual experience. Stevens's "heaven" is reality itself, the reality of pure experience, which one may enter by freeing oneself of human illusions and false interpretations of experience. In this respect Stevens welcomes the "death" of all gods as an event that helps to cleanse man's perceptual faculties of images that counterfeit the real. Phoebus, the Greek god of the sun—an anthropomorphic representation—is "a name for something that never could be named." This "something" is the reality of basic fact, the reality of being (the truth of being), the experience of which defies our human attempts to circumscribe its nature with manmade labels. For "The sun / Must bear no name, gold flourisher, but be / In the difficulty of what it is to be" (CP 381). In other words, the sun must be known not merely by means of symbolic reduction, but as fact, that is, directly "in its idea."

Ironically the *Notes* themselves represent Stevens's own effort to "name" that very primordial intuition of "being" which he says "must bear no name." But the naming process in which he is engaged is an "abstract" one, as indicated in the title of the poem's first section, "It Must Be Abstract." It is a naming primarily intended to define the mental conditions that make possible the enlarged awareness of fact that takes away the necessity for human names or metaphors. The supreme fiction, which is supreme by virtue of its fundamental agreement with reality, is thus not so much a "name" (or metaphor) as a state of mind, which one may move "toward," but perhaps never realize entirely, as suggested in the canto beginning "Not to be realized . . . " (CP 385). Though both Stevens and James understood the need for metaphor as a means of exploring the processes of consciousness, Stevens seems to have been more aware of the need eventually to move beyond metaphor in order to articulate the growth of consciousness beyond the limits of cultural beliefs. The abstract states of mind that he presents as the form of the supreme fiction are meditative states of silence in which the truth of being is allowed to come into the foreground of conscious awareness, and speak for itself through the revelations of pure experience.

THE IMAGINATION AS WILL TO BELIEVE

Earlier in the poem, Stevens writes:

> It is the celestial ennui of apartments
> That sends us back to the first idea, the quick
> Of this invention . . . [CP 381].

In one of his letters he explains: "If you take the varnish and dirt of generations off a picture, you see it in its first idea. If you think about the world without its varnish and dirt, you are a thinker of the first idea."[16] The first idea is "first" in the sense that it involves perceptual activity anterior to both reason and sensation as ordinarily understood. The first idea is thus Stevens's term for the perception of fact prior to the historical accumulation of more or less inaccurate human opinions, "varnish and dirt," about it.

In a series of lines that suggest the Jamesian notions imbibed by Stevens in his earlier years, we are told:

> The poem refreshes life so that we share,
> For a moment, the first idea. . . . It satisfies
> Belief in an immaculate beginning
>
> And sends us, winged by an unconscious will,
> To an immaculate end [CP 382].

The reference to "belief," followed in the next line by a mention of the "will," may recall to the student of James the famous doctrine of the *will to believe*. And in two letters Stevens suggests that this doctrine may have had a germinal influence on him during the writing of the poem. To Henry Church, to whom the poem is dedicated, he wrote, in 1942 (the year the poem was published):

> There are things with respect to which we willingly suspend disbelief; if there is instinctive in us a will to believe, or if there is a will to believe, whether or not it is instinctive, it seems to me that we can suspend disbelief with reference to a fiction as easily as we can suspend it with reference to anything else. There are fictions that are extensions of reality.[17]

These remarks represent Stevens's awareness of Samuel Taylor Coleridge's argument that a "willing suspension of disbelief" is necessary to a correct understanding of the literature of the supernatural, and its conjunction in Stevens's mind with James's more current phrase "the will to believe." In a letter to his friend Gilbert Montague, Stevens gives more specific hints of an affinity between the *Notes* and James's doctrine. Embodied in the *Notes*, he says,

> is the idea that, in the various predicaments of belief, it might be possible to yield, or to try to yield, ourselves to a declared fiction.
>
> This is the same thing as saying that it might be possible for us to believe in something that we know to be untrue. Of course, we do that every day, but we don't make the most of the fact that we do it out of the need to believe, what in your day, and mine, in Cambridge was called the will to believe.[18]

Stevens's "day" as a student in Cambridge was for three years (1897 to 1900) concurrent with James's long and distinguished career as a Harvard professor, though the Stevens files in the Harvard archives show that the poet never enrolled in a course from James. Yet James's influence was clearly felt by the young Stevens and appears to have been long-lived. The philosopher's ideas were part of the intellectual currency of Cambridge in those years, and there is little doubt that Stevens was well aware of them, and to a degree came under their spell.[19]

"The Will to Believe" was delivered by James as an address to the Philosophical Clubs of Yale and Brown Universities early in 1896, and published in the June issue of the *New World* that same year. In 1897, the first of Stevens's three years as a special student at Harvard, James's address appeared in book form as the first of ten essays, in *The Will to Believe and Other Essays in Popular Philosophy*. Is it likely that Stevens read these essays? Though one can only speculate, the letters cited above suggest that he did.[20]

James argues in "The Will to Believe" that consciousness is organized according to a principle of intentionality, characterized by "passional tendencies and volitions."[21] These are typically experienced not as inward and private mental phenomena, but as fundamental means of orienting thought to the world. He claims that the will is a natural tendency inherent in the structures of experience. It is ultimately a naturalistic principle of creativity, not unlike the imagination which, for Stevens, has the revelatory power of opening up consciousness to previously undiscovered aspects of reality. For James, the disposition of our "willing nature" is a force, operating to some extent prior to our conscious awareness of it, which actually contributes to the structures and contours of fact as we experience them. Concrete evidence is not always sufficient to justify belief in a thing's factuality on intellectual grounds alone, according to James. Thus it often becomes necessary (perhaps "every day," in Stevens's words) to rely on the emotionally charged volitions that animate the deeper levels of our psychic life as guides to belief and action. "There are, then, cases where a fact cannot come at all unless a preliminary faith exists in its coming,"[22] James contends. And in many situations "*faith in a fact can help create the fact*."[23] For a man's faith "acts on the powers above him as a claim, and creates its own verification."[24] On the basis of its observable consequences, James declares the validity of holding to a "voluntarily adopted faith"[25] in possibilities that may at first lie beyond the range of one's immediate awareness.

The "passional tendencies and volitions" at the heart of James's psychology of belief Stevens calls (in the lines quoted above) "an unconscious will," a will that is "unconscious" by virtue of its independence from the judgments of conscious intellect and reason. "The poem" according to Stevens "satisfies / Belief in an immaculate beginning"—immaculate because poetry or the act of imagination probes behind the "varnish and dirt" with which history and culture cloud the first idea. And that same imaginative energy of the poem "sends us, winged by an unconscious will, / To an immaculate end." For Stevens the concept of will is a form of creative imagination, analogous to the Jamesian will to believe—a power to actualize in experience what initially exists only as potential.

REVELATION AS THE DISCOVERY
OF A NEW STANDPOINT

At a later point in the poem Stevens asserts that

> The first idea was not our own. Adam
> In Eden was the father of Descartes
> And Eve made air the mirror of herself,
>
> Of her sons and of her daughters [CP 383].

A limited perceiver does not experience the fact immediately, but treats the subjective images of what he perceives as things in themselves. In other words, he treats appearances, whether individual or collective representations, as basic reality. But according to Stevens's principles of perception, only the fact is basic. The first idea "was not our own," since it has an ontological status prior to the projections or constructions of the human mind. Yet Stevens tells us later that "The first idea is an imagined thing" (CP 387). If the "first idea" is not constructed by the human mind ("not our own"), and yet is a product of imagination ("an imagined thing"), the imagination itself must work beyond the limits of human or subjective consciousness. When in another poem Stevens writes "We say God and the imagination are one" (CP 524), the reader may sense that he is eliminating God from his universe, and replacing divinity with the human imagination. This reading follows a conventional humanistic interpretation of Stevens's thought as it touches on religious matters. But the meaning of this controversial line is not so unambiguous. In another sense, Stevens is redefining both the human mind, or imagination, and what traditional religion has called God, claiming that both are aspects of a larger inclusive order of being, beyond the grasp of conceptual formulas. The human mind has the capability of attaining a Godlike perspective toward reality, by uniting with the "central mind" (CP 524)—centered in the concrete reality of experience—named in the same poem. The true (i.e., experiential) meaning of the idea of *God*, then, is found in this very experience of an exalted perceptual standpoint, arrived at directly by the exercise of that inner power that the poet calls *imagination*.

Stevens's reference to Descartes recalls the philosopher's subjective I-think, proclaimed as his first principle of philosophic certainty. Adam, who in the allegory of Genesis was given the job of naming all the living creatures, imposed a subjective interpretation on them, thereby "fathering" the tendency toward subjectivism manifested in Descartes's philosophy. By making "air the mirror of herself" Eve projected a humanly contrived form onto nature. Eve and her sons and daughters, we are told, "found themselves / In heaven as in a glass" (CP 383). This "heaven" is not an actual experience, but rather the projection of idealized human thought on the environment. The phrase "inhabitants of a very varnished green" (CP 383) recalls the lines quoted above from Stevens's letters suggesting that the "first idea" is what is left after the "varnish and dirt" have been eliminated from perception. This "varnished" dwelling place is a "second earth," whose secondary quality involves the human imposition of form on it—as opposed to the first idea, or man's primal experience of the basic structure of being.

In his reference to a "seeing and unseeing in the eye" (CP 385), the poet distinguishes between appearance (seeing) and creative discernment of fact (unseeing). The distinction between inner or subjective awareness and reality is common to Western philosophic tradition since Descartes. But the creative process called "unseeing" is another term for what Stevens also calls "decreation," whereby the "thing seen becomes the thing unseen" (OP 167). This is a process in which ego-centered attention is loosened to allow fact to come directly to light, without having to leap the gap presumed to exist between objective and subjective realms. Such unmediated perception can take place only after the human disposition to impose order on the data of perception has been relaxed.

In a seminal canto later in the *Notes* Stevens clarifies these points further by declaring that

> [T]o impose is not
> To discover. To discover an order as of
> A season, to discover summer and know it,
>
> To discover winter and know it well, to find,
> Not to impose, not to have reasoned at all,
> Out of nothing to have come on major weather.
>
> It is possible, possible, possible. It must
> Be possible. It must be that in time
> The real will from its crude compoundings come,
>
> Seeming, at first, a beast disgorged, unlike,
> Warmed by a desperate milk. To find the real,
> To be stripped of every fiction except one,
>
> The fiction of an absolute—Angel,
> Be silent in your luminous cloud and hear
> The luminous melody of proper sound [CP 403–404].

The act of creative "discovery"—distinguished in Jamesian fashion from the tendency to "impose" our cherished private images or collective representations on the real—requires one to hold in abeyance the exercise of "reason," which inhibits the revelatory action of imagination. Such action entails catching from the "[i]rrational moment" its "unreasoning," "As when the sun comes rising" (CP 398), that is, when fact as such is permitted to appear in consciousness, without subjective distortion.

Though we may reason of such things "with later reason" (CP 401), the poet's true task is to discover "the instant field of the present," as described by James. That is ultimately what it means "to find the real," for reality to Stevens is above all the "fluent mundo" (CP 407) that must be grasped in its "living changingness" (CP 380). "To find / Not to impose" means "not to have reasoned at all," where reason implies thought dualistically cut off from fact and accepting its own rational constructions ("later reason") as basic reality. Like the process of "unseeing," a perceptual activity prior to the images that arise from either private sensation or social construction, Stevens's "unreasoning" involves a mental action anterior to the function called reason. But "to discover an order" is, for Stevens as for James, a radically different kind of act from imposing a rational scheme on things and events. For the "order" that is discovered through the imagination is the basic structure of all fact.

Stevens's approach to perception, like James's, involves as a first step the effort to strip false concepts from the mind. For Stevens this is a means to prepare the soil of consciousness for the seed of poetic revelation. That preparation is finally achieved not by speaking but by being "silent." Can Stevens be referring to the silence of Zen-like meditative states, in which all "thoughts" and their accompanying anxieties are not repressed but willingly relinquished, in favor of a higher standpoint?[26] One seemingly innocent hint about the poet's practice of a personal form of meditation appears briefly in a letter in which Stevens late in his life explained to a friend that his was a quiet existence, given to "meditation and prayer."[27] To what could the anti-religious Stevens be referring by this phrase, except the practice of a natural inner discipline, training himself like the Zen practitioner to "Exile desire / For what is not" (CP 373)—i.e., the fabrications of a human mind divorced from its own potentially fecund intercourse with the real. Only by such meditative silence can the "Angel" of the poem hear the "luminous melody of proper sound"—the sound that emanates directly from fact, and leads the attentive poet to his "final poem," which is "the poem of fact in the language of fact" (OP 164). The "beast disgorged, unlike" suggests the "real," which is "not our own" and "not ourselves" (CP 383). The "beast," much like the psychic apparition that is so devastatingly revelatory to the protagonist of Henry James's story "The Beast in the Jungle" (1901) yet so "unlike" anything within the range of ordinary human perception that its appearance could not be humanly contrived, is an image for that ultimate revelation of reality sought by the poet of the *Notes*. Stevens's Angel, not unlike the angels of Biblical religion, here representing a naturalistic though ecstatic state of consciousness, is an agent of that expanded perception of the real which the poet calls revelation.

THE PERSPECTIVE OF TRUTH

Stevens's poetry represents a journey to find a right way of seeing, a perspective toward the real that is not limited and conditioned by finite or personal perspectives. In one poem he speaks of a passion to "step barefoot into reality" ("Large Red Man Reading"). And in the magnificent late work *Credences of Summer* (1946), he approaches his ultimate standpoint of perception in the following eloquent words:

> Let's see the very thing and nothing else.
> Let's see it with the hottest fire of sight.
> Burn everything not part of it to ash.
>
> Trace the gold sun about the whitened sky
> Without evasion by a single metaphor.
> Look at it in its essential barrenness
> And say, this, this is the centre that I seek [CP 373].

The impassioned desire to "see the very thing"—the reality of being— "and nothing else" requires the "hottest fire of sight," a vehemence in seeing, capable of burning "everything not part of it to ash." Such perception involves a certain elevation of thought, moving to "the centre" of being (experience) that Stevens elsewhere calls a "central purity." In one of his late essays, he speaks of an "elevation and elation on the part of the poet, which he communicates to the reader" (NA 60). This "may not be so much elevation as an incandescence of the intelligence and so more than ever a triumph over the incredible" (NA 60). Through the experience of poetry, we come to identify with the process of seeing experienced and documented by the poet, and so find the "purification that all of us undergo as we approach any central purity" (NA 60). Philosophically, Stevens's experience of central purity may be understood as a form of James's "pure experience."

Such a high standpoint, from which truth appears, perceptible as fact, as something more than a conception in the mind, is presented in the poem by images of the tower and the mountain, in the following lines:

> It is the natural tower of all the world,
> The point of survey, green's green apogee,
> But a tower more precious than the view beyond,
> A point of survey squatting like a throne
> Axis of everything, green's apogee. . . .
>
> It is the mountain on which the tower stands,
> It is the final mountain. Here the sun,
> Sleepless, inhales his proper air, and rests,
> This is the refuge that the end creates [CP 373].

In contrast to the use of *green* in the early poems of *Harmonium* (1923) symbolizing an enhancement of physical sight—"the green freedom of a cockatoo," and "pungent oranges and bright green wings" of "Sunday Morning," for example—the later Stevens of *Credences of Summer* uses green as a means of defining a heightened and centered perspective toward the real. This new perspective is the standpoint of truth: the ultimate "point of survey," "green's green apogee," the highest point of view, sensitive not just to such things as the "bright green wings" of finite sense experience, but to ultimate reality. This high standpoint, "the axis of everything," "the final mountain," is the perspective of ultimate revelation for Stevens. Having achieved "the end," the poet as seer, as well as his attentive reader, finds the "refuge" of truth, as suggested in a later line from the same poem: "The rock cannot be broken. It is the truth" (CP 375).

NOTES

1. J. Hillis Miller, "Wallace Stevens' Poetry of Being," in *The Act of the Mind: Essays on the Poetry of Wallace Stevens*, edd. Roy Harvey Pearce and J. Hillis Miller (Baltimore: The Johns Hopkins University Press, 1964), p. 154. Though he does not rely on sources in the American philosophic tradition, I am indebted to Miller for his ground-breaking treatment of philosophic themes in the writings of Stevens, Eliot, and Williams, in *Poets of Reality: Six Twentieth-Century Writers* (Cambridge: Harvard University Press, 1965).

2. *Saving the Appearances*, pp. 40–45.

3. *Collected Poems*, pp. 380–408; hereafter cited as CP. For one example of Stevens's direct engagement of some of James's ideas, see the essay entitled "The Figure of the Youth as Virile Poet" in *The Necessary Angel: Essays on Reality and the Imagination* (New York: Vintage, 1951), pp. 39–67; hereafter cited as NA.

4. This study of the relationship between Stevens and James is an expanded version of my essay "Wallace Stevens and William James: The Poetics of Pure Experience," published in *Philosophy and Literature*, 1 (1977), 183–91. Since that time other scholars have found the scent of this relationship worth following. Noteworthy among them is David M. LaGuardia, author of *Advance on Chaos: The Sanctifying Imagination of Wallace Stevens* (Hanover, N.H.: University Press of New England, for Brown University Press, 1983). LaGuardia gives detailed analysis of Stevens's thought as it relates to the ideas of both James and Emerson, but is not concerned with the issue of Stevens's or James's advance beyond the horizons of the Cartesian paradigm.

5. See, for example, Nicolai Berdyaev, *Truth and Revelation*, trans. R. M. French (New York: Harper & Row, 1953); and H. Richard Niebuhr, *The Meaning of Revelation* (New York: Macmillan, 1941).

6. For a naturalistic account of the idea of the core religious experience, by one of the heirs of William James in American psychology who worked beyond the limits of the Cartesian paradigm toward a holistic view of experience, see Abraham H. Maslow, *Religions, Values, and Peak Experiences* (New York: Penguin, 1976), esp. the chapter "The 'Core Religious,' or 'Transcendent' Experience," pp. 19–29.

7. For a valuable study that makes a strong case for a specifically religious

dimension in Stevens's art and thought without reference to James, see Leonora Woodman, *Stanza My Stone: Wallace Stevens and the Hermetic Tradition* (West Lafayette, Ind.: Purdue University Press, 1983).

8. *Opus Posthumous*, ed. Samuel French Morse (New York: Knopf, 1957), pp. 190–91; hereafter cited as OP.

9. A study of Stevens which treats his connections to the idealist tradition beginning with Coleridge, and also contains several helpful pages about views of the Absolute shared by Stevens and James, is Margaret Peterson's *Wallace Stevens and the Idealist Tradition* (Ann Arbor, Mich.: UMI Research Press, 1983), esp. pp. 94–110.

10. James had used the very phrase "agreement with reality" as his essential definition of "truth" in *The Meaning of Truth* in 1909. See esp. chap. 9, "The Meaning of the Word Truth" (*The Meaning of Truth*, ed. Fredson Bowers, The Works of William James 2 [Cambridge: Harvard University Press, 1975], pp. 117–19). James regarded truth not as an abstract idea cut off from experience, but as a *working agreement* between fact and idea going into action. Thus he writes, in *Pragmatism*, p. 102, "To 'agree' in the widest sense with a reality, *can only mean to be guided either straight up to it or into its surroundings, or to be put into such working touch with it as to handle either it or something connected with it better than if we disagreed.*" Though Stevens may not have stressed the working aspect of ideas to this same degree, it is likely that he would concur with James's conviction that our ideas need to "touch" the solid ground of actuality in order to validate themselves.

Stevens's nondualistic way of construing the idea of "fact" also bears an important resemblance not only to Dewey's sense of fact (see below, pp. 104–106), but also to that of an earlier holistic thinker in the American philosophic tradition, Ralph Waldo Emerson. In his seminal essay *Nature* (1836), Emerson argued that all natural facts are linked as symbols to what he called "spiritual facts." The category of "spiritual fact" in Emerson is not a conception of some ethereal or supernatural entity. It is precisely the connection between what traditional epistemology called "spirit" (mind) and "fact" (thing), in the concrete realization of a natural experience that is fully awake. Only that realization reveals the factual truth about both nature and experience that Emerson calls the spiritual fact.

11. See James's *Principles of Psychology*, I 221–23; and Wild's *Radical Empiricism of William James*, pp. 29–31, 50–51.

12. P. 4.

13. Ibid., p. 13.

14. Ibid., pp. 36–37.

15. Ibid., p. 7.

16. *Letters*, ed. Holly Stevens (New York: Knopf, 1966), pp. 426–27.

17. Ibid., p. 430.

18. Ibid., p. 443.

19. During this period Stevens also came more explicitly under the influence of the European-born George Santayana. A study treating in detail Santayana's influence on both Stevens and Eliot is Lois Hughson's *Thresholds of Reality: George Santayana and Modernist Poetics* (Port Washington, N.Y.: Kennikat, 1977). Though Stevens acknowledged Santayana's influence more consciously than that

of James, in my opinion the former had little to do with the development of Stevens's thinking beyond the boundaries of the Cartesian paradigm. See also Stevens's poem "To an Old Philosopher in Rome" (CP 508–10) written in memory of Santayana.

20. See Milton J. Bates's valuable biography *Wallace Stevens: A Mythology of Self* (Berkeley: University of California Press, 1985), pp. 205–207.

21. *The Will to Believe and Other Essays in Popular Philosophy*, ed. Fredson Bowers, The Works of William James 6 (Cambridge: Harvard University Press, 1979), p. 19. See also Robert J. O'Connell, s.j., *William James on the Courage to Believe* (New York: Fordham University Press, 1984), esp. chap. 8, "Metaphors of Belief," pp. 107–22.

22. *Will to Believe*, p. 29.

23. Ibid.

24. Ibid., pp. 28–29.

25. Ibid., p. 13.

26. See D. T. Suzuki, *Studies in Zen Buddhism* (New York: Dell, 1978), esp. chap. 4, "Reason and Intuition in Buddhist Philosophy," pp. 85–128, where Suzuki makes prominent use of the Jamesian phrase "pure experience" to describe the quality of *prajna* consciousness, or Buddhist intuition. For an alternate (and basically Western) view of Stevens's approach to meditation, see Louis L. Martz's excellent article "Wallace Stevens: The World as Meditation" in *The Achievement of Wallace Stevens*, edd. Ashley Brown and Robert S. Haller (Philadelphia: Lippincott, 1962), pp. 211–31.

27. *Letters*, p. 841; see also Woodman, *Stanza My Stone*, p. 1; and for an account of Stevens's late "conversion" to Christianity, see Bates, *Wallace Stevens*, pp. 296–97.

5

Toward Conscious Creativity:
The New Empiricism
of John Dewey

1. The Problem of New England Culture

BORN IN VERMONT IN 1859, of flinty New England stock like that which in earlier eras had produced such giants in the American intellectual landscape as Jonathan Edwards and Ralph Waldo Emerson, John Dewey carved a philosophy—like theirs deeply in the American grain—out of the hard granite of lived experience.[1] By his own account, "a heritage of New England culture" had created in him a sense of "inward laceration" concerning the "isolation of self from the world, of soul from body, of nature from God." This unusually poignant autobiographical statement from Dewey points to a central problem that would occupy him as a philosopher for the rest of his life: the problem of how to overcome the disposition to dichotomize experience that seemed hereditary to anyone raised in his native New England. Having identified his central problem early, he worked tirelessly to reconstruct the basic principles of philosophy and to reorient its methods so that it could regain something of its anciently acclaimed ability to care for the lacerated soul, an ability that might contribute to the healing and reconstruction of man's individual and collective experience. Among the earliest steps in Dewey's philosophic odyssey was his conversion to a form of Hegelian idealism expounded by his mentor, George Sylvester Morris of Johns Hopkins University where Dewey took his doctorate in 1884. Though the formalism of Hegelian dialectics held little interest even for the young Dewey, the "synthesis of subject and object, matter and spirit, the divine and the human" which he found in Hegel and his followers was "no mere intellectual formula," but "an immense release, a liberation."[2]

Wary of the tendency of conceptual analysis to distort lived experience, Dewey sought throughout his career to liberate himself and his readers from the snares of conceptualization. Every concept is a reduction—even, he would eventually discover, the conceptual structures of Hegelian philosophy—whereby some raw experienced phenomenon is brought under intellectual control. The great virtue of the uniquely human capacity to form abstract concepts out of the raw materials of experience may be the glory of rational thought. The danger is that the abstractions of the rational mind may become ends in themselves, losing touch with the vibrant generative tissue of experience that gave them birth in the first place. If we compare the fixed structures and categories of philosophic analysis to a series of photographs of a town, taken from various points of view, the photographs, no matter how well executed, would never be equivalent to the reality of the town in which we walk about. Dewey's reconstructed empiricism attempts to get as close as possible to original experience, to sense its texture and organization. In the process, he tries to shape philosophy into a discipline that accounts for the walk through the town, not merely for conceptual "photographs" of it.[3] And because he conceived of philosophy as not merely descriptive, but as having transformative effects on experience, the empirical method that Dewey evolved would become a means of finding one's way and in effect expanding experience by clarifying it and working out increasingly significant patterns of organization within it.

Rendering the patterns and energies of experience in human language, without resorting to Western philosophy's arsenal of abstract concepts, has traditionally been the office of the poet or fiction writer. The sense of an intuited connection between poetry and the dynamics of lived experience prompted the poet Charles Olson to remark: "He who possesses rhythm possesses the universe, . . . [which is] why art is the only twin life has—its only valid metaphysic. Art does not seek to describe but to enact."[4] Because it is an attempt to articulate living experience, regardless of the cost in abandoning doctrine and conceptualization, Dewey's philosophy fulfills some of the same functions Olson ascribed to poetry. While historic empiricism stemming from Locke had reduced experience to its lowest common denominator of sensation, leading directly to the skepticism of Hume, which systematically excludes values and meanings, Dewey's philosophy evolved in time into a new empiricism that encompasses all the concrete empirical data of experience, as well as meanings and values like those found in the arts. At its fullest development his philosophy became an empirical naturalism that is, or strove to be, like the work of the poet as defined by Olson, a true metaphysic of experience. Like Olson, Dewey recognized that the artist is uniquely qualified to bring about the vivid qualitative "realization" of experience, that is, to awaken more immediate contact with sensory experience, but also, by the transfer of its energies to the viewer, to aid our growth into more organized stages of conscious experience. Because of his high estimate of the qualitative experience embodied in works of art, Dewey looked upon art and literature as primary resources for the philosopher (and others) to become fully engaged in the clarifying and transformative energies inherent in experience itself. Though Dewey never elevated philosophy to the status he accords to the arts, as a medium for rendering (and expanding) experience, we perceive in his naturalistic empiricism, as in James's, a desire to enact as much as to describe the dynamics of the complex energy fields we call experience. If "nature" is a name for the universal context in which experience takes place, Dewey concurs with Olson's assessment of the role of the poet when he states that poets are the "true metaphysicians of nature."[5]

MIND IS IMMANENT IN NATURE AND EXPERIENCE

In *The Quest for Certainty* (1929) Dewey described an historical shift in perspectives toward the world, which he compared to the Copernican revolution in sixteenth-century astronomy. During his lifetime Dewey observed in American philosophy, and participated in, a shift from a primary concern with the epistemological subject to an emphasis on the experiential context of life-activity. This change of emphasis, evident in his own philosophy, was as momentous as the historic reorientation of cosmological perspectives called the Copernican revolution. Nicolaus Copernicus (1473–1543) offered his age a new understanding of planetary movements, and promoted a revolutionary change in man's sense of his place in nature by exchanging a "given" terrestrial point of view for an imagined solar standpoint. The imaginative projection of the sun as a center of perspective reference opened new avenues of understanding to the discerning inquirer that remained closed to those still held within the conceptual boundaries of the earth-centered Ptolemaic cosmology. In a chapter of *The Quest for Certainty* titled "The Copernican Revolution," Dewey develops an analogy between the geocentric cosmos of Ptolemy (A.D. ca. 100–ca. 178) and the subjectivism of modern philosophy, and compares Copernicus's heliocentric perspective to the contextualistic outlook emerging early in twentieth-century philosophy.

Copernicus had reoriented the human understanding by observing the revolutions of the heavenly spheres *as if* he were at the standpoint of the sun. Inspired by this magnificent theoretical achievement, Immanuel Kant in 1787 proclaimed that he had accomplished a "second Copernican revolution"—in critical philosophy. He believed he had discovered the true nature of knowledge by shifting his own attention, and that of his age, from the objective material world to the cognitive subject. Kantian idealism, progenitor of Romantic idealism in nineteenth-century philosophy and literature, made the knowing subject a primary agent in the construction of the world. By imposing its *a priori* "categories" of understanding— as well as the "forms of intuition" that we call schematic time and space—

on the raw materials of sense experience, the mind became an ordering principle, contributing rational structure to all observed phenomena. Instead of playing a merely passive role as the receiver of sense data, as in the empiricism of Locke and Hume, mind assumed a legislative function in the knowing process. In Kant's own words, "the understanding does not draw its laws (*apriori*) from nature, but prescribes them to nature."[6]

Ancient classical tradition, according to Dewey, had asserted that "knowledge is determined by the objective constitution of the universe." But, he claims, it did so "only after it had first assumed that the universe is itself constituted after the pattern of reason. Philosophers first constructed a rational system of nature and then borrowed from it the features by which to characterize their knowledge of it." Kant, in effect, did no more than "[call] attention to the borrowing."[7] Convinced by the skepticism of Hume that the order of our world is inherent neither in objects themselves nor in objective physical laws, including the principle of causality, Kant turned to the knowing mind to find the source of the world's apparent unity and order. The world of things as they *appear* would not in fact *be* a world for us, Kant argued, if observed phenomena did not conform to the innate categories of the human understanding. Casuality was just one of twelve such categories, regarded by Kant as *a priori* forms imposed by the mind on the data of perception to create unity out of an otherwise chaotic "sensuous manifold." The transcendental ego, a lineal descendant of Descartes's *cogito*, but unlike the passive "subject" of empirical psychology, contributed—by imposing—form on all experience and knowledge. The Kantian assertion that the mind is central in shaping knowledge became equivalent to the claim that it effects the organization of nature itself.

Acknowledgment of the mind's office as a shaping instrument within experience is a key factor in the experimentalist position defended by Dewey. But Kant's way of cutting off the subject from the object of knowledge, in rigorous accord with Cartesian tradition, was regarded by Dewey as highly conservative, and even retrograde. Hence Kant's "endeavor to make the known world turn on the constitution of the knowing mind" was in Dewey's view no revolution at all, but a retreat to an "ultra-Ptolemaic" position in epistemology (QC 228).

From the Copernican revolution two possible lessons can be learned about the relations between the knower and the known. On the one hand, we learn to distrust the evidence of the senses—i.e., not to accept at face value the apparent "rising" and "setting" of the sun on the earth's horizons—and instead, as Kant argued, to lean more heavily for our picture of the universe on the conceptual powers of reason. Such powers proved capable, in Kant's interpretation, of defying the senses and conceiving the sun as the center around which the earth and other planets revolve. From Copernicus Kant derived the principle that reason acts by its own autonomous power to organize and give rational significance to the manifold of sense. But Kantian rationalism sustained its subjectivist bias so rigorously that it denied the mind direct access to anything outside the mind's own conceptual sphere. Though we could not "know" them directly, external objects were still held by Kant to cause stimulation of the five senses. All that could be unequivocally known were the phenomenal appearances of sense, on display within the mind's self-enclosed theater. From the Cartesian paradigm, which separated subject from object at the outset, was bred another insidious dichotomy: the separation between unknowable "things-in-themselves," or *noumena*, and immediate sense data, called *phenomena*.

On the other hand, beyond Kantian subjectivism, Dewey drew a second kind of conclusion from the Copernican revolution. To him, that revolution suggested the possibility of shifting philosophic perspectives not merely from the senses to the reason, or, as Kant expressed it, from the object to the subject, but also from the conception of mind as a spectator located in an internal psychic space to a new conception of mind as an active "character" participating constructively in the shaping of events. Mind performs an "instrumentalist" function, contributing intelligent energies to the ongoing process of ordering and unifying the problematic situations that constitute experience in its raw state.[8] Consciousness is not confined within a subjective sanctuary. Dewey insists on philosophy's potential by its application of critical and constructive thinking to move us away from the artificially secure framework of subjectivism—comparable to the earthbound Ptolemaic perspective—not to a converse "objectivity," but to a new framework, which rejects the categorical opposition between subject and object. In this new framework the mind pecks open its subjective shell and assumes the authority of a guide, participating in events by bringing order to the contexts of experience. Like Copernicus, Dewey made clear that we can reject the limitation of mind to a "given" perspective. As Copernicus led the way beyond the Ptolemaic outlook toward his heliocentric perspective, looking down upon earth from the sun, Dewey replaced the egocentric perspective common to both Descartes and Kant with a new orientation of consciousness, an orientation that he called "contextual."

The revolutionary turn in philosophy involves a "genuine reversal of traditional ideas about the mind, reason, conceptions, and mental processes" (QC 231). This "reversal" is a displacement of the modern conception of consciousness, and the discovery of a new form of mind, which we may term *postmodern*. As Dewey argues, the "old centre" of human and philosophic insight—first disclosed by Descartes and accepted implicitly by Kant—was "mind knowing by means of an equipment of powers complete within itself . . ." (QC 232). The "new centre" is "[n]either self nor world, neither soul nor nature (in the sense of something isolated and finished in its isolation) . . . , any more than either earth or sun is the absolute centre of a single universal and necessary frame of reference" (QC 232). The new center is the *context* of man's existence—his existential relation to a total situation in the world, a relation characterized by affectional, as well as rational, understanding of nature and the social environment. "There is a moving whole of interacting parts; a centre emerges wherever there is effort to change them in a particular direction" (QC 232). The "new centre," or new conception of mind, is the point of creative encounter between these parts, whereby "changes take place in a *directed* way, so that a movement . . . from the doubtful and confused to the clear, resolved and settled . . . takes place." Mind for Dewey is "no longer a spectator beholding the world from without. . . . The mind is within the world as a part of the latter's on-going process." Thus the "historical transition" for which Dewey accounts is a shift from "knowing as an outside beholding to knowing as an active participant in the drama of an on-moving world . . ." (QC 232). The world is an "on-moving" organic whole, and what we call mind is a phase of this dynamic but "unfinished" continuum. The act of knowing is not a matter of the entry through the senses of mental contents into a substantive consciousness. Genuine mental activity is a transformational act, the "transformation of disturbed and unsettled situations into those more controlled and more significant" (QC 236). By means of such a knowing process, the experienced world takes on "more luminous and organized meaning" (QC 236). Mind—and its functional equivalents, knowing, imagining, intelligent action—is in the last analysis immanent in the contexts of experience, which are in turn aspects of that inclusive category, nature.

TRUE KNOWING INCLUDES THE AFFECTIONS

Conventional rationality typically involves the application of fixed intellectual structures, like the principles of logic and mathematics to various objects, and a disposition to judge concepts and cognitive objects by rational criteria, like Descartes's clarity and distinctness. The ascendancy of rational analysis over other forms and methods of knowing is a keynote of modernity. It functions by means of intellectual distancing of the object. But an alternate mode of knowing embraced by Dewey, identified by such terms as *intuition* and *affection*, involves placing oneself at the center of the known object in order to look out from its point of view, so to speak, to participate by sympathetic identification with the object—and thereby comprehend by entering into its uniqueness and inner dynamics. A major aspect of Dewey's revolution in empirical philosophy is the increased valuation of this affectional or, as he also called it, "qualitative" mode of understanding:

> the idea that [rational and analytical] cognition is the measure of the reality found in other modes of experience is the most widely distributed premise of philosophies. The equation of the real and the known comes to explicit statement in idealistic theories. If we remind ourselves of the landscape with trees and grasses waving in the wind and waves dancing in sunlight, we recall how scientific thought of these things strips off the qualities significant in perception and direct enjoyment, leaving only certain physical constants stated in mathematical formulae. What is more natural, then, than to call upon mind to reclothe by some contributory act of thought or consciousness the grim skeleton offered by science [QC 235]?

This reclothing process is typical of the cognitive method of idealism in the Kantian mold. On the other hand, "realistic theories" have protested against this tendency, proclaiming that "Knowledge must be the grasp or vision of the real as it 'is in itself,' while emotions and affections deal with it as it is affected with an alien element supplied by the feeling and desiring subject" (QC 235). The distorting tendencies of both modes of knowing are evident to Dewey. "When real objects are identified, point for point, with knowledge-objects," he contends, "all affectional and volitional objects are inevitably excluded from the 'real' world, and are compelled to find refuge in the privacy of an experiencing subject or mind" (EN 30). The notion of a private experiencing subject is the offspring of purely cognitive approaches to knowledge. Affectional and volitional approaches, on the other hand, leave the door open to a nonsubjective process of knowing.

Basing his argument on an appeal to experience and to qualitative modes of knowing, Dewey attacks the postulates of both the idealist and the realist. "The meaning of a Copernican reversal" is that we do not have to go to the rational "knowledge" of either the realist or the idealist "to obtain an exclusive hold on reality," for the "world as we experience it is a real world" (QC 235). *Experience*, in its qualitative configuration, and *reality*, he suggests, are the same. One is not a subjective copy of the other. Nor is experience a controlling or beautifying lens through which reality is perceived. *Experience* and *reality* are terms that describe a *contextual field*, from differing points of view. The field itself Dewey calls a "situation" or "context," a structural integer that cannot be arbitrarily divided into subjective and objective parts. It is one existential fact, a "contextual whole," whose integration or wholeness includes both consciousness and its environment, and is known by the only means available to discern qualitative meaning, the affections.

The term "situation" suggests "a complex existence that is held together in spite of its internal complexity by the fact that it is dominated

and characterized throughout by a single quality." By "object," on the
other hand, is meant "some element in the complex whole that is defined
in abstraction from the whole. . . ."⁹ Valid thinking, that which takes its
bearings from existential facts, is a matter of "selective determination" of
objects "controlled by reference to a situation—to that which is constituted by a pervasive and internally integrating quality . . ." (QT 246).
Failure to discern the ontological reality called a situation "leaves, in the
end, the logical force of objects and their relations inexplicable" (QT 246).
While Kant and the empiricists saw primal experience as a mass of raw
perceptual data, which could be processed, and hence organized, by our
mental machinery—whether the *a priori* categories of Kant, or the associ-
ational mechanisms of the empiricists—Dewey saw experience as events
occurring in the already partially organized form of complex situations or
contexts. The main principle of contextual organization for Dewey is the
presence of a unifying quality, inherent not in a "mind" as such, but in
the situation—in the developing relations and interactions between the live
creature and other facts. The facts in any situation are inevitably disparate
in character and type, including the physical characteristics of a man's
environment, the behavior and perspectives of other individuals, and a
host of other variables likely to change over time. The situational complex
is "held together" by its dominant quality, a fact as discernible within the
terms of Dewey's new empiricism as simple ideas and sense data were to
the sensory mechanisms of traditional empiricism.

The historian, for example, who attempts to analyze such phenomena
as wars, revolutions, depressions, etc., without reference to the pervasive
quality of the situation he is dealing with, will from Dewey's perspective
inevitably get stuck in a quagmire of meaningless nominalistic detail (the
equivalent of undigested sense data). But the historian who has a strong
intuition of the dominant quality that gives an historical situation identity
not only will write more perceptively and persuasively but will manifest
insight that comes closer to the "reality" of the situation than could ever
be achieved by a linear accumulation of facts. History is a field that clearly
cannot be divorced from the contexts that include persons, ideas, relationships, laws, influences, decisions, actions, etc. But the principle of context
is so important to Dewey's vision of the world that he claims one can
never think accurately in any discipline—whether it be mathematics,
agriculture, or poetry—without intuiting the concrete reality of contexts.
In other words, the context with its pervasive quality is always the most
fundamental reality. "Quality" has a concrete ontological status and is not
a matter of mere subjective imposition.

The principle of intuition, a power that involves the direct apprehension
of quality, prior to and guiding rational inference, is essential to Dewey's
reconstruction of philosophic method. Though philosophers, like histori-

ans, social scientists, and others, have shown a tendency to ignore the pervasively qualitative aspects of the situations they study, poets and artists have consistently given us examples of thinking processes in possession of the intuitive method. Poetic and artistic creativity stems precisely from the intuition of quality, and is manifested in the largely intuitive integration of formal elements in the canvas, the musical performance, or the poetic text. The value of works of art is not so much the beauty they add to our lives as the instruction they give us in the life-enhancing powers and methods of intuition. As articulated by Dewey, the idea of intuition forms a link between the thinking of the contextualist in any field and that of the artist or poet. "[I]ntuition precedes conception and goes deeper . . ." (QT 249), he says. The process of intuition "is closely connected with the single qualitativeness underlying all the details of explicit reasoning. It may be relatively dumb and inarticulate and yet penetrating . . ." (QT 249). (Compare James's emphasis on the forming process involved in the relatively inarticulate transitive states of consciousness that move the thinker-as-artist toward the realization of form. See pp. 63–67, above). The intuition may be "unexpressed in definite ideas which form reasons and justifications" and yet be "profoundly right." "Reflection and rational elaboration spring from and make explicit a prior intuition. But there is nothing mystical about this fact, and it does not signify that there are two modes of knowledge, one of which is appropriate to one kind of subject-matter, and the other mode to the other kind" (QT 249).

Since there is no valid ontological distinction between subject and object, there is no need for imposition of subjectively generated qualities on objective fact. So Dewey also saw no ultimate dichotomy between rational and intuitive modes of knowing. All thinking, that of the artist as well as the scientist, originates in intuition, and each embodies in its own way a form of "logic." The "thinking of the artist" is the intuitive "logic of . . . qualitative thinking" (QT 251). "The logic of artistic construction" is significant because it exemplifies "in accentuated and purified form the control of selection of detail and of mode of relation, or integration, by a qualitative whole" (QT 251). The creative process manifested in the work of art, and then reiterated in the consciousness of the experiencer of art, exemplifies in a heightened and purified way the qualitative nature of all valid thought processes. For the poet and the artist are individuals gifted with extraordinary sensitivity to the conceptually vague yet ontologically significant qualities that govern the contexts of every experience, and that are apprehended by intuitive or affectional modes of knowing.

NATURE AS CONTEXT

The experiential metaphysics implied in the above paragraph first came to complete expression in *Experience and Nature* (1929).[10] *Nature* is a name for the ground and condition in which all experience takes place. It is a counterpart to Martin Heidegger's idea of Being (*Sein*), while Dewey's idea of experience corresponds to Heidegger's lower case "being" (*Dasein*), which refers to one's concrete human existence in a specific time and place.[11] The elusiveness of the idea of experience, when set free of the dichotomized conception of subject and object, never distracted Dewey from recognizing its critical importance to the new structure of philosophic understanding he sought to establish. Despite the metaphysical imponderables involved in its theory of two substances, the Cartesian paradigm provided modern philosophy with a conceptual framework in which the questions of epistemology could be handled with supreme clarity. In *Experience and Nature,* on the other hand, we observe an epoch-making attempt to confront these questions without the benefit of the incisive (but ultimately debilitating) conceptual tools of dualism, and in the process to shift attention to a new set of questions that could not be asked or that made little sense within the old paradigm of consciousness. Dewey describes his work as "a critique of prejudices," "a kind of intellectual disrobing," and an effort to "divest ourselves of the intellectual habits we take on and wear when we assimilate the culture of our own time and place" (EN 40). From this standpoint, which employs an empirical attitude in the service of cultural criticism, Dewey saw the fallacy involved in the metaphysical presuppositions of Cartesian dualism. The duality of physical and psychical worlds, Dewey holds, is an "inevitable result" of failing to acknowledge "the primacy and ultimacy of the material of ordinary experience" (EN 26). To arrive at such an acknowledgment is an intellectual disrobing of the most radical kind. According to Richard Rorty, Dewey "is one of the few philosophers of our century whose imagination was expansive enough to envisage a culture shaped along lines different from those we have developed in the West during the last three hundred years."[12] The first step toward that imaginative vision was to strip away the invisible but mesmeric image of man and his relation (or disrelation) to nature that had been the heritage of Cartesian culture.

In the late phase of his career—which, in addition to *Experience and Nature,* saw the publication (among other things) of *The Quest for Certainty* (1929), *Art as Experience* (1934), *Logic: The Theory of Inquiry* (1938), and (with Arthur F. Bentley) *Knowing and the Known* (1949)—Dewey's concern for context shapes his definitions of experience and mind. The central premise of contextualism is that the universe is composed not of substances, but of *events.* "Every existence is an event," he writes. This brief statement is a microcosm of his contextualist position. The word *event* implies action: the discharge of energy in an organized framework of facts. It implies a situation with a multiplicity of components, which cannot be treated as independent units, but must be understood in their changing, relational character. Organization of some sort is indigenous to all events in nature—that is, to all existence. Part of the unique significance of each event, seen in and with its complex setting, is the measure of its state of relative coherence, or, as Dewey calls it, "fusion."[13] There is no such thing as a completely chaotic event. In an article published in 1925 Dewey wrote:

> Wherever there is an event, there is interaction, and interaction entails the concept of a *field*. No "field" can be precisely delimited; it extends wherever the energies involved in the interaction operate and as far as any redistributions of energy are effected. The field can be limited *practically*, as can all matters of degree; it can not be existentially located with literal exactness.[14]

The concept of the contextual field, like the historic event, is a metaphor that for Dewey applies to every occasion and every occurrence. Nature itself is a process of constant interactions, with varying durations, in a multitude of facts. When we speak of the "experiential field," we call attention to the fact that all experience, including both knowing and acting, is in and of a situation, context, or field of facts. Mind and matter, traditionally defined as substantial and independent existences, become in Dewey's view "significant characters of events, presented in different contexts, rather than underlying and ultimate substances" (EN 5).

Consciousness and its environment are "characters," but the contextual event has an ontological primacy for Dewey. In an article composed while Dewey was still in his early Hegelian period, he wrote: ". . . the psychological standpoint is necessarily a universal standpoint and consciousness necessarily the only absolute. . . . [I]t is only because the individual consciousness is, in its ultimate reality, the universal consciousness that it affords any basis whatever for philosophy."[15] The concept of a "psychological standpoint" still retains a residue of subjectivistic bias, which Dewey attempts here to expand by identifying it with an Hegelian Universal Mind, or Absolute. In *Experience and Nature*, the mature Dewey would shift his focus from the relation between finite and universal consciousness to consciousness defined naturalistically as a mode of interaction or transaction between the live creature and the open universe of events. Because it is grounded in the realm of experienced events, and not in a realm of abstract thought, consciousness shows its potential for authentic universality. The universe of natural occurrences, and the human consciousness of it, are included in the one authentic context called nature. The mark of the presence of consciousness is the transformation of an existential situation from relative incoherence or "indeterminacy" to a higher state of qualitative meaning and unity. Concrete experience in its "inclusive integrity" (EN 19) is the key to Dewey's radical redefinition of consciousness. If "consciousness is the only absolute" for the younger Dewey, "experience," conceived ultimately as in a state of "integrated unity," is the only absolute for the mature Dewey. The ideal of experience "recognizes in its primary integrity no division between act and material, subject and object, but contains them both in unanalyzed totality" (EN 18). Such a totality is not a preconceived universal. It is a situational whole, whose integrity is experienced and made intelligible by the intuitive discernment, not analysis, of a pervasive quality.

In modern thought, the neglect of context bred a tendency to conceive of objects as rigidly isolated from one another and from the mind doing the conceiving, rather than as aspects of an infinite series of interpenetrating natural contexts. By contrast, the contextualist always begins inquiry by putting himself at the standpoint of experience. The experiential standpoint involves that participation of the perceiver in the objects of perception. It constitutes a new metaphysical perspective toward the world. It is the "new centre" of Dewey's Copernican revolution. "We never experience nor form judgments about objects and events in isolation," he maintains, "but only in connection with a contextual whole. This latter is what is called a 'situation.' "[16] As a man comes to identify himself with the contextual or situational perspective—to recognize himself as in and of the contexts of experience, with all their natural and social constituents—the presupposition of ontological duality of mind and world, which haunted the great modern systems of idealism and empiricism, vanishes as the epicycles of Ptolemy did before Copernican astronomy. "When objects are isolated from the experience through which they are reached . . . experiencing is . . . treated as if it were also complete in itself," and we get, in philosophy, as in literature, the "absurdity" of a consciousness that experiences only its own states and processes. "Since the seventeenth century [the] conception of experience as the equivalent of subjective private consciousness set over against nature, which consists wholly of physical objects, has wrought havoc in philosophy" (EN 21). Consciousness is inextricable from the experiential event in which it participates and which calls it to perform its transformative function. To ignore the field is to perform a piece of metaphysical surgery, extracting a vital organ from the living body of experience, for arbitrary analytical purposes. "One cannot decline to *have* a situation," for as experienced fact the situation is the one impregnable absolute of the contextualist world view; "a qualitative and qualifying situation is present as the background and control of *every* experience."[17]

Though it is often treated by linguists as a highly artificial product of culture, language to Dewey is necessarily a part of the contextual structure of all experience. "Discourse that is not controlled by reference to a situation is not discourse, but a meaningless jumble, just as a mass of pied type is not a font much less a sentence."[18] Language that transmits empirically perceivable meaning is that which is "controlled" by its "reference to a situation." "A universe of experience is the precondition of a universe of discourse." As the various contexts of experience overlap and exhibit "strands" of reference that extend into other contexts, so the inherently contextual structures of language depend for their meaning on the surrounding experiential field. "The universe [i.e., contextual field] of experience surrounds and regulates the universe of discourse. . . ."[19]

ART AS TRANSACTIONAL EXPERIENCE

In a famous definition of the poetic "image," Ezra Pound summarizes characteristics of modernist poetry that show a basic affinity with Deweyan contextualist aesthetics. "An image," Pound writes, "is that which presents an intellectual and emotional complex in an instant of time."[20] For Pound the image is not defined as a word picture designed to stimulate a mental representation of an object. It is a "complex" of intellectual and emotional elements, presented and perceived in a nonlinear way, that is, instantaneously. These characteristics suggest the qualitative integration of experience that Dewey calls "fusion." A given event is composed of details and, in Stephen Pepper's words, "always exhibits some degree of fusion of the details of its texture."[21] The tonic triad C–E–G, for example, has a distinctive quality that may be fused, when heard as a chord, or relatively unfused, when the tones are heard as related, but at certain time-intervals apart. Where fusion occurs, the details coalesce in the fused quality of the whole. "Where fusion is relaxed, the details take on qualities of their own, which may in turn be fusions of details lying within these latter qualities. Fusion, in other words, is an agency of qualitative simplification and organization."[22]

Every event, in Dewey's world view, exhibits some such degree of qualitative integration in time. Its temporal "duration" constitutes the event's actual (i.e., experiential) present. Some occasions possess a relatively high degree of such integration, or are completely fused, as in mystical or highly integrated aesthetic experiences. Similarly, the poetic image is an instantaneous presentation of a complex which, in Pound's words, "gives us that sense of sudden liberation; that sense of freedom from time limits and space limits; that sense of sudden growth, which we experience in the presence of the greatest works of art."[23] The "limits" of time and space referred to here are the conceptual construction of a mechanistic world view. To be free of the limits imposed by patterns of schematic time and space is to be released into the experiential present moment, known through the direct intuition of its durational and immediate spatial qualities. The early modernist poetry of Pound, Eliot, Williams, and, later, Olson showed, in the words of one critic, a "capacity to form new wholes, to *fuse* seemingly disparate experiences into an organic unity.''[24] Williams's definition of the poem as a "field of action" and Olson's discussion of "composition by field" (cited by Williams in his *Autobiography*) both suggest that poetic structure involves the interaction of verbal signs representing an open experiential field. In Dewey's conception—as in the work of Eliot, Pound, and Williams—art is characterized by the "unexpected combination" of structural elements, and by a "consequent revelation of possibilities hitherto unrealized" (EN 270).

Understanding language, including the language of poetry, "brings with it the sense of sharing and merging in a whole"—a contextual field in which the elements of language serve as "strands," or connecting links between the participating consciousness and the field of experience. "Forms of language are unrivalled in ability to create this sense [of wholeness], at first with direct participation on the part of an audience; and then, as literary forms develop, through imaginative identification" (EN 145). The imaginative participation and identification stressed by Dewey is a basic aspect of all literature, but has a specific relevance to the experience of modernist poetry. Language is "a form of action," in Dewey's phrase. The language of poetry is not different in kind from ordinary language, but it is different in its degree of density of meaning. If ordinary language involves interaction between a speaker and a hearer, poetic language involves an interaction of a higher order of intensity which Pound called *first intensity*. It involves what Plato called *mimesis*—the immersion of the consciousness of the hearer in the poetic performance, in such a way that the subject–object dichotomy breaks down, and the perceiver becomes identified with the form and qualities of experience expressed in the poem.[25] To such higher orders of interaction Dewey in his later works gives the name "transaction."

When the elements of an interaction, the perceiver and the perceived, become especially well integrated or coordinated, the form of their relation takes on a *transactional* character. The idea of transaction is central to Dewey's theory of language, and to the radicalism of his contextualist orientation to knowing, but also to his conception of art.[26] In *Knowing and the Known*, Dewey and Bentley outline three approaches to the problem of knowing, which they call respectively *self-action*, *interaction*, and *transaction*—the latter two terms often hyphenated to emphasize the *action* involved in the knowing process, and in other kinds of relations. "Trans-action" stresses the idea of action *across* the boundaries usually (but erroneously) conceived to separate knower from known, while "inter-action" emphasizes the belief that knower and known, though related, remain essentially distinct entities with an action running *between* them, and are not intertwined in each other's existence. The term "self-action" identifies a point of view in which independent agents, or substances (including such distinct entities as knowers and knowns), are conceived (again, erroneously) to act under their own powers.

"Transaction" is defined by Dewey and Bentley as the "knowing–known taken as one process," while "in older discussions, the knowings and knowns are separated and viewed as in interaction."[27] The Cartesian paradigm was fundamentally interactional, stressing the distinction between the thought and its object, yet claiming that somehow action takes place "between" their separate ontological spheres. In the new approach offered by Dewey and Bentley, knowing and the known are (or may be) completely fused in the coordinated event. By reorienting our cognitive and perceptual standpoint, moving away from an artificial sense of the separateness of subjects and objects, we see the knowing situation in its totality as "one process," of which the self and its environment are aspects.[28]

There is only one field of experience, and this experience embraces the naming or sign-processes of language. The term "fact," regarded by Dewey and Bentley as preferable to "nature" though it covers the same subject matter, is defined as the "cosmos in course of being known through naming by organisms, themselves among its phases. It is knowings-knowns, durationally and extensionally spread. . . . Fact is under way among organisms advancing in a cosmos, itself under advance as known."[29] Etymologically, the English word "fact" (from Latin *factum*, something done) suggests the transaction involved in knowing and naming. This approach maintains neither a mystical identity nor a rationalistic separation of knowing and the known, but rather their contextual unity, accomplished partly by the action of naming.

Like language, art is inherently transactional. While language exists only when it is both spoken and heard, the "work of art is complete only as it *works* in the experience of others than the one who created it."[30] The work of art "works" by embodying and communicating organized energies; it does more than lead to an experience—it constitutes an immediate realization of qualitative experience, which can be re-created in its general form by the attentive perceiver. "The thoroughgoing integration of what philosophy discriminates as 'subject' and 'object' (in more direct language, organism and environment) is the characteristic of every work of art" (AE 281). Because aesthetic experience not merely involves an interaction between a perceiving subject and an art object, but is rather a matter of "total seizure" (AE 195) in which the perceiver becomes immersed in the energy field of the art work, object and subject are embraced in transactional unity. This is one meaning of the concept of *fusion* in Dewey's philosophy. "[E]sthetic experience is experience in its integrity," and so becomes the model for understanding all experience.

Had not the term "pure" been so often abused in philosophic literature, had it not been so often employed to suggest that there is something alloyed, impure, in the very nature of experience and to denote something beyond experience, we might say [echoing James] that esthetic experience is pure experience. For it is experience freed from the forces that impede and confuse its development as experience; freed, that is, from factors that subordinate an experience as it is directly had to something beyond itself. To esthetic experience . . . the philosopher must go to understand what experience is. . . . [A]ll the elements of our being that are displayed in special emphases and partial realizations in other experiences are merged in esthetic experience [AE 278].

The elements of subject, object, and idea are "merged" in the contextual wholeness of aesthetic experience. Each is subordinated to the whole, and thus does not appear "in consciousness as a distinct element." Ultimately, "no experience of whatever sort is a unity unless it has esthetic quality" (AE 47).

Aesthetic "form" for Dewey does not merely concern the internal coherence of formal elements in an art object. It concerns the structure of the experiential field made possible by the work of art for each perceiver. The art object makes a certain range of qualitative experiences possible; the perceiver makes those possibilities actual by his contribution of attention and mental energies. "Experience," Dewey maintains, "is the result, the sign, and the reward of that interaction of organism and environment which, when it is carried to the full, is a transformation of interaction into participation and communication" (AE 28). Such original participation is the essential characteristic of aesthetic experience. For this reason, aesthetic experience becomes a guide to understanding correctly the participatory (i.e., transactional) nature of all experience. The value of the aesthetic is its ability to reveal the "dynamic organization" of experience. Works of art make such revelations possible, not by communicating esoteric truths, but by inviting participation in the higher densities of experience touched by the artist and embodied in genuine works of art.

The most important characteristic of aesthetic experience is not pleasure or beauty, but the sense of completeness or wholeness that it may generate in the perceiver. "Every work of art follows the plan of, and pattern of, a complete experience, rendering it more intensely and concentratedly felt" (AE 58). A work of art is instrumental in creating a situation with a dominantly aesthetic quality. Such a situation involves a transaction of energies between a text and a perceiver. It involves a pattern of "doing" and "undergoing." To undergo an experience is to become receptive. "It involves surrender. But adequate yielding of the self is possible only through a controlled activity that may well be intense" (AE 59). Such intentional receptivity is not passive, but involves "a series of responsive acts that accumulate toward objective fulfillment" (AE 58). Without such a series of acts there is not perception but mere recognition of previously known features of experience. Perception is defined as an "act of the going-out of energy in order to receive, not a withholding of energy." To respond adequately to a work of art, and to participate in the revelations it makes possible, "We must summon energy and pitch it at a responsive key in order to *take* in" (AE 60). The transaction leads to "an integrated complete experience" (AE 62). Aesthetic experience is "conversion of resistance and tensions" between the observer and the work "into a movement toward an inclusive and fulfilling close" (AE 62).

Dewey could be describing the poetics of such works as *The Waste Land*, *The Cantos*, and *Paterson* when he writes that "The *form* of the whole is . . . present in every member. Fulfilling, consummating, are continuous functions, not mere ends, located at one place only" (AE 62–63). In the radical poetics of Pound's, Eliot's, and Williams's poems there is no effort to build aesthetic structure to a single consummatory climax. Instead, the poets operate by producing a contextual sign-process with a pattern of dramatic moments of varying intensities. This process of developing poetic significance relies much more heavily than traditional literary forms do on the intimate participation of the alert and responsive reader. Though the text is an occasion that calls for intuitive participation, the reader performs the vital intuitive act of integrating the sometimes dissonant parts.

The creativity contributed by the reader and needed for such participation is captured by Dewey in passages like the following:

> . . . to perceive, a beholder must *create* his own experience. . . . But with the perceiver, . . . there must be an ordering of the elements of the whole that is in form, although not in details, the same as the process of organization the creator of the work consciously experienced. Without an act of recreation the object is not perceived as a work of art [AE 60].

Dewey's philosophy of experience culminates in a principle of creativity. All genuine experience is creative and leads to action that has the potential to transform both the self and the social context by moving one beyond the boundaries of what the old paradigm called subjective consciousness.

NOTES

1. George Dykhuizen, *The Life and Mind of John Dewey* (Carbondale and Edwardsville: Southern Illinois University Press, 1973), pp. 1–18.

2. John Dewey, "From Absolutism to Experimentalism," *John Dewey: The Later Works, 1925–1953. V. 1929–1930*, ed. Kathleen E. Poulos (Carbondale and Edwardsville: Southern Illinois University Press, 1984), p. 153.

3. For a discussion of the "spatializing" tendency of rational concepts, as opposed to the fluidity of immediate experience, presented in terms of a similar image of photographic abstraction, see Bergson, *Introduction to Metaphysics*, pp. 159–200.

4. Charles Olson, "The Human Universe" in *Selected Writings* (New York: New Directions, 1966), p. 61.

5. *Experience and Nature*, *John Dewey: The Later Works, 1925–1953*. I. *1925*, edd. Patricia Baysinger and Barbara Levine (Carbondale and Edwardsville: Southern Illinois University Press, 1981), p. 96; hereafter cited as EN.

6. *Prolegomena to Any Future Metaphysics*, trans. Peter G. Lucas (Manchester: Manchester University Press, 1953), no. 36, p. 82. On "second Copernican revolution," see second preface (1787) to *The Critique of Pure Reason*.

7. *The Quest for Certainty: A Study of the Relation of Knowledge and Action*, *John Dewey: The Later Works, 1925–1953*. IV. *1929*, ed. Harriet Furst Simon (Carbondale and Edwardsville: Southern Illinois University Press, 1984), p. 229; hereafter cited as QC.

8. See Gail Kennedy, "Dewey's Concept of Experience: Determinate, Indeterminate, and Problematic," *The Journal of Philosophy*, 56 (1959), 801–14; Felix Kaufmann, "John Dewey's Theory of Inquiry," ibid., 826–36; Elizabeth Flower and Murray G. Murphey, *A History of Philosophy in America* II (New York: Putnam's, 1977), pp. 851ff.; John E. Smith, *Purpose and Thought: The Meaning of Pragmatism* (New Haven: Yale University Press, 1978), esp. chap. 3, "The New Conception of Experience," pp. 78–95; and Richard J. Bernstein, "Action, Conduct, and Inquiry: Peirce and Dewey," in *Praxis and Action: Contemporary Philosophies of Human Activity* (Philadelphia: University of Pennsylvania Press, 1971), pp. 165–229.

9. "Qualitative Thought," *John Dewey: The Later Works, 1925–1953*. V. *1929–1930*, ed. Kathleen E. Poulos (Carbondale and Edwardsville: Southern Illinois University Press, 1984), p. 246; hereafter cited as QT.

10. See Richard Rorty, "Dewey's Metaphysics," *Consequences of Pragmatism (Essays: 1972–1980)* (Minneapolis: University of Minnesota Press, 1982), pp. 72–89.

11. Heidegger, "What Is Metaphysics?" pp. 95–112.

12. "Dewey's Metaphysics," p. 85.

13. Stephen C. Pepper, "The Concept of Fusion in Dewey's Aesthetic Theory," *The Work of Art* (Bloomington: Indiana University Press, 1955), pp. 151–72.

14. "A Naturalistic Theory of Sense-Perception," *John Dewey: The Later Works, 1925–1953*. II. *1925–1927*, ed. Bridget A. Walsh (Carbondale and Edwardsville: Southern Illinois University Press, 1984), p. 52.

15. "The Psychological Standpoint," *John Dewey: The Early Works, 1882–1889*. I. *1882–1888* (Carbondale and Edwardsville: Southern Illinois University Press, 1969), pp. 141–42.

16. *Logic: The Theory of Inquiry*, *John Dewey: The Later Works, 1925–1953*. XII. *1938*, ed. Kathleen Poulos (Carbondale and Edwardsville: Southern Illinois University Press, 1986), p. 72.

17. Ibid., pp. 72, 76.

18. Ibid., p. 74.

19. Ibid.

20. *Make It New* (London: Faber & Faber, 1934), p. 336.

21. "Contextualism," p. 243.

22. Ibid., pp. 243–44.

23. *Make It New*, p. 336.

24. Joseph Frank, "Spatial Form in Modern Literature," *The Widening Gyre:*

Crisis and Mastery in Modern Literature (New Brunswick, N.J.: Rutgers University Press, 1963), p. 10; emphasis added.

25. Havelock, *Preface to Plato*, esp. chap. 2, "Mimesis," pp. 20–35, and chap. 9, "The Psychology of the Poetic Performance," pp. 145–64.

26. Bertram Morris, in his article "Dewey's Theory of Art," in *Guide to the Works of John Dewey*, ed. Jo Ann Boydston (Carbondale and Edwardsville: Southern Illinois University Press, 1970), pp. 156–82, gives an excellent general account of Dewey's aesthetics. But like many similar studies, his does not stress the implications of the idea of transaction for Dewey's view of art.

27. *Knowing and the Known, John Dewey: The Later Works, 1925–1953*. XVI. *1949–1952*, edd. Harriet Furst Simon and Richard W. Field (Carbondale and Edwardsville: Southern Illinois University Press, 1989), p. 272.

28. Ibid.

29. Ibid., p. 263.

30. Dewey, *Art as Experience, John Dewey: The Later Works, 1925–1953*. X. *1934*, ed. Harriet Furst Simon (Carbondale and Edwardsville: Southern Illinois University Press, 1987), p. 111; emphasis added. Hereafter cited as AE.

6

William Carlos Williams: *Paterson* and the Poetics of Contextualism

AN EXPERIENTIAL POETICS

AN ELOQUENT IF UNSYSTEMATIC SPOKESMAN for the poetics of American modernism, William Carlos Williams saw poetry as a way of uncovering by imaginative means the "radiant gist" that lies immanent though hidden in the things of ordinary experience.[1] By his own account, Williams's poetics grows out of his sense of immediate experience. His earliest articulated theory, which we may call imagism, suggests that the poet is primarily occupied with rendering direct sensory experience—"what actually impinges on the senses . . . untouched."[2] Poetry according to this view is concerned with "a relation to the immediate conditions of the matter in hand, and a determination to assert them in opposition to all intermediate authority" (SE 143). The poem comes from the "contact with experience" (SE 32), "by paying naked attention first to the thing itself" (SE 35), to "those things which lie under the direct scrutiny of the senses, close to the nose" (SE 11). The poem is a result of the poet's being "attached with integrity to actual experience" (SE 118). Williams's second major theory, objectivism, claims that the poem is not a report about experience but an object of experience. Yet when Williams defines the poem as "a small (or large) machine made of words" (SE 256), he means to emphasize not so much the thingness of the poem as its power to enhance the experiential energies of the reader. "Prose may carry a load of ill-defined matter like a ship. But poetry is the machine which drives it, pruned to a perfect economy. . . . its movement is intrinsic, undulant, a physical more than a literary character" (SE 256). In his third theory, Williams conceives of poetry as a means of capturing the actual rhythms of ordinary American speech, and hence as a means of uncovering in its unheralded richness the universal values inherent in common experience. In order to do this accurately, without the imposition of literary form on his material, Williams experimented with poetic language until he found what he called a "new measure."

If I am right in suggesting that each of these three poetic theories—imagism, objectivism, and the new measure—rests on Williams's conception of concrete experience, and if we take the term poetics, in addition to the poet's explicit theorizing, to mean the basic structures of experience implicit in the way his art is organized, then we ought to ask: What is the conception of experience underlying both his poetry and his theories? One way to answer this question is to explore the affinity, hinted at repeatedly by Williams, between his poetics and the philosophy of John Dewey. From the vantage point of Dewey's contextualism and experiential aesthetics we see in Williams's work, perhaps most specifically in *Paterson* (1946–1951), evidence of what might be called a *poetics of contextualism*. Dewey's contextualism—and that of others in the American philosophic tradition who followed him—though largely ignored by Williams's critics, provides—by significant analogy, if not direct influence—an instructive method of approaching the problem of structure in *Paterson*.

What does the problem of structure really mean? In any poem or literary work, the writer is not simply presenting a pattern of images and ideas with a formal structure completely extrinsic to the reader. He is in effect giving us a series of instructions about how to have a certain kind of experience. We read the signs and symbols of poetry in the same way we "read" other elements of our experience such as houses, cars, trees, animals, the ordinary speech of our neighbors, and the very presence of our neighbors as human beings.[3] Everything we encounter is an opportunity to "see," participate in, and create what Dewey calls *an experience*, with a form and content specific to the occasion.[4] Certainly it would be an exaggeration from Dewey's point of view to argue as Kant had that we create the forms of nature by imposing rationalistic categories on them. But by means of mind and imagination (here Williams and Dewey would agree) we contribute a vital element to the process of shaping our individual and collective experience of the world. Mind and imagination are names for the vital forming powers within experience. As we follow the "instructions" of the poetic text, we may feel that we are entering an imaginative realm separate from our own experience. But what can be said with greater empirical credibility is that we are encountering a certain frequency (like a radio frequency) of conscious experience which the poet has had in some way, and which is now offered to us as a shared experience through the symbols of poetry. In poetry written according to implicit contextualist principles, the shared aspect of the experience is made into a focal concern. As we read we participate in a specific way in a constructive process, using the materials of the poem to generate an experiential context.

Reading a work like *Paradise Lost* is an experience different in kind from reading modernist epics like *The Cantos, The Waste Land,* or

Paterson. Why? Because Milton gives us a more finished literary gestalt to work with. It has a finished quality, which consists, partly, of such things as a regular iambic pentameter blank verse line, consistency in the handling of point of view, a narrative structure that moves with relative clarity from point A to point B in both time and space, and with devices of smooth narrative transition kept relatively intact. In the modernist works, on the other hand, those much-needed transitions are conspicuously absent, and the logical presentation of point of view shattered, as in the multiple planes and perspectives of a Cubist painting, by the poet's experimentation with structure. One critic has argued that the true center of Milton's *Paradise Lost* is neither its central characters nor any of its objective contents, but "the reader's consciousness of the poem's *personal* relevance"—specifically the drama of sin and redemption enacted in the reader's consciousness by the experience of reading the poem.[5] In modernist poetry like that of Pound, Eliot, and Williams, the center of gravity shifts, not from an objective literary gestalt to the reader's subjective consciousness, but precisely to the interrelation between them—to the experienced reality which Martin Buber calls "the between."[6] So, as Buber might argue, the act of reading becomes a matter of the mutuality of genuine dialogue, or "meeting." The text and the reader's consciousness are elements in a contextual whole which, though never "finished" as a perfected literary form, becomes a unified experience as a completed stage in an ongoing process of experiential growth. The "unfinished" quality of the poetic performance in a work like *Paterson*—at least as judged by premodernist standards of formal structure—is a mirror to us of the incompleteness of experience apart from the organizing powers of a centered mind and imagination. Like other modernist poems, and unlike the premodernist *Paradist Lost*, *The Prelude*, or *The Iliad*, *Paterson* functions according to an experiential poetics that challenges us in a specific way to acknowledge the contextual nature of experience and to enter with the poet into a shared constructive effort to actualize new forms of experience. The reader is called upon to become a co-creator with the poet.

DEWEY AND WILLIAMS

In various essays and letters Williams left traces of an interest in Dewey's ideas. In the last chapter of his *Autobiography* (1951), for example, concerning the writing of *Paterson*, Williams suggests that the basic method of the poem has roots in Dewey's philosophy of experience. "The poet's business," says Williams, is "not to talk in vague categories but to write particularly, as a physician works, upon the thing before him, in the particular to discover the universal. John Dewey had said (I discovered it quite by chance), 'The local is the only universal, upon that all art builds.' '"[7]

Although the most casual reading of *Paterson* reveals, beginning with the title, Williams's preoccupation with "local" events and "particular" facts, the impulse to convey ideas of universal scope seems less evident in the poem. Perhaps a key to the universality of *Paterson* is suggested by Williams's pregnant remarks: "A work of art is important only as evidence, in its structure, of a new world which it has been created to affirm. . . . Look at the structure if you will truly grasp the significance of a poem" (SE 196, 207). Williams's advice, to grasp the meaning of poetry by looking at its structure, has rarely been taken seriously by readers of *Paterson*, partly because the poem presents such radical departures from conventional poetic or narrative structure that it often seems formless. Within the new poetic modes he invented, Williams was attempting to articulate the patterns of natural experience as they actually unfold. One result is the delineation of a "new world," or new view of the world. Williams discovers "the universal" by demonstrating, through the peculiar interrelation of particulars in the poem, the way experience is organized according to the premises of that new world view. Despite the seemingly random way materials are combined in the text, my contention is that there is a structural principle at work in the poem, a principle that is an expression of universal ideas, and that the poem and its principle of organization become clearer when examined in the light of Deweyan contextualism.

For Dewey experience always takes the form of complex "wholes" called *situations*, *events*, or *contexts* (see above, pp. 99–102). The perceiving subject thus can never be set apart from the objects of perception, for both are phases of the one primal fact: the experiential context. The subjective and objective are phases of experience necessarily implicated in each other's existence. There is no disjunction between the fact and the idea that reflects it, or between facts and values, in contextualism. Both are aspects of a single experiential whole, termed "the situation." The word *situation* designates the complex of interpenetrating elements making up experience—which may include disparate objects, qualities, ideas, signs, relations, the minds and perspectives of others.

A situation, according to Dewey, is never a "singular object or event. . . ." We experience objects and events only as they are related to "a contextual whole." In actual experience an object or event is

> always a special part, phase, or aspect, of an environing experienced world—
> a situation. The singular object stands out conspicuously because of its
> especially focal and crucial position at a given time in determination of some
> problem . . . which the *total* complex environment presents. There is always
> a *field* in which observation of *this* or *that* object or event occurs.

Every context or situation "is a whole in virtue of its immediately pervasive quality."[8] Another writer on the philosophy of contextualism stresses that "a situation includes both agents and circumstances, so action and the situation go together. The agent is faced by circumstances within the situation, and the act is his response to the problem they present. Through it the total situation, including both agent and circumstances, is changed in some way."[9] Characteristically, situations are either problematic or stable. And when one is confronted by a problematic situation, the response that Dewey advocates is called "inquiry." This term implies creativity, which involves the "directed transformation" of the facts of the situation into an integrated whole.[10]

As if in explanation of the slogan "the local is the only universal" cited by Williams, Stephen Pepper argues that on contextualist premises "one does not need to hunt for a distant cosmological truth, since every present event gives it as fully as it can be given."[11] In the situation as immediately experienced, the "local" or "present event," we find evidences of the basic structures of all events. Every event is a constellation of fused details, held together by what Pepper calls "strands."[12] Every experiential context is embedded in some larger context or field. And just as a context comes into being by the interaction and transaction of particular facts, whole contexts may be in interaction with one another, may intersect with each other in various complex ways, and a smaller context may take on some special significance when understood in relation to a larger context.

Though the contextualist denies the premise of a closed or "block" universe, he nevertheless accepts the idea of the totality of facts "transactionally" related to each other.[13] Whenever a fact is perceived as in and of the unfolding relations that constitute its context, it is evidence of the overall structural interrelation of facts called "nature" or "cosmos."[14] Because of its ability as a theory to account for the universe of facts in an unrestricted way, Pepper designates contextualism as a "world hypothesis" comparable in scope and explanatory potential to the other major world theories, called mechanism, organicism, and formism. In the modern world, Newtonian physics and astronomy, as well as Lockean empiricism, are examples of theories worked out within the parameters of the world hypothesis called mechanism. Einstein's theory of relativity, as well as the philosophies of Dewey and James, are based on an alternative cosmological paradigm that Pepper calls contextualism. Pepper believes that each of the major world hypotheses is based on a "root metaphor," a familiar image drawn from common experience that has an application to all other areas of fact and experience. As the name suggests, the root metaphor for mechanism is the machine. The root metaphor for contextualism is the historic event, with a stress on the "temporal actuality of the event, i.e., the act in its context."[15]

The concept of poetry captured in the title of Williams's essay "The Poem as a Field of Action" is implicitly rooted in a contextualist outlook, though it is unlikely that Williams deliberately formulated a contextual approach to his art on the basis of his reading of Dewey or other philosophers. The title implies two principles basic to the philosophy of contextualism: (a) that experience happens in an open field of facts and events; and (b) that through action, an individual may effect change in the overall structure of the field and in the quality of interactions taking place within it. While the philosopher (like the social scientist, the working man, or the housewife) undertakes inquiry in order to transform a problematic situation, the poet, according to Williams, steps into a similar "field" of experienced fact, not in order to impose an aesthetic vision on it, but to "transmute" those existential materials through imagination, "to lift the world of the senses to the level of the imagination and so give it new currency" (SE 213). And while the aim of Deweyan inquiry is to convert the elements of an indeterminate situation into a "unified whole," the purpose of Williams's art is to exercise the powers of creative invention, and thereby to bring about "*a dispersal and a metamorphosis*," as stated in the headnote to *Paterson*.[16] That "dispersal" implies the breaking up of the gestalt tendencies of the normal conscious mind which ordinarily govern and limit perception. And "metamorphosis" implies a reintegration of the facts of experience, as Williams says, on a "new ground."

CONTEXTUALIST STRUCTURE OF *Paterson*

The uninitiated reader, or the reader who approaches *Paterson* with a preconception of formal design, may find the poem disconcertingly diffuse if not chaotic in structure. In a famous remark Randall Jarrell speaks of the "organization of irrelevance" in the poem. "Such organization," he writes, "is *ex post facto* organization: if something is somewhere, one can always find Some Good Reason for its being there, but if it had not been there, would one reader have guessed where it should 'really' have gone?"[17] If we can bracket the disparaging tone of Jarrell's remarks, and interpret *ex post facto* to mean the opposite of *a priori*, then his comments take on a precision that may lead us to a clearer grasp of the poem's structure. The poem consists of an aggregate of disparate elements fused in a common poetic "field," as the term is used by Williams. The process of composition involved, in the words of Book I,

> . . a mass of detail
> to interrelate on a new ground, difficultly
> an assonance, a homologue
> > triple piled
> pulling the disparate together to clarify
> and compress [p. 20].

The terms *assonance* and *homologue* suggest a state of mind responsive to the potential relatedness of particular facts in "disparate" contexts, and thus to the possibility of their "compression" (or "fusion") in the structure of the poem. Pulling disparate factors of experience together appears at first to be an unpromising means to achieve the density and clarity of expression expected of poetry. And Williams's relative success has been a subject of debate since the publication of Book I of *Paterson* in 1946.[18] However, the "new ground" on which facts are "interrelated" in the poem is, I would argue, the contextual field of awareness and conforms in broad outlines to a contextualist world view. Observing Williams's poetic experiment in the light of the view implicit in its structure, rather than in terms of an arbitrary (and perhaps irrelevant) formalist standard, should at least enable one to evaluate his achievement by appropriate criteria.

Paterson (Books I–IV, 1946–1951) was at first considered by both Williams and his critics to be a complete work. The addition of Book V in 1958 and the fragmentary notes for a sixth book found among Williams's papers after his death called that original impression of completeness into question and underscored a basic feature of the poem: its open-ended quality. But evidence of structural openness is not exhausted in the fact of Williams's inability (like Pound's in the *Cantos*) to conclude his poem. A deliberate dispersion of narrative elements deprives the poem of a coherent surface form that might have made it more easily accessible to the reader. Williams's method allows him freedom to incorporate into the work any facts that enter his field of experience, including material that often seems eccentric or accidental to its central threads of meaning. Into this fluid field the reader is asked to enter to discover whatever order *she* can. Thus the reader's active engagement with the work is indispensable to its structure, to a degree that is unnecessary in literary works with well-articulated characters, images, ideas, and the connections between them.

The poem is composed of semantic units of both verse and prose ranging in length from a word or phrase to several pages. These units of meaning are logically disjoined from the other units to which they are immediately juxtaposed. Though each block of material is distinct from adjoining blocks, it is likely to be connected with other more remote parts of the poem, so that the reader is asked to be attentive to structural connections between passages that are not related by their placement in a causal or linear series. The poem is organized in terms of a poetic field in which the relationship of the parts is neither logical nor given in advance. The structure of the field is worked out by the poet, and subsequently by the reader, on an intuitive basis. The diffuse attention required of the reader from the start must be sustained until he or she has been exposed to the entire poetic field. Then she can begin the creative work "to "interrelate" the given "mass of detail" in terms of the contexts of awareness that she brings to the poem. It is the organization of parts as a "field" rather than a linear sequence that gives *Paterson* its contextual structure, and makes a specific kind of demand upon us for creative interaction with the text.

Book I is dominated by the images of Paterson, as a mythical giant, a "man-city," representing the unity and interdependence of man and his environment; as an actual modern city with an historical past; and as a human character, Dr. Paterson, a thin mask for Williams himself. Like an historical event, each book forms a contextual whole. The unifying quality of the book is made by interrelated strands of meaning. These point beyond themselves and beyond the immediate contexts in which they are found, making their influence felt in other contexts and often reaching beyond the expected limits of the poem into the poet's (or the reader's) actual experience. One example of the use of such strands is the series of letters from "C" to Dr. Paterson (actual letters to Williams), the first of which appears in Book I and the last of which concludes Book II. The felt connectedness between the letters is precisely what the contextualist defines as a strand. The letters are concerned with the blockage of creative energies when the ego of the artist prevents her from confronting reality directly. The content of the letters as a whole forms a continuous strand, which, among other strands, ties the separate contexts of Books I and II together. This structural principle applies to the interrelation of parts throughout *Paterson*. The continuity between such relatively large blocks of material marks them as major strands.

A close reading of the poem reveals networks of briefer references whose interconnections generate patterns of meaning that might be called minor strands. A typical minor strand is Williams's repetition of the phrase "great beast" as a link tying together the three sections of Book II. The meaning of the phrase is most fully clarified in a passage located near the middle of section ii. Enclosed within Klaus Ehrens's sermon in the park on Sunday, the following prose segment appears:

> Hamilton saw more clearly than anyone else with what urgency the new government must assume authority over the states if it was to survive. He never trusted the people, "a great beast," as he saw them and held Jefferson to be little better if not worse than any [p. 67].

Passages dealing with Hamiltin, Jefferson, and Madison figure as details in a major strand running through Book II, concerned with early developments in American government and economic policies. The reference in this passage to the "great beast," as Hamilton's view of the mass of common people, recalls two previous uses of the term in Book II. The first of these occurs near the beginning of section i in an historical anecdote from nineteenth-century Paterson. On the first Sunday in May 1880, it is related, the "German Singing Societies of Paterson met on Garret Mountain." This proved a "fatal day" for one John Joseph Van Houten who was shot by William Dalzell when he attempted to cross Dalzell's garden near the scene of the festivities.

> Immediately after the shot the quiet group
> of singers was turned into an infuriated mob
> who would take Dalzell into their own hands.
> The mob then proceeded to burn the barn into
> which Dalzell had retreated from the angry group. . . .
> The crowd now numbered some ten thousand,
> "a great beast!"
> for many had come from the city to
> join the conflict . . . [p. 46].

The second appearance of the key phrase is also in section i, in a verse passage which describes further aspects of the park scene on Sunday, through the eyes of the wandering Dr. Paterson.

> Thus she finds what peace there is, reclines,
> before his approach, stroked
> by their clambering feet—for pleasure
> It is all for
> pleasure . their feet . aimlessly
> wandering
> The "great beast" come to sun himself
> as he may
> . . their dreams mingling,
> aloof [pp. 54–55].

The phrase appears for a fourth time in section iii, after the passage (section ii) dealing with Hamilton.

> At nine o'clock the park closes. You
> must be out of the lake, dressed, in
> your cars and going: they change into
> their street clothes in the back seats
> and move out among the trees .
>
> The "great beast" all removed
> before the plunging night, the crickets'
> black wings and hylas wake . [p. 80]

While the great beast references do not form a series, they yet form a strand, linking disparate contexts together, and helping to create a unified poetic field. The whole of *Paterson* is made up of tissues of such interwoven strands, consisting not simply of semantic blocks or of short phrases like those described, but of images, ideas, fragments of actual speech, and other seemingly random data.

THE CONCEPTION OF MIND IN *Paterson*

Among the various elements that enter and recede from the focus of our attention as we read the poem are many references to the activities of mind. These references function together contextually as contributing details in a major strand. Four key passages in which references to the mind's activities occur are the following:

> (1)—Say it, no ideas but in things—
> nothing but the blank faces of the houses
> and cylindrical trees
> bent, forked by preconception and accident—
> [Book I, p. 6]

> (2) —his mind a red stone carved to be
> endless flight   .
> [Book II, p. 49]

> (3) Books will give rest sometimes against
> the uproar of water falling
> and righting itself to refall filling
> the mind with its reverberation
>   shaking stone.
> [Book III, p. 97]

> (4) And love, bitterly contesting, waits
> that the mind shall declare itself not
> alone in dreams   .
> [Book IV, p. 178]

Each of the four passages illustrates an aspect of Williams's nondualistic conception of mind. The first contains the fragmentary slogan "no ideas but in things," repeated verbatim a few pages later (p. 9) in a different context, and restated still later in the words

> —No ideas but
> in the facts   .   .   [p. 28]

These repetitions constitute a minor strand in the contextual organization of Book I. The slogan makes a cryptic assault on the dualistic principle of rational thought which conceives of "ideas" and "things" as categorical opposites. Williams displays his nonrational instinct to displace this traditional way of thinking by simply denying the conventional opposition between the subjective consciousness and objective fact. Similarly, as we have seen, in contextualism there can be no absolute or categorical separation between mind and the facts it confronts, for both are bound together by their inclusion in an experienced contextual whole. The wider significance of Wiliams's slogan may be understood on the basis of the conception of experience developed by Dewey and other contextualists.

Passage (2) contains a metaphor representing mind as a carved "stone." But the passage refers back to an incident (on the preceding pages) in which Dr. Paterson, walking through the park, experiences a moment of epiphany:

> When! from before his feet, half tripping,
> picking a way, there starts
> > a flight of empurpled wings!
> —invisibly created (their
> jackets dust-grey) from the dust kindled
> to sudden ardor!
> > They fly away, churring! until
> their strength spent they plunge
> to the coarse cover again and disappear
> —but leave, livening the mind, a flashing
> of wings and a churring song . [p. 47]

The "endless flight" of passage (2) echoes the "flight" of grasshoppers in the park which "livens" and transports Paterson's mind to its own imaginative flight. Paterson at this point is moved to the recollection of a large sculpted insect:

> . . . a grasshopper of red basalt, boot-long,
> tumbles from the core of his mind,
> a rubble-bank disintegrating beneath a
> tropic downpour
>
> > . . . .
>
> —a matt stone solicitously instructed
> to bear away some rumor
> of the living presence that has preceded
> it, out-precedented its breath   .
>
> These wings do not unfold for flight—
> no need!
> the weight (to the hand) finding
> a counter-weight or counter buoyancy
> by the mind's wings   .   [pp. 47–48]

The boot-long grasshooper carved in basalt is a metaphor for art, giving one "some rumor" of "living presence." The stone wings of the sculpture do not need to "unfold for flight" because the work of art has its dynamic effect on the perceiver's mind. The physical "weight" of the object finds a "counter-weight or counter buoyancy" in the mind's "wings" (thinking as a form of action), for both are part of one integral experience.

The radical identification of mind and thing is made explicit in passage (2), in which Paterson's "mind" itself becomes a "red stone carved to be / endless flight." These lines, like the phrase "no ideas but in things," affirm the essential continuity between the kinds of experiences called percepts and those called concepts, a continuity that is clarified in the light of contextualist epistemology. In a chapter titled "A Situational Approach to Cognitive Experience" in his book *Experience and the Analytic*, the American philosopher Alan Pasch claims that

> abstract conceptual thinking does in fact occur contextually, and . . . so far as this matter of contexts is concerned there is an epistemological continuum including both the most primitive or immediate experiences discernible and the highest flights of abstract cognitive experience.
>
> To speak of such a continuum is, of course, to deny in one important respect, at least, the sharp and radical distinction usually said to exist between cognitive experience which is perceptual and that which is conceptual. *All* cognitive experience occurs within contexts. . . .[19]

The contexts of knowing, like all contexts of experience, are pervaded by a sense of qualitative unity. What this means is that subject and object— Williams's "mind" and "stone," "ideas" and "things"—are bound together as aspects of one integral experience, though man's integrity as a creative agent is inviolable in Williams's view, for "stones invent nothing, only a man invents" (p. 82).

Passage (3), forming part of the same strand, continues to develop the relation between "mind" and "stone": "the mind with its reverberation / shaking stone." The pronoun "its" here is ambiguous and may refer either to "the uproar of water falling" or to "the mind." In the former sense it is this uproar whose "reverberation" shakes stone; in the latter sense it is the mind's reverberation that does the shaking. Because mind and reality (stone) are in Williams's view parts of a continuum of experience, not divided into separate ontological spheres, mind assumes an unprecedented authority and ability to effect changes in its environment.

Passage (4) develops this thought further, from another perspective. As a detail in the strand constituting a definition of mind, the passage expresses an antisubjectivist conception of mind—capable of declaring itself "not / alone in dreams." The principle of Williams's affirmation is the power of "love," which makes imaginative "contact" with reality possible. The dream, as a literal psychic phenomenon, may be the most private of the mind's functions, according to the Cartesian paradigm. But Williams implies that this preconception is a fallacy. References to dreams appear at various points throughout *Paterson* and thus form another minor strand. One such reference occurs in Book III after a description of a fire in late nineteenth-century Paterson. The poet speaks of

> the awesome sight of a tin roof (1880)
> entire, half a block long, lifted like a
> skirt, held by the fire—. . .
>
> While we stand with our mouths open,

> shaking our heads and saying, My God, did
> you ever see anything like that? As though
> it were wholly out of our dreams, as
> indeed it is, unparalleled in our most sanguine
> dreams   .
>   The person submerged
> in wonder, the fire become the person   .
>   [pp. 121–22]

Here the dream is equated with the sense of wonder experienced by those witnessing the awesome power of the fire. In this collective "dream" state, the objective reality of the fire is merged with the perceivers in one experience.

The four passages operate contextually as an aggregate, though not an isolated one. Together they add up to a redefinition of mind that repudiates conventional Cartesian definitions. This redefinition is fundamentally in accord with Dewey's description of mental functioning in transactional and contextualist terms.

In view of this analysis of Williams's conception of mind in *Paterson*, we may ask, why should Williams, Dewey, and other contextualists be so interested in overturning the authority of the dualistic paradigm and replacing it with what today might be called a holistic view of mind and experience? Obviously they believed they were stating the truth of experience more accurately than was possible under the terms of the old paradigm. So they were motivated by simple honesty to break down the prejudices inherent in our Western social construction of reality. Many astute critics of our culture have noted, often passionately and with some sense of anguish, that when experience is dichotomized (to use Abraham Maslow's term) all things in nature or human culture are degraded to the level of mere objects of sensation or use.[20] Stars, animals, trees, lakes, the ozone layer have no significance or value in themselves. Value becomes something that only sentimentalists out of their (misguided) subjective feeling impose on the things of nature. There is no question that the Cartesian paradigm has been enormously useful to modern Western man in his quest for dominance over nature. But by its downgrading of nature to the status of value-free objectification, it is a short step from the premises of the Cartesian paradigm to the almost mindless exploitation and pollution of nature (recall "the filthy Passaic" of *Paterson*) that we witness at ever-increasing rates today, and an even shorter step from there to the crisis of nuclear annihilation facing the planet. The extent to which Dewey and Williams were aware of all these issues is debatable. But there is no question that their works have practical significance, as tools to overcome the spiritual paralysis of dualism—even when it presents itself in the guise of technological progress.

As a poet, Williams saw the problem of modern man as a matter of rediscovering the values implicit in the things of present experience, and of finding a path of escape from the bondage of the mechanistic world view inevitably engendered by the presuppositions of Cartesianism. In the "Prologue to *Kora in Hell*" (1920) he writes:

> It is to the inventive imagination we look for deliverance from every other misfortune as from the desolation of a flat Hellenic perfection of style. What good then to turn to art from the atavistic religionists, from a science doing slavery service upon gas engines, from a philosophy tangled in a miserable sort of dialect that means nothing if the full power of initiative be denied at the beginning by a lot of baying and snapping scholiasts? If the inventive imagination must look, as I think, to the field of art for its richest discoveries today it will best make its way by compass and follow no path.
>
> But before any material progress can be accomplished there must be someone to draw a discriminating line between true and false values.
>
> The true value is that peculiarity which gives an object a character by itself. The associational or sentimental value is the false. Its imposition is due to lack of imagination, to an easy lateral sliding. The attention has been held too rigid on the one plane instead of following a more flexible, jagged resort. It is to loosen the attention, my attention since I occupy part of the field, that I write these improvisations [SE 10–11].

Williams's comment about the improvisations of *Kora in Hell* pertains to his method and purpose in *Paterson* as well. The diffuseness of structure that we feel in the poem is a result of the desire to "loosen the attention" from the objectified world of things and turn it to the fluid field of experience.

In a later passage from the same prologue Williams addresses the need to use the imagination to unpack the rigidity of ordinary sense perception.

> The senses witnessing what is immediately before them in detail see a finality which they cling to in despair, not knowing which way to turn. Thus the so-called natural or scientific array becomes fixed, the walking devil of modern life. He who even nicks the solidity of this apparition does a piece of work superior to that of Hercules when he cleaned the Augean stables [SE 11–12].

Is there a contradiction between Williams's desire for immersion in "the contacts of experience" and his distrust of the senses? Not if the term "senses" is understood as the kind of mechanical sensory interaction between mind and world outlined in Lockean empiricism, and "experience" is understood in the way contextualists like Dewey defined it—as creative and transactional participation in events. A book filled with that kind of experience " 'would feed the hungry,' " says Wallace Stevens in a letter quoted by Williams (SE 13). Not only would it feed the hungry, it would "nick the solidity" of the mechanistic world view—"the so-called natural or scientific array"—that because of its ability to paralyze the unaided senses has become "the walking devil of modern life." Williams saw as his own purpose and that of the imagination in general to shatter the influence of this "apparition" of modern culture called the Cartesian (or Cartesian–Newtonian) paradigm that still inhibits our ability to come into the fullness of experience today.

Consciousness as Field or Stream

The form of *Paterson* has often been described as following the literary convention of the stream of consciousness. For example, Sister M. Bernetta Quinn states that

> the Passaic River is used in the poem to represent the giant Paterson's stream of consciousness. . . . The parallel between the currents of the Passaic and Paterson's thoughts (their interlacing, repulsion, advance, eddying, coalescence, leap and fall, retaking of the course) is worked out with a clarity of invention that brings the vehicle of the metaphor sharply before the eyes and into the ears in the best objectivist manner.[21]

In a similar vein, James Breslin argues that "Paterson's thoughts throughout the poem, instead of moving in a linear progression, 'interlace, repel and cut under, / rise rockthwarted and turn aside / but forever strain forward.' The form of the poem is the stream of his consciousness."[22] In one sense the use of this phrase, borrowed by the critics from William James, to describe the structure of *Paterson*, has some obvious validity. Whether the critic is referring to the giant Paterson whose "dreams," personified as citizens, "walk about the city" (p. 6); to the poet–doctor Paterson who himself is one of these citizens, and whose "thoughts" can be seen "inside the bus" "sitting and standing" ("His / thoughts alight and scatter—" p. 9); or to Williams himself, who often speaks in the first person, and who asks "why even speak of 'I' . . . which / interests me almost not at all?" (p. 19); the poem's looseness of form may be attributed to the poet's attempt to render directly the stream of human consciousness. If we accept the principle of "metamorphosis," stated by Quinn, as the method Williams used to "interchange man and certain aspects of his environment"[23] and to mingle the identities of certain characters, it is possible that the bulk of material presented in the poem appears within the framework of a multifaceted stream of consciousness.

But a significant problem regarding the depiction of the stream of consciousness in Book II, as in the rest of *Paterson*, concerns the interjection of the voices of other characters, materials such as the letters from "C," and public documents, ranging from contemporary newspaper clippings to instructions from an exercise manual, into an otherwise continuously flowing interior monologue. The thread of Klaus Ehrens's sermon at one point appears as follows:

> And the Lord said to me, Klaus, get rid of your
> money. You'll never be happy until you do that.

These lines are immediately followed by a passage dealing with the historical subject of assumption by the Federal Government of the national debt.

> As a corollary to the famous struggle for assumption lay the realization among many leading minds in the young republic that unless industry were set upon its feet, unless manufactured goods could be produced income from taxation would be a myth. . . .
> Even during the Revolution Hamilton had been impressed by the site of the Great Falls of the Passaic. His fertile imagination envisioned a great manufacturing center, a great Federal City, to supply the needs of the country. Here was water-power to turn the mill wheels and the navigable river to carry manufactured goods to the market centers: a national manufactury [p. 69].

The irony in the juxtaposition of sentimental verse with such clear expository prose is typical of many such juxtapositions in the poem. Ehrens's sermon could enter Paterson's stream of consciousness as he walks through the park on a Sunday afternoon. But can the latter prose passage be an element in that same stream of consciousness? An individual is hardly likely to *think* in successive expository paragraphs in such circumstances. Moments like these seem like temporary interruptions, from an outside source, of the immediate flow of Paterson's thought. But by shifting our metaphors slightly we see that the structure of consciousness portrayed in the poem is less like a *stream* of successive mental events within a private perspective than a complex *field*, capable of including a variety of perspectives and attitudes. This may ultimately be the significance of the "objectivism" that sets Williams's work apart from the subjectivism of the modern interior monologue. "The poem is made of things—on a field," Williams writes.[24] And *Paterson* bears witness to the conception of consciousness as a nonlinear field, rather than a stream, by its way of juxtaposing elements like those cited above. If there is a central consciousness in *Paterson*, it has the form and latitude of a contextual field of awareness.

In *Paterson*, Williams implicitly attempts to break out of the limits of the literary method called stream of consciousness, based on the principle of subjectivity. In doing so he developed a poetic form that reflects the contextual structure of thought, which because of its active involvement in a changing world, includes more than private subjectivity.

> Drawn from the streets we break off
> our minds' seclusion . . . [p. 96]

Paterson says upon entering the library in Book III. Throughout the poem this thread of Paterson's individual awareness is sustained, though often eclipsed by passages relating to his environment. The organization of consciousness in the poem is best described not as a "stream," but in terms of the experiential field in its plurality of aspects. *Paterson* is a poetic enactment of contextualist principles of the function of consciousness.

CONTEXTUALIST POETICS AND RELATIVITY

If the absolute point of view implied by the use of the omniscient narrator in literature and by Renaissance perspective in painting finds a counterpart in the absolute structures of space and time in Newtonian mechanics, the multiple and relative space–time systems of modern physics find a counterpart in the use of multiple perspectives in Williams's art and in the idea of the relativity of contexts at the heart of contextualist philosophy. Williams himself makes the connection between the theory of relativity in physics and modern poetry explicit in the essay "The Poem as a Field of Action." He writes: "How can we accept Einstein's theory of relativity, affecting our very conception of the heavens about us of which poets write so much, without incorporating its essential fact—the relativity of measurements—into our own category of activity: the poem. Do we think we stand outside the universe" (SE 283)?

We have seen that *Paterson* incorporates multiple perspectives in its structure. In what way, then, does the poem embody this "relativity of measurements" that reflects the new conception of the universe enunciated by modern physics? Verse, Williams says, "has always been associated in men's minds with 'measure,' i.e., mathematics" (SE 337), by which he means the counting of syllables and poetic feet. Williams found the metrics of conventional verse to be too rigid for his purposes. But he also felt that "No verse can be free, it must be governed by some measure, but not by the old measure. . . . We have no measure by which to guide ourselves except a purely intuitive one which we feel but do not name" (SE 339). This intuitive measure Williams associated with the sense of musical time.

In Williams's view high degrees of metrical regularity in poetry belong to older modes of consciousness. The feeling of one engaged in developing a new poetics "is similar to what must have been the early feelings of Einstein toward the laws of Isaac Newton in physics. Thus from being fixed, our prosodic values should rightly be seen as only relatively true. Einstein had the speed of light as a constant—his only constant—What have we? Perhaps our concept of musical time" (SE 286). The difference between Williams's metrics and those of more conventional verse lies in the fact that "the stated syllables, as in the best of present day free verse, have become entirely divorced from the beat, that is the measure. The musical pace proceeds without them. Therefore the measure, that is to say, the count, having got rid of the words, which held it down, is returned to the *music*" (SL 326).

In a letter of 1954, Williams cites the following example of his new practice of poetic measure:

> (1)   the smell of the heat is boxwood
>   (2)   when rousing us
>   (3)   a movement of the air
> (4)   stirs our thoughts
>   (5)   that had no life in them
>   (6)   to a life, a life in which   .   .   .   .

"Count a single beat to each numeral . . ." he explains. "Over the whole poem it gives a pattern to the meter that can be felt as a new measure. It gives resources to the ear which result in a language which we hear spoken about us every day" (SL 326–27). In *Paterson* he used a meter that had not been pre-established but, like the organization of content, was worked out intuitively in the process of writing. He discovered in the poem, after the fact, a relatively stable metrical structure that he termed "the variable foot." The concept of the variable foot emphasizes not the syllable, as in older verse forms, but a musical time period denoted by being written as a line fragment. Each fragment is, therefore, one foot, variable in that it may contain almost any number of words, or syllables, but constant in its time duration. Divided into three "feet," each "line" becomes a unit in a formal symmetry.[25]

As in the following lines from *Paterson*, Williams attempted to get away from the quantitative measurement of conventional verse and to employ a qualitative sense of measure, in accord (however loosely) with his understanding of relativity theory.

> The descent beckons
>   as the ascent beckoned
>   Memory is a kind
> of accomplishment
>   a sort of renewal
>   even
> an initiation, since the spaces it opens are new
> places
>   inhabited by hordes
>   heretofore unrealized,
> of new kinds—
>   since their movements
>   are towards new objectives
> (even though formerly they were abandoned)
>   [pp. 77–78].

The metrical "foot" that is made to count as a single "beat" also presents one idea-fragment toward the accretion of the whole. The foot thus is no longer a fixed quantity but can only be described as variable, in conformity with the relativistic world view it reflects.

Williams's use of the idea of physical relativity as a metaphor for the metrics of his poetry is an aspect of his contextualist orientation to experience. The poetic line based on the variable foot, like the structural deployment of disparate semantic elements in *Paterson*, points to a contextualist view of the world. These aspects of the poem's structure constitute evidence of the "new world which it has been created to affirm" (SE 196). The structure of the poem, including both its metrics and the organization of its meaning elements, corresponds to Williams's experience of the structure of that "new world."

Williams's poetics, which supports a contextualist world theory, is a sign of the revolutionary disposition in his thought. For it registers a shift from the traditional belief that mind is centered in a subjective ego to a new conception of mind as immersed in transactional relationships with other facts, a conception that corresponds to the contextualist definition of the way mind operates in the field of lived experience. Reading *Paterson* is an experience that can help us to conceive the shape of the contextualist's universe.

NOTES

1. Carl Rapp's excellent book *William Carlos Williams and Romantic Idealism* (Hanover, N.H.: University Press of New England, for Brown University Press, 1984) is the most valuable full-length study of Williams from a philosophical perspective to appear in recent years. Rapp places Williams's poetry and poetics in the context of philosophical idealism, both its indigenous American variety stemming from Emerson and its Hegelian form. In his fourth chapter, "Poetry as Power" (pp. 79–119), Rapp unravels the complexities and clarifies much of the misunderstanding that has surrounded Williams's poetic theories. The three theories that Rapp identifies, imagism, objectivism, and the search for a new measure, are all, he says, expressions of the same basic principle—"the principle of subjectivity" (p. 82). Rapp's argument is a compelling statement of Williams's kinship with idealistic philosophers. My thesis in this study regarding the relationship between Williams's poetics and Dewey's contextualistic aesthetics is a counterpart to Rapp's. But this study arrives at a different conclusion: namely, that Williams did break away from the paradigm of subjectivity in the process of discovering his own experiential naturalism.

2. *Selected Essays* (New York: New Directions, 1969), p. 119; hereafter cited as SE.

3. Langer, *Philosophy in a New Key*, chap. 3, "The Logic of Signs and Symbols," pp. 53–78.

4. *Art as Experience*, chap. 3, "Having an Experience," pp. 42–63.

5. Stanley E. Fish, *Surprised by Sin: The Reader in* PARADISE LOST (Berkeley: University of California Press, 1971), esp. pp. 340–56.

6. See "What is Common to All," *The Knowledge of Man: A Philosophy of the Interhuman*, trans. Maurice Friedman and Ronald Gregor Smith (New York: Harper & Row, 1965), pp. 89–109.

7. (New York: New Directions, 1967), p. 391. For a statement resembling Williams's "quotation" from Dewey, see Dewey's "Americanism and Localism," *John Dewey: The Middle Works, 1899–1924. XII. 1920*, ed. Bridget A. Walsh (Carbondale and Edwardsville: Southern Illinois University Press, 1982), p. 15. And for other references by Williams to Dewey, see: Williams, *Selected Letters*, ed. John C. Thirwall (New York: McDowell, Oblensky, 1957), pp. 138 and 224 (hereafter cited as SL); SE 132; and an article by Williams in *Contact*, 2 (January, 1921), 7. Williams's respect for Dewey and interest in his philosophy have been topics for comment by many critics, though no one has to date attempted either a comparison or a reading of Williams's work from a Deweyan standpoint. Among the critics who have noted Williams's kinship with Dewey are: Thomas R. Whitaker, *William Carlos Williams* (New York: Twayne, 1968); James Guimond, *The Art of William Carlos Williams* (Urbana: University of Illinois Press, 1968); and Vivienne Koch, *William Carlos Williams* (New York: New Directions, 1950). Each of them regards the alliance as of some (at least potential) importance, yet each relegates the issue to peripheral status in his or her study of Williams's work. Their comments are suggestive if relatively undeveloped. Ms. Koch's position is the most strongly stated. She suggests that "Williams might . . . be usefully described as a Deweyan instrumentalist in his approach to art" (p. 261). Though such comments are significant, Ms. Koch's exposition includes neither a specific examination of Williams's instrumentalist tendencies as a critic nor an application of instrumentalist principles to his poetry. Guimond emphasizes only that "Williams derived the vocabulary for his conception of the universality of the local from John Dewey" (p. 55). Whitaker presents evidence to demonstrate a pragmatic orientation to Williams's thought but does not make extensive use of this insight in the analysis of his poetry. Paul Mariani, in his biography *William Carlos Williams: A New World Naked* (New York: McGraw-Hill, 1981), makes numerous references to Dewey, which illustrate the fact that Williams wrestled with Dewey's ideas over a period of many years.

8. *Logic*, pp. 72, 73.

9. Otis Lee, "Value and the Situation," *The Journal of Philosophy*, 41 (1944), 338.

10. *Logic*, pp. 107–108.

11. "Contextualism," p. 251.

12. Ibid., pp. 246–64.

13. See Dewey and Bentley, "Interaction and Transaction," *Knowing and the Known*, pp. 96–109.

14. Ibid., p. 261.

15. Andrew J. Reck, *Speculative Philosophy: A Study of Its Nature, Types, and Uses* (Albuquerque: University of New Mexico Press, 1972), p. 47.

16. (New York: New Directions, 1963), p. 2; hereafter cited by page number.

17. *Poetry and the Age* (New York: Vintage, 1962), pp. 238–39.

18. See James E. Breslin, *William Carlos Williams: An American Artist* (New York: Oxford University Press, 1970), p. 169.

19. (Chicago: The University of Chicago Press, 1958), p. 160.

20. See, for example, Berman's *Reenchantment of the World*.

21. *The Metamorphic Tradition in Modern Poetry* (New Brunswick, N.J.: Rutgers University Press, 1955), p. 95.

22. *William Carlos Williams*, p. 182.

23. *Metamorphic Tradition*, p. 103.

24. *Autobiography*, p. 333.

25. Alan Ostrom, *William Carlos Williams* (Carbondale and Edwardsville: Southern Illinois University Press, 1966), p. 145.

CONCLUSION:

Participating Consciousness—
A Way Beyond
Authoritarianism

THE PHILOSOPHERS AND POETS examined in these studies were passionately committed to a process that I have called a return to experience. In Western society, and in Western philosophy, the idea of experience historically has meant either conscious observation of or conscious participation in events. The principles of observation and participation form a polarity of philosophical views about what experience is and how it happens. Though experience is obviously difficult to grasp by the tools of reflective thought, as humans we have a natural drive to understand the structures of experience. To grow in our understanding of experience is to develop our ability to orient our lives meaningfully to others and to gain increasing powers of self-awareness. The philosophers and poets under examination here were evidently pursuing the paradoxical goal of attaining self-awareness of the meaning of the stream of experience by abandoning the very principle of ego-consciousness that in previous eras had been the primary source of meaning. These studies trace tendencies in their work toward the realization of this goal, not merely in individual lives, but also in the context of social transactions. Their works involve instructions to readers about the kinds of thought, action, and experiment that bring us, as James Joyce said, to encounter "the reality of experience"[1] and to the educative process that Dewey called the "reconstruction of experience."[2] One conclusion we are drawn to by the evidence in these studies is that, departing from the mainstream of modern Western culture, these thinkers made a revolutionary turn, away from observation, and toward participation, as the most effective way to attain this goal.

Since ancient times, the tendency to grasp experience by means of observation, as distinct from participation, has dominated Western philosophy. In "The Invention of the Mind," the opening chapter of his epoch-making book *Philosophy and the Mirror of Nature* (1979), Richard Rorty argues that in the pursuit of universal objects of knowledge, like the idea of the Good, philosophy "undertook to examine the difference," for example, "between knowing that there were parallel mountain ranges to the west and knowing that infinitely extended parallel lines never meet, the difference between knowing that Socrates was good and knowing what goodness was."[3] When the question of the difference between the particular man Socrates and the universal idea of goodness "was answered in terms of the distinction between the eye of the body and the Eye of the Mind, νοῦς—thought, intellect, insight—was identified as what separates men from beasts,"[4] according to Rorty. "There was, we moderns may say with the ingratitude of hindsight, no particular reason why this ocular metaphor seized the imagination of the founders of Western thought. But it did, and contemporary philosophers are still working out its consequences, analyzing the problems it created, and asking whether there may not be something to it after all."[5] In a note, Rorty cites Dewey's argument that the metaphor of the Eye of the Mind originated "as the result of the prior notion that knowledge must be of the unchangeable."[6] And in *The Quest for Certainty* Dewey writes:

> The theory of knowing is modeled after what was supposed to take place in the act of vision. The object refracts light to the eye and is seen; it makes a difference to the eye and to the person having an optical apparatus, but none to the thing seen. The real object is the object so fixed in its regal aloofness that it is a king to any beholding mind that may gaze upon it. A spectator theory of knowledge is the inevitable outcome.[7]

Rorty is highly skeptical of the view that there may be something valid in the ocular metaphor or the spectator theory, and his neo-pragmatism represents a potent revolt in its own right against the epistemology based on the root metaphor of the mind as "mirror of nature." In "The World Well Lost" (1972), Rorty's argument, as Cornel West puts it, is that "We cannot isolate 'the world' from theories of the world, then compare these theories of the world with a theory-free world. We cannot compare theories with anything that is not a product of another theory. So any talk about 'the world' is relative to the theories available."[8] Rorty explains: "I can now express the same point by saying that the notion of 'the world' that is correlative with the notion of 'conceptual framework' is simply the Kantian notion of a thing-in-itself . . ."[9]—in other words, an unknowable noumenon beyond experience, born of Kant's particular brand of the spectator theory, that Rorty finds unacceptable. Instead of attempting, as James and Dewey do, to resolve this dilemma by returning to the field of experience as defined by radical empiricism, Rorty opts to hold tight to language use as the one part of the field that we can grasp with a minimum of ambiguity.

By pulling the pegs out from under the mirror-of-nature theory of mind, Rorty develops a linguistic and epistemological behaviorism that makes its own contribution to the deconstruction of the Cartesian paradigm. "Can

we treat the study of 'the nature of human knowledge' just as the study of
certain ways in which human beings interact, or does it require an
ontological foundation?'' Rorty asks. His answer is another question:

> Shall we take "S knows that p" . . . as a remark about the status of S's
> reports among his peers, or shall we take it as a remark about the relation
> between subject and object, between nature and its mirror? The first alterna-
> tive leads to a pragmatic view of truth and a therapeutic approach to ontology.
> . . . The second alternative leads to "ontological" explanations of the relations
> between minds and meanings, minds and immediate data of awareness,
> universals and particulars, thought and language, consciousness and brains,
> and so on. . . . The aim of all such explanations is to make truth something
> more than what Dewey called "warranted assertability": more than what our
> peers will . . . let us get away with saying.[10]

Opposed to hierarchical systems of authority that claim privileges for one
set of values, one language, one society, or one philosophical point of
view over others, Rorty explains "rationality and epistemic authority by
reference to what society lets us say"[11] rather than the other way around.
Such a method of explanation is the essence of what he calls "epistemological behaviorism," a method that he says is common to both Dewey
and Wittgenstein. The tendency to justify such privileged authority by
appealing to philosophical criteria alone, as West explains, "is a species
of the more traditional philosophical temptation to think of the world,
society, self, or language as possessing an intrinsic nature or an essence,"[12]
a temptation that Rorty resolutely resists.

> Since truth is a property of sentences, and languages are made rather than
> found, the results of appealing to philosophical criteria will be but viciously
> circular and apologetic arguments, rhetorical self-compliments regarding
> one's own perspective, "attempts to eternalize a certain contemporary lan-
> guage-game, social practice, or self-image."[13]

From a general acceptance of Dewey's instrumental approach to mind and
knowing, Rorty proceeds to an antifoundationalist view of epistemology,
focused heavily on the issue of language use. In Rorty's view, there is no
beginning or final ground to the knowing process, such as a material (or
mental) substance, but only an endless series of possible statements. This
antifoundationalism "precludes the notion of privileged representations
because it views knowledge as relations to propositions rather than as
privileged relations to the objects certain propositions are about."[14] There
is, in other words, neither an ascertainable correspondence between ideas
and objects, nor ultimately a pragmatic vision of truth as the validation of
ideas by their results in experience and action, for Rorty. Though according to him, " 'Language' may be a more suitable notion than 'experience'
for saying the holistic and anti-foundationalist things which James and
Dewey had wanted to say,"[15] many will disagree. Though both James and

Dewey were disposed to reject any kind of specious "foundations," neither found an acceptable substitute for the concept of experience, because both were looking for a resolution to the dilemma of Cartesian dualism from a motive of participation. Though admittedly vague, the concept of experience served an indispensable function of enabling one to embrace the contrasting or conflicting elements of existence in a unity of contextual wholeness.[16]

The claim that truth is a property of the way sentences hang together, or a function of linguistic behavior, bypasses the anomaly of subject–object dualism implicit in some correspondence theories of truth. But it misses the constructive principle in James's pragmatic concept of truth, defined as the quality of an idea that lets us get into satisfactory relation to facts within the field of experience. Though Rorty disparages Dewey's use of the term "experience" as "an incantatory device for blurring every possible distinction,"[17] the principles of return to experience and reconstruction of experience prescribed by Dewey as the cure for modernity's pathological subjectivism are tools that help us break down the mindset of dualistic epistemology. But they help us at the same time to avoid the relativism of the "potentially infinite regress of propositions-brought-forward-in-defense-of-other-propositions" that Rorty accepts as an inevitable "consequence" of his own linguistic behaviorism.[18]

Why did the ocular metaphor seize the imaginations of the founders of Western thought? Why did the spectator theory of knowledge come to dominate the modern philosophical imagination? And why have philosophers persistently viewed knowledge as, in Rorty's works, "*looking* at something (rather than, say, rubbing up against it, or crushing it underfoot, or having sexual intercourse with it)"[19]—the way "knowledge" is conceived in the Hebrew scriptures, for example? One possible approach to this line of questioning is given by Huston Smith in an article entitled "Beyond the Modern Western Mind-set" (1981). Smith argues that the Modern Western Mind-set, with the spectator theory of knowledge at its heart, was driven by a motive to control things. The principle of observation, as the fundamental definition of knowledge, led to a practice of psychologically distancing the mind from the objects it encounters in the process of knowing. Though as Rorty stresses, it is far from clear what motivated the ancient philosophers' quest for certainty and led to their preoccupation with the root metaphor of sight to describe the knowing situation, Smith's argument leads one to conclude that the centrality of the spectator theory of knowledge in modern philosophy resulted from a motivation not just to know things or to find out the truth in a disinterested way, but also to manipulate the objects of thought.

If a root metaphor (or gestalt image) of mind and knowing, like that of the mirror of nature, comes about because of a specific motivation, that same motivation will tend in a philosophical culture like modernity to become reified in the conceptual structures of epistemology and metaphysics. From the motivation to control and manipulate the material world for human ends, modernity generated its own dichotomized image of experience which it reinforced through its powerful dominant epistemology, expressed most fully in classic empiricism. With sources as deep in Western history as Plato's dialogues, the philosophic tendency to dichotomize experience, to reduce mind to a role of spectatorship, and the world to an observed object, evolved in the philosophies of Descartes, Locke, Hume, Kant, and many others into a potent analytical formula. The power of consciousness to set itself at a (psychological) distance from nature was soon recognized in the dawning of the modern age as the key to domination of the natural world. For by eliminating subjective elements such as emotion and religious interpretation from the human perception of the objects of nature, modernity was able to reduce nature to a purely "objectified" status, thus rendering it susceptible to the analytical inroads of modern science. Despite the dangers of subjectivism, the distancing of consciousness from the object, which might have simply been acknowledged as one of the mind's many powers for generating meaning, was instead reified, first in modern epistemological dualism and then (as in Descartes's *Meditations*) in a dualistic ontology, as a permanent image of the human condition. From the mental power of distancing, reinforced and legitimated, so to speak, by modern epistemology and ontology, came the more literal scientific and technological power to control, with increasing effectiveness, the objects analyzed.

Though James, Dewey, Peirce, and Royce all saw their philosophies as fundamentally in accord with the aims of modern science, in some crucial aspects of their work they pursued a motive contrary to that of control. They had an acute perception that the power over the objective world that came with intellectual and analytical distancing also brought along with it the potential psychosis of subjectivism. It was largely a desire to cure pathological subjectivism in modern philosophy and modern life that moved the American philosophers to spurn the spectator theory of knowledge, and I would argue not merely to evade the kind of epistemology represented in modern empiricism, but also to reject the motive of control that lay behind it. In the course of their reflections about experience, James and Dewey (and, to a lesser extent, Peirce and Royce) encountered the equivalent of a gestalt-switch. Instead of an image of a spectator-consciousness observing an external object-world, they came to see with increasing clarity a single experiential continuum, with consciousness detranscendentalized, yet persistently valued because it was redefined in terms of what James called "its equivalent in realities of experience." To the builders in American philosophy the return to experience meant the recovery, within philosophic understanding, of actual experience (or pure experience) as opposed to the highly rationalized, dichotomized image of experience found in modern epistemology. To accomplish this end, each in his own way pursued the motive of participation—evident in a new image of the human mind engaged in the processes that Royce called interpreting and Dewey called reconstructing things and events, from a standpoint other than the private psychic sphere that modernity had called "consciousness." Counterbalancing the debilitating effects of subjectivism, their desire for participation rather than observation entailed a process of creative reconstruction of experience.

Though Rorty helps us to see why epistemology based on the mirror-of-nature concept of mind is no longer a viable path of inquiry, to see what is wrong with the observation model of experience, his work is more valuable as a diagnosis of cultural ills than as a prescription for their cure. Because of his preoccupation with linguistic behavior, and because of his skepticism about epistemological or ontological foundations, he is in effect only incompletely able to turn his thinking back to experience in the way mapped out by James, Dewey, and others in the period of the builders. Though his *Philosophy and the Mirror of Nature* has an air of finality about its deconstruction of the spectator gestalt, it gives only incomplete hints about the territory beyond the frontiers defined by Cartesian epistemology. By equating knowledge (and "epistemic authority") with linguistic behavior, Rorty paradoxically rejects the principle of observation, but maintains a posture of distancing. Since objects and "the world" seem to have no status apart from linguistic expressions, the motivation to control seems strangely absent from his thinking.

To remedy modernity's pathological egocentricity and sociocentricity, we need to recognize the validity and pragmatic significance of the power of distancing, but also to nurture the motives of participation and relation. In addition to the trail of reasoning and poetic insight we have followed in these studies, tools for this nurturing process may be found in a variety of sources. In his powerful essay on "Distance and Relation," for example, Martin Buber writes

> Man can set at a distance without coming into real relation with what has been set at a distance. He can fill the act of setting at a distance with the will to relation, relation having been made possible only by that act; he can accomplish the act of relation in the acknowledgment of the fundamental actuality of the distance. But the two movements can also contend with one another, each seeing in the other the obstacle to its own realization. And finally, in moments and forms of grace, unity can arise from the extreme tension of the contradiction as the overcoming of it, which is granted only now and in this way.[20]

The holistic point of view expressed by Buber resembles an attitude implicit in radical empiricism: though twofold in its (mental and physical) functions and in its movements (distancing and relation), experience emerges into integrity and participatory relations with others through its own powers of creative synthesis. Working to a degree under Buber's influence, Dwayne Huebner argues that "every mode of knowing is a mode of being in relationship. It is a relationship of mutual care and love, often distorted into mere attentiveness and sometimes distorted into control and oppression."[21] Furthermore, Huebner maintains,

> Every mode of knowing is participation in the continual creation of the universe—of one's self, of others, of the dwelling places of the world. It is co-creation. If knowing is in language forms, then the events between self and the other create new language forms. If knowing is in visual and plastic forms, then co-creation is change in the qualitative and sensory aspects of the world. If knowing is practical and technical, it modifies the forms of the ever present but changing relationship between the human and the other than human. If it is knowing of the other, it is creation of new relationships—of exclusion or inclusion, of love or enmity, of dialogue or control.[22]

The co-creation with the other of transactional relationships is also a theme we have observed in American philosophy and poetry. According to Huston Smith, the motive to participate is capable of generating forms of knowing based on metaphoric and intuitive thinking, which remain inaccessible within the logic of modernity's dominant paradigm of knowing: the observation model, based on the empiricism of sense data. "[I]f we were to approach the world with intent other than to control it, it would show us a different guise," Smith writes.[23] "The opposite of the will-to-control is the wish to participate—a genuine desire to accent embracing yin over abrasive yang so that domination will not preclude partnership or assertiveness stymie cooperation."[24] To choose consciously to make this shift of intent is "[t]o move from captivity toward a freedom we have yet to understand. . . ."[25] It is to move beyond the frontiers of consciousness accessible to modernity, beyond the epistemology of a mechanistic empiricism based solely on sensory deposits, perhaps beyond an anti-epistemological disposition that acknowledges no "other" apart from what language allows us to say, toward what Hocking calls an "empiricism of meaning."[26]

For such a new empiricism experience is understood to include "meaning"—i.e., intrinsic relatedness between knowing and the known that must be realized by conscious acts of embracing the other. Such relatedness, in Hocking's view, is progressively made actual as the boundaries of the old subjectivity give way to the motive of "intersubjectivity."[27] With its focus on the "*participation* of each I-think in the experience of an intersubjective Thou-art,"[28] Hocking's empiricism of meaning offers significant clues to what lies beyond the frontiers of Cartesian consciousness and to the aspects of the philosophy of the builders that are concerned with passage beyond modernity. For while Hocking, like James and Dewey, maintains an ethical and existential grounding in individual experience, he also takes a critical step that Rorty seems reluctant to take. That is the step toward a reconstruction of experience based on the motive of participation, which Smith conceives as a radical alternative to the motive of control.

The instrumentalist view of mind in the thought of James and Dewey might be regarded as in accord with the Western drive for analytical control of the objects of perception and experience. But this would be an oversimplification and misconstruction of their thought. James and Dewey (and to varying degrees, Peirce and Royce) sensed the critical limitations of the dualistic mindset of modernity, and ran aground intellectually against what Dewey called its "alleged epistemological predicament."[29] In order to extricate themselves and their readers from this predicament they were confronted with a paradox. Despite their enthusiasm for science, including James's desire to put psychology on scientific foundations, and Dewey's zeal to apply scientific methods to social problems, they found themselves, almost involuntarily, developing methods of thinking—unlike the cognitive logic of science—that decidedly emphasize affective strategies. James's use of metaphor, as we have seen, was not simply a matter of a linguistic factor occasionally punctuating an otherwise analytical form of discourse. Because metaphor represents a form of thinking that has synthesizing effects, linking disparate parts of experience, it proved to be a crucial tool in James's redefinition of consciousness as a function within holistic experiential contexts. Though lacking James's literary gifts, in parts of his philosophy Dewey emphasized the intuitive and affectional aspects of thought as more fundamental than the cognitive and analytical, recognizing art as the most complete model of integrated experience, and bringing his own new empiricism to focus near the end of his life in the concept of transactional experience. As Dewey writes in *Democracy and Education* (1916) "If the living, experiencing being is an intimate participant in the activities of the world to which it belongs, then knowledge is a mode of participation, valuable in the degree in which it is effective. It cannot be the idle view of an unconcerned spectator."[30] Royce's empirical idealism, which relies on Peirce's theory of signs and meaning, culminates in a hermeneutical theory capable of taking into account the full range of meanings, from the rational to the metaphorical, as aspects of an experiential continuum. What I have described as a gestalt-switch in American philosophy, which established the rudiments of a new paradigm of consciousness, results from a shift of motive from control to participation.

If, with Rorty, we can regard poetry as a form of inquiry on an equal footing with science and philosophy,[31] we see that Dewey, James, Peirce, and Royce, despite their many differences, shared with the poets a recognition of the arbitrariness of the authority of the Cartesian paradigm, and (like the poets) strove for a recovery of the sense of integration of mind in nature, a recovery of what Gregory Bateson called the "necessary unity" of mind and nature.[32] Recovering this unity is a large part of the meaning of the return to experience pursued by all these American writers. The new gestalt of experience, as redefined by James, Dewey, Royce, and Peirce, is no longer dualistic. This new image of a pure experience, common to all men and women, deconstructs elitist or hierarchist views of existence and therefore of social relations. Like pragmatism and Rorty's neo-pragmatism, it carries the implication that there is no privileged authority for the claims of knowledge or truth, apart from the transactional fields of experience that all men and women share equally. Ironically, the modern idea of individual human consciousness, recognized by Descartes as a means of dispelling the false "authority" of ancient traditions, became in the modern tradition a domain of its own kind of privileged authority. The return to experience in one respect has the effect of shattering this subjective authority.

Poetry is intrinsically a participatory art, as critics from Aristotle to Stanley Fish have shown, moving readers and audiences to catharsis, epiphany, and experiential identification with fictional characters, states of consciousness, and events. Clearly the power of the written word to move readers emotionally and intellectually to new sight and new understanding is due in part to the alchemy of metaphor to connect otherwise divergent parts of experience and make them one. As Dewey insists in *Art as Experience,* in order to "work" in the lives of readers, literature demands the readers' creative participation. But I have emphasized in these studies the peculiar experiential participation demanded by the poetry of Eliot, Stevens, and Williams, among other twentieth-century poets. Sensing the crisis of alienation to which Cartesian culture had brought Western society in their time, and evidently moved by the drive to develop and portray a post-Cartesian participating consciousness in their works, the poets sought to articulate a return to experience by the method of metaphor as well as through deliberate and historically unprecedented structural and linguistic experimentation.

I am not suggesting that the motives of James, Dewey, Peirce, Royce, and of the poets Eliot, Stevens, and Williams were uniformly clear (either to themselves or to others) or that these thinkers all agreed with one another in the details of their objectives. But these studies trace a pattern that illustrates their collective desire to break through the boundaries of the cultural definition of mind within the Cartesian paradigm. Instead of dualism the philosophers proposed the image of unified experience; instead of mental and material substances in mechanistic interaction they proposed an organic process-model of experiential relations, leading to creative transactionalism, as the basis of a redefinition of mind. Instead of a passive receptacle for sensory (or intellectual) deposits, called *knowledge*, consciousness is redefined on the basis of a new empiricism as a creative instrument engaged in risk-taking and ethical initiatives, which bring individuals into more and more significant relation to each other and to the natural environment. The emphasis in the new paradigm of consciousness is on *knowing* as a constructive act, rather than knowledge as static content of consciousness. Working more explicitly, as artists, in terms of qualitative and affective thinking, the poets struggled to clarify the experiential form of post-Cartesian points of view. Notably this struggle results in the literary expression of expanded points of perspective reference that are no longer merely subjective, but intersubjective and contextual.

The texts of philosophy and poetry examined here, and to a lesser degree these studies themselves, may become instruments of the return to experience as redefined in a post-Cartesian frame of thought. The texts do not merely embody descriptions of a new epistemology, or a new paradigmatic conception of mind. They may have the effect of enabling readers to undergo the gestalt-switch from a dichotomized image to an integrated process-based model of the way mind works. Achieving the effect of a return to experience, by means of poetic and philosophic discourse, entails reliance on metaphorical (more than analytical) thinking, and affective and hermeneutical strategies. For this reason, I have emphasized the theories of meaning and interpretation in Peirce and Royce rather than their scientific and logical studies. I have developed the idea of an experiential hermeneutics in Royce and Peirce that may have more concrete relevance to American poetry of the twentieth century than theories of interpretation that retain a grounding in the Cartesian paradigm. I have focused on what I have called a metaphorical method in James's work. And I have stressed Dewey's transactional approach to language and creativity rather than his attempts to apply scientific method to problems of knowledge and society.

In his perceptive reassessment of American philosophy from Emerson to Rorty, *The American Evasion of Philosophy* (1989), Cornel West argues that American philosophers have consistently evaded the epistemology-centered philosophy of the Cartesian tradition in favor of "accenting human powers, and transforming antiquated modes of social hierarchies in light of religious and/or ethical ideals. . . ."[33] This evasion and transformation "results in a conception of philosophy as a form of cultural criticism" that responds to "distinct social and cultural crises."[34] West describes the work of the American pragmatists as "an indigenous mode of thought that subordinates knowledge to power, tradition to invention, instruction to provocation, community to personality, and immediate problems to utopian possibilities."[35] Its common denominator consists of "a future-oriented instrumentalism that tries to deploy thought as a weapon to enable more effective action. Its basic impulse is a plebeian radicalism that fuels an antipatrician rebelliousness for the moral aim of enriching individuals and expanding democracy.''[36] These comments about pragmatism also apply to a degree to radical empiricism.

Because it represents an holistic orientation, the idea of pure experience is itself a pragmatic tool of reflective thought that enables one to work out the experiential linkages between conflicting factors in our existence, and to overcome arbitrary intellectual hierarchies. If experience is no longer dichotomized, every person in a given social environment is understood as participating equally in the field of experience, and no point of view can claim privileged status over others, apart from the pragmatic authority of experience itself. Not only is there no more necessity, in radical empiricism, to accept arbitary lines of hierarchical social, political, or religious authority, but conflicting existential opposites, symbolized by the subject and object of Cartesian epistemology, are given a chance to become pragmatically integrated with each other. Other contraries are embraced in pragmatic and experiential unity according to the post-Cartesian paradigm of mind we have been tracing in these studies. These include: self and society, rigor and imagination, ethical ideals and actual circumstances, theory and practice, reason and intuition, philosophy and poetry, mind and nature.

The contrast in perspectives represented by Hocking and Rorty symbolizes contrasting impulses inherent in the major creative achievements of American pragmatism and radical empiricism. These contrasting impulses, one toward Rorty's epistemological behaviorism, and the other toward the kind of constructive empirical idealism found in Hocking, both lead toward a breakdown of the authority of the Cartesian paradigm, and both are anti-authoritarian in the broader sense of working to dissolve the arbitrariness of any privileged authority. But while Rorty's antifoundationalism challenges arbitrary authority only at the cost of embracing relativism in the knowing process and in ethics, Hocking's principle of intersubjectivity and historical sense of passage beyond modernity (which is the thread of American philosophy and poetry followed in these studies) leads one toward values inherent in Dewey's idea of creative democracy.

While his behaviorism and materialistic bias[37] lead Rorty to reject mind as a legitimate sphere of inquiry, and to be interested mainly in discussing how linguistic expressions hang together with other linguistic expressions, Hocking's new principle of historical advance—intersubjectivity—begins with the concept of meaning as the actual connectedness of facts, including subjective facts, and defines truth as the human awareness of that connectedness. To be authentically connected to others through the power of intersubjectivity is to be a conscious participant in existence and in the co-creation with others of meaning. When James says that ideas are made true by events, he means that ideas have served a progressive or educative function, providing clues to success in survival and to significant relation to others. Since existence is a continuous process (an experiential continuum, in Dewey's terms), those individual experiences that enable the process to flow from one phase to another uninhibitedly serve end-values that are intrinsic to existence. Though it is possible for some events to be miseducative, if they block or inhibit the natural transactions that make up the experiential continuum, nurturing that uninhibited growth process, in oneself and in others, is Dewey's definition of the essential gesture of our existence, education. To serve the primal educational ends of existence as envisioned by Dewey, Rorty's behavioristic approach to knowing may be good therapy to liberate some individuals from the disease of ontological subjectivism. But such liberation can be genuine only if Rorty's argument is used, not as a stopping place, but as a ladder that helps us climb up to intersubjective points of view (as in Hocking's "empiricism of meaning") from which our genuine relatedness to others is empirically confirmed, and meanings in experience are progressively realized.

NOTES

1. *A Portrait of the Artist as a Young Man* (New York: Viking, 1972), p. 253.

2. *Experience and Education, John Dewey: The Later Works, 1925–1953*. XIII. *1938–1939*, ed. Barbara Levine (Carbondale and Edwardsville: Southern Illinois University Press, 1988), p. 28 and passim.

3. P. 38.

4. Ibid.

5. Ibid.

6. Ibid., p. 39n6.

7. P. 19.

8. *The American Evasion of Philosophy: A Genealogy of Pragmatism* (Madison: University of Wisconsin Press, 1989), p. 197.

9. "The World Well Lost," *Consequences of Pragmatism (Essays: 1972–1980)* (Minneapolis: University of Minnesota Press, 1982), p. 16.

10. *Philosophy and the Mirror of Nature*, pp. 175–76.

11. Ibid., p. 174.

12. West, *American Evasion of Philosophy*, p. 200.

13. Ibid. West is citing Rorty's *Philosophy and the Mirror of Nature*, p. 10.

14. West, *American Evasion of Philosophy*, p. 201.

15. "Symposium on Rorty's *Consequences of Pragmatism*: Comments on Sleeper and Edel," *Transactions of the Charles S. Peirce Society*, 21, No. 1 (Winter 1985), 40.

16. See John J. McDermott, "Symposium on Rorty's *Consequences of Pragmatism*: Introduction," ibid., 1–7.

17. "World Well Lost," p. 16.

18. *Philosophy and the Mirror of Nature*, p. 159.

19. Ibid., p. 39.

20. P. 64.

21. "Spirituality and Knowing," in *Learning and Teaching the Ways of Knowing*, ed. Elliot Eisner (Chicago: National Society for the Study of Education, 1985), pp. 170–71.

22. Ibid., p. 172.

23. "Beyond the Modern Western Mind-set," p. 143.

24. Ibid.

25. Ibid.

26. Hocking, *Coming World Civilization*, p. 70.

27. Ibid.

28. Ibid., p. 32.

29. "The Need for a Recovery of Philosophy," *John Dewey: The Middle Works, 1899–1924*. X. *1916–1917*, ed. Anne Sharpe (Carbondale and Edwardsville: Southern Illinois University Press, 1980), p. 29.

30. In *John Dewey: The Middle Works, 1899–1924*. IX. *1916*, edd. Patricia R. Baysinger and Barbara Levine (Carbondale and Edwardsville: Southern Illinois University Press, 1980), p. 347.

31. "Introduction: Pragmatism and Philosophy," *Consequences of Pragmatism (Essays: 1972–1980)* Minneapolis: University of Minnesota Press, 1982), p. xliii.

32. See his *Mind and Nature: A Necessary Unity*.

33. P. 4.

34. Ibid., p. 5.

35. Ibid.

36. Ibid.

37. See Robert Schwartz, Review of Richard Rorty, *Philosophy and the Mirror of Nature*, *The Journal of Philosophy*, 80, No. 1 (January 1983), 52.

BIBLIOGRAPHY

Allan, Mowbray. *T. S. Eliot's Impersonal Theory of Poetry*. Lewisburg, Pa.: Bucknell University Press, 1974.

Barfield, Owen. *Saving the Appearances: A Study in Idolatry*. New York: Harcourt, Brace & World [1965].

Barzun, Jacques. "William James and the Clue to Art." *The Energies of Art: Studies of Authors Classic and Modern*. New York: Harper & Row, 1956. Pp. 325–55.

Bates, Milton J. *Wallace Stevens: A Mythology of Self*. Berkeley: University of California Press, 1985.

Bateson, Gregory. *Mind and Nature: A Necessary Unity*. New York: Dutton, 1979.

Berdyaev, Nicolai. *Truth and Revelation*. Trans. R. M. French. New York: Harper & Row, 1953.

Berger, Peter L., and Luckman, Thomas. *The Social Construction of Reality: A Treatise in the Sociology of Knowledge*. Garden City, N.Y.: Doubleday, 1966.

Bergson, Henri. *Introduction to Metaphysics*. Trans. Mabelle L. Andison. Totowa, N.J.: Littlefield, Adams, 1975.

Bergsten, Staffan. *Time and Eternity: A Study in the Structure and Symbolism of T. S. Eliot's* FOUR QUARTETS. Stockholm: Svenska, 1960.

Berman, Art. *From the New Criticism to Deconstruction*. Urbana: University of Illinois Press, 1988.

Berman, Morris. *The Reenchantment of the World*. Ithaca: Cornell University Press, 1980.

Bernstein, Richard J. "Action, Conduct, and Inquiry: Peirce and Dewey." *Praxis and Action: Contemporary Philosophies of Human Activity*. Philadelphia: University of Pennsylvania Press, 1971. Pp. 165–229.

Berry, Wendell. "The Loss of the University." In *Home Economics*. San Francisco: North Point Press, 1987.

Bordo, Susan. *The Flight to Objectivity: Essays in Cartesianism and Culture*. Albany: SUNY Press, 1987.

Breslin, James E. *William Carlos Williams: An American Artist*. New York: Oxford University Press, 1970.

Buber, Martin. "Distance and Relation." *The Knowledge of Man: A Philosophy of the Interhuman*. Trans. Maurice Friedman and Ronald Gregor Smith. New York: Harper & Row, 1965. Pp. 59–71.

——. *I and Thou.* Trans. Ronald Gregor Smith. 2nd ed. New York: Macmillan, 1987.

——. "What Is Common to All." *The Knowledge of Man: A Philosophy of the Interhuman.* Trans. Maurice Friedman and Ronald Gregor Smith. New York: Harper & Row, 1965. Pp. 89–109.

Burnham, Jack. *The Structure of Art.* New York: Braziller, 1971.

Cavell, Stanley. "Aesthetic Problems of Modern Philosophy." *Must We Mean What We Say? A Book of Essays.* New York: Scribner's, 1969. Pp. 73–96.

Chomsky, Noam. *Language and Mind.* New York: Harcourt, Brace & World, 1968.

Clendenning, John. *The Life and Thought of Josiah Royce.* Madison: University of Wisconsin Press, 1985.

Cobb, John, Jr. *The Structure of Christian Existence.* New York: Seabury, 1979.

Conrad, Joseph. *The Nigger of the Narcissus.* New York: Doubleday, Doran, 1930.

Cooper, Douglas. *The Cubist Epoch.* London: Phaidon, 1970.

Corrington, Robert S. *The Community of Interpreters: On the Hermeneutics of Nature and the Bible in the American Philosophical Tradition.* Macon, Ga.: Mercer University Press, 1987.

Cotton, James Harry. *Royce on the Human Self.* New York: Greenwood, 1968.

Descartes, René. *Meditations.* In *Discourse on Method and Other Writings.* Trans. J. Wollastrom. Harmondsworth: Penguin, 1970.

——. *Principles of Philosophy I.* Trans. John Cottingham. *The Philosophical Writings of Descartes* I. Trans. John Cottingham, Robert Stoothoff, and Dugald Murdoch. Cambridge: Cambridge University Press, 1985. Pp. 177–222.

Dewey, John. "Americanism and Localism." *John Dewey: The Middle Works, 1899–1924.* XII. *1920.* Ed. Bridget A. Walsh. Carbondale and Edwardsville: Southern Illinois University Press, 1982. Pp. 12–16.

——. *Art as Experience. John Dewey: The Later Works, 1925–1953.* X. *1934.* Ed. Harriet Furst Simon. Carbondale and Edwardsville: Southern Illinois University Press, 1987.

——. *Democracy and Education. John Dewey: The Middle Works, 1899–1924.* IX. *1916.* Edd. Patricia R. Baysinger and Barbara Levine. Carbondale and Edwardsville: Southern Illinois University Press, 1980.

——. *Experience and Education. John Dewey: The Later Works, 1925–1953.* XIII. *1938–1939.* Ed. Barbara Levine. Carbondale and Edwardsville: Southern Illinois University Press, 1988. Pp. 1–62.

——. *Experience and Nature. John Dewey: The Later Works, 1925–1953.* I. *1925.* Edd. Patricia Baysinger and Barbara Levine. Carbondale and Edwardsville: Southern Illinois University Press, 1981.

——. "From Absolutism to Experimentalism." *John Dewey: The Later Works, 1925–1953.* V. *1929–1930.* Ed. Kathleen E. Poulos. Carbondale and Edwardsville: Southern Illinois University Press, 1984. Pp. 147–60.

——. *Logic: The Theory of Inquiry. John Dewey: The Later Works, 1925–1953.* XII. *1938.* Ed. Kathleen Poulos. Carbondale and Edwardsville: Southern Illinois University Press, 1986.

——. "A Naturalistic Theory of Sense-Perception." *John Dewey: The Later Works, 1925–1953.* II. *1925–1927.* Ed. Bridget A. Walsh. Carbondale and Edwardsville: Southern Illinois University Press, 1984. Pp. 44–54.

——. "The Need for a Recovery of Philosophy." *John Dewey: The Middle Works, 1899–1924.* X. *1916–1917.* Ed. Anne Sharpe. Carbondale and Edwardsville: Southern Illinois University Press, 1980. Pp. 3–48.

——. "Qualitative Thought." *John Dewey: The Later Works, 1925–1953.* V. *1929–1930.* Ed. Kathleen E. Poulos. Carbondale and Edwardsville: Southern Illinois University Press, 1984. Pp. 243–62.

——. "The Psychological Standpoint." *John Dewey: The Early Works, 1882–1889.* I. *1882–1888.* Carbondale and Edwardsville: Southern Illinois University Press, 1969. Pp. 122–43.

——. *The Quest for Certainty: A Study of the Relation of Knowledge and Action. John Dewey: The Later Works, 1925–1953.* IV. *1929.* Ed. Harriet Furst Simon. Carbondale and Edwardsville: Southern Illinois University Press, 1984.

——, with Bentley, Arthur F. *Knowing and the Known. John Dewey: The Later Works, 1925–1953.* XVI. *1949–1952.* Edd. Harriet Furst Simon and Richard W. Field. Carbondale and Edwardsville: Southern Illinois University Press, 1989. Pp. 1–294.

Dykhuizen, George. *The Life and Mind of John Dewey.* Carbondale and Edwardsville: Southern Illinois University Press, 1973.

Edie, James. "William James and Phenomenology." *The Review of Metaphysics*, 23 (1970), 481–526.

Edwards, Jonathan. *Treatise on Religious Affections.* Ed. John E. Smith. The Works of Jonathan Edwards 2. New Haven: Yale University Press, 1959.

Ehrenzweig, Anton. "The Hidden Order of Art." *British Journal of Aesthetics*, 1 (1961).

——. *The Psycho-Analysis of Artistic Vision and Hearing.* New York: Braziller, 1965.

Eliot, T. S. *The Complete Poems and Plays.* London: Faber & Faber, 1969.

——. *Knowledge and Experience in the Philosophy of F. H. Bradley.* New York: Farrar, Straus, 1964.

——. "The Metaphysical Poets." *Selected Essays.* New York: Harcourt, Brace & World, 1964. Pp. 241–50.

———. "The Music of Poetry." *On Poetry and Poets*. New York: Farrar, Straus & Giroux/Noonday, 1973. Pp. 17–33.

———. *The Use of Poetry and the Use of Criticism*. Cambridge: Harvard University Press, 1933.

Emerson, Ralph Waldo. "Nature." *Ralph Waldo Emerson: Essays and Lectures*. Ed. Joel Porte. The Library of America 15. New York: Viking, 1983. Pp. 5–230.

———. "Self-Reliance." *The Essays of Ralph Waldo Emerson*. Cambridge: The Belknap Press of Harvard University Press, 1987. Pp. 27–51.

Feibleman, James K. *An Introduction to the Philosophy of Charles S. Peirce*. Cambridge: The MIT Press, 1969.

Fish, Stanley E. *Surprised by Sin: The Reader in* PARADISE LOST. Berkeley: University of California Press, 1971.

Flower, Elizabeth, and Murphey, Murray G. *A History of Philosophy in America* II. New York: Putnam's, 1977.

Frank, Joseph. "Spatial Form in Modern Literature." *The Widening Gyre: Crisis and Mastery in Modern Literature*. New Brunswick, N.J.: Rutgers University Press, 1963. Pp. 3–9.

Freed, Lewis. *T. S. Eliot: Aesthetics and History*. LaSalle, Ill.: Open Court, 1962.

Fuss, Peter, "Royce on the Concept of the Self: An Historical and Critical Perspective." In *American Philosophy from Edwards to Quine*. Edd. Robert W. Shahan and Kenneth R. Merrill. Norman: University of Oklahoma Press, 1977. Pp. 111–47.

Gavin, William J. "Modern Art and William James." *Science, Technology, and Human Values*, 1 (1978), 45–54.

Goldstein, Michael. "Paradigm Shifts in Deep Ecology." Unpublished.

Goudge, Thomas A. *The Thought of C. S. Peirce*. New York: Dover, 1969.

Guimond, James. *The Art of William Carlos Williams*. Urbana: University of Illinois Press, 1968.

Gray, Piers. *T. S. Eliot's Intellectual and Poetic Development, 1909–1922*. Atlantic Highlands, N.J.: Humanities, 1982.

Hartshorne, Charles. *Creative Synthesis and Philosophic Method*. Lanham, Md.: University Press of America, 1983.

———. *Reality as a Social Process: Studies in Metaphysics and Religion*. Boston: Beacon, 1953.

Havelock, Eric A. *Preface to Plato*. Cambridge: Harvard University Press, 1963.

Heidegger, Martin. *Discourse on Thinking*. Trans. John Anderson and E. Hans Freund. New York: Harper & Row, 1966.

———. "What Is Metaphysics?" *Basic Writings from* BEING AND TIME *(1927) to* THE TASK OF THINKING *(1964)*. Ed. David Farrell Krell. New York: Harper & Row, 1977. Pp. 91–112.

Heraclitus: The Cosmic Fragments. Ed. G. S. Kirk. Cambridge: Cambridge University Press, 1962.

Hocking, William Ernest. *The Coming World Civilization*. London: George Allen & Unwin, 1958.

——. "On Royce's Empiricism." *The Journal of Philosophy*, 53 (1956), 57–63.

——. Foreword to *Reality as a Social Process: Studies in Metaphysics and Religion* by Charles Hartshorne. Boston: Beacon, 1953. Pp. 11–16.

Huebner, Dwayne. "Spirituality and Knowing." in *Learning and Teaching the Ways of Knowing*. Ed. Elliot Eisner. Chicago: National Society for the Study of Education, 1985. Pp. 159–73.

Hughson, Lois. *Thresholds of Reality: George Santayana and Modernist Poetics*. Port Washington, N.Y.: Kennikat, 1977.

James, William. *Essays in Radical Empiricism*. Ed. Fredson Bowers. The Works of William James 3. Cambridge: Harvard University Press, 1976.

——. *The Letters of William James*. Ed. Henry James. 2 vols. Boston: Atlantic Monthly Press, 1920.

——. *The Meaning of Truth*. Ed. Fredson Bowers. The Works of William James 2. Cambridge: Harvard University Press, 1975.

——. *Pragmatism*. Ed. Fredson Bowers. The Works of William James 1. Cambridge: Harvard University Press, 1975.

——. *The Principles of Psychology*. Ed. Fredson Bowers. 3 vols. The Works of William James 8. Cambridge: Harvard University Press, 1981.

——. *Psychology: Briefer Course*. Ed. Fredson Bowers. The Works of William James 12. Cambridge: Harvard University Press, 1984.

——. "Remarks on Spencer's Definition of Mind." *Essays in Philosophy*. Ed. Fredson Bowers. The Works of William James 5. Cambridge: Harvard University Press, 1978. Pp. 7–22.

——. *The Varieties of Religious Experience*. Ed. Fredson Bowers. The Works of William James 13. Cambridge: Harvard University Press, 1985.

——. *The Will to Believe and Other Essays in Popular Philosophy*. Ed. Fredson Bowers. The Works of William James 6. Cambridge: Harvard University Press, 1979.

Jarrell, Randall. *Poetry and the Age*. New York: Vintage, 1962.

Jaynes, Julian. *The Origin of Consciousness in the Breakdown of the Bicameral Mind*. Boston: Houghton Mifflin, 1976.

Joyce, James. *A Portrait of the Artist as a Young Man*. New York: Viking, 1972.

Kant, Immanuel. *Prolegomena to Any Future Metaphysics*. Trans. Peter G. Lucas. Manchester: Manchester University Press, 1953.

Kaufman, Felix. "John Dewey's Theory of Inquiry." *The Journal of Philosophy*, 56 (1959), 826–36.

Kennedy, Gail. "Dewey's Concept of Experience: Determinate, Indeterminate, and Problematic." *The Journal of Philosophy*, 56 (1959), 801–14.

Koch, Vivienne. *William Carlos Williams*. New York: New Directions, 1950.

Kuhn, Thomas. *The Structure of Scientific Revolutions*. Chicago: The University of Chicago Press, 1970.

Kuklick, Bruce. *The Rise of American Philosophy: Cambridge, Massachusetts, 1860–1930*. New Haven: Yale University Press, 1977.

LaGuardia, David M. *Advance on Chaos: The Sanctifying Imagination of Wallace Stevens*. Hanover, N.H.: University Press of New England, for Brown University Press, 1983.

Laing, R. D. *The Divided Self: An Existential Study in Sanity and Madness*. Harmondsworth: Penguin, 1971.

Langbaum, Robert. *The Mysteries of Identity: A Theme in Modern Literature*. Chicago: The University of Chicago Press/Phoenix, 1982.

——. *The Poetry of Experience: The Dramatic Monologue in Modern Literary Tradition*. New York: Norton, 1963.

Langer, Suzanne. *Philosophy in a New Key: A Study in the Symbolism of Reason, Rite, and Art*. 3rd ed. Cambridge: Harvard University Press, 1980.

Leavis, F. R. "*The Waste Land*." In *T. S. Eliot: A Collection of Critical Essays*. Ed. Hugh Kenner. Englewood Cliffs, N.J.: Prentice-Hall, 1962.

Lee, Otis. "Value and the Situation." *The Journal of Philosophy*, 41 (1944).

Linschoten, Hans. *On the Way Toward a Phenomenological Psychology: The Psychology of William James*. Trans. Amedeo Giorgi. Pittsburgh: Duquesne University Press, 1968.

McDermott, John J. *The Culture of Experience: Philosophical Essays in the American Grain*. New York: New York University Press, 1976.

——. "Symposium on Rorty's *Consequences of Pragmatism*: Introduction." *Transactions of the Charles S. Peirce Society*, 21, No. 1 (Winter 1985), 1–7.

Marcel, Gabriel. *Royce's Metaphysics*. Trans. Virginia Ringer and Gordon Ringer. Chicago: Regnery, 1956.

Mariani, Paul. *William Carlos Williams: A New World Naked*. New York: McGraw-Hill, 1981.

Martz, Louis L. "Wallace Stevens: The World as Meditation." In *The Achievement of Wallace Stevens*. Edd. Ashley Brown and Robert S. Haller. Philadelphia: Lippincott, 1962. Pp. 211–31.

Maslow, Abraham H. *Religions, Values, and Peak Experiences*. New York: Penguin, 1976.

Miller, J. Hillis. *Poets of Reality: Six Twentieth-Century Writers*. Cambridge: Harvard University Press, 1965.

——. "Wallace Stevens' Poetry of Being." *The Act of the Mind: Essays on the Poetry of Wallace Stevens*. Edd. Roy Harvey Pearce and J. Hillis Miller. Baltimore: The Johns Hopkins University Press, 1964. Pp. 143–62.

Morris, Bertram. "Dewey's Theory of Art." *Guide to the Works of John Dewey*. Ed. JoAnn Boydston. Carbondale and Edwardsville: Southern Illinois University Press, 1970. Pp. 156–82.

News of the Universe: Poems of Twofold Consciousness. Ed. Robert Bly. San Francisco: Sierra Club, 1980.

Niebuhr, H. Richard. *The Meaning of Revelation*. New York: Macmillan, 1941.

O'Connell, Robert J., s.j. *William James on the Courage to Believe*. New York: Fordham University Press, 1984.

Olson, Charles. "The Human Universe." *Selected Writings*. New York: New Directions, 1966.

Ostrom, Alan. *William Carlos Williams*. Carbondale and Edwardsville: Southern Illinois University Press, 1966.

Palmer, Richard. "Post-Modernity and Hermeneutics." *Boundary 2* (1977), 363–93.

Pasch, Alan. *Experience and the Analytic*. Chicago: The University of Chicago Press, 1958.

Peirce, Charles Sanders. *Collected Papers of Charles Sanders Peirce*. Edd. Charles Hartshorne, Paul Weiss, and Arthur Burks. 8 vols. Cambridge: The Belknap Press of Harvard University Press, 1931–1958.

Pepper, Stephen. "The Concept of Fusion in Dewey's Aesthetic Theory." *The Work of Art*. Bloomington: Indiana University Press, 1955. Pp. 151–72.

——. "Contextualism." *World Hypotheses: A Study in Evidence*. Berkeley: University of California Press, 1942. Pp. 232–79.

——. "Root Metaphors." *World Hypotheses: A Study in Evidence*. Berkeley: University of California Press, 1942. Pp. 84–114.

Perle, George. *Serial Composition and Atonality: An Introduction to the Music of Schoenberg, Berg, and Webern*. Berkeley: University of California Press, 1963.

Peterson, Margaret. *Wallace Stevens and the Idealist Tradition*. Ann Arbor: UMI Research Press, 1983.

Pound, Ezra. *Make It New*. London: Faber & Faber, 1934.

Quinn, M. Bernetta. *The Metamorphic Tradition in Modern Poetry*. New Brunswick, n.j.: Rutgers University Press, 1955.

Rapp, Carl. *William Carlos Williams and Romantic Idealism*. Hanover, n.h.: University Press of New England, for Brown University Press, 1984.

Read, Herbert. *A Concise History of Modern Painting*. New York: Praeger, 1959.

Reck, Andrew J. *Speculative Philosophy: A Study of Its Nature, Types, and Uses*. Albuquerque: University of New Mexico Press, 1972.

Robinson, Daniel S. *Royce and Hocking: American Idealists*. Boston: Christophers, 1968.

Rorty, Richard. "Dewey's Metaphysics." *The Consequences of Pragmatism (Essays: 1972–1980)*. Minneapolis: University of Minnesota Press, 1982. Pp. 72–89.

———. "Introduction: Pragmatism and Philosophy." *The Consequences of Pragmatism (Essays: 1972–1980)*. Minneapolis: University of Minnesota Press, 1982. Pp. xiii–xlvii.

———. *Philosophy and the Mirror of Nature*. Princeton: Princeton University Press, 1979.

———. "Symposium on Rorty's *Consequences of Pragmatism*: Comments on Sleeper and Edel." *Transactions of the Charles S. Peirce Society*, 21, No. 1 (Winter 1985), 39–48.

———. "The World Well Lost." *The Consequences of Pragmatism (Essays: 1972–1980)*. Minneapolis: University of Minnesota Press, 1982. Pp. 3–18.

Royce, Josiah. *The Basic Writings of Josiah Royce*. Ed. John J. McDermott. 2 vols. Chicago: The University of Chicago Press, 1969.

———. *Josiah Royce's Seminar, 1913–1914*. Ed. Grover Smith. New Brunswick, N.J.: Rutgers University Press, 1963.

———. *The Problem of Christianity*. Chicago: The University of Chicago Press, 1968.

———. *The World and the Individual*. New York: Dover, 1959.

Schuetz, Alfred. "William James' Concept of the Stream of Thought Phenomenologically Interpreted." *Philosophy and Phenomenological Research*, 1 (1941), 442–52.

Schwartz, Robert. Review of *Philosophy and the Mirror of Nature* by Richard Rorty. *The Journal of Philosophy*, 80, No. 1 (January 1983), 51–67.

Scott, Stanley. "Beyond Modern Subjectivism: T. S. Eliot and American Philosophy." *Thought*, 51, No. 203 (December 1976), 409–27.

———. "Wallace Stevens and William James; The Poetics of Pure Experience." *Philosophy and Literature*, 1 (1977), 183–91.

Smidt, Kristian. *Poetry and Belief in the Work of T. S. Eliot*. London: Routledge & Kegan Paul, 1961.

Smith, Grover. *T. S. Eliot's Poetry and Plays: A Study in Sources and Meaning*. Chicago: The University of Chicago Press, 1956.

Smith, Huston. "Beyond the Modern Western Mind-set." *Beyond the Post-Modern Mind*. New York: Crossroad, 1982. Pp. 132–61.

Smith, John E. "Community and Reality. In *Perspectives on Peirce*. Ed. Richard J. Bernstein. New Haven: Yale University Press, 1965. Pp. 92–119.

——. *Purpose and Thought: The Meaning of Pragmatism.* New Haven: Yale University Press, 1978.

——. *Royce's Social Infinite.* New York: Liberal Arts Press, 1950.

——. *Themes in American Philosophy: Purpose, Experience, and Community.* New York: Harper & Row, 1970.

Spiegelberg, H. *The Phenomenological Movement: An Introduction* I. The Hague: Nijhoff, 1976.

Stevens, Wallace. *The Collected Poems of Wallace Stevens.* New York: Knopf, 1967.

——. "The Figure of the Youth as Virile Poet." *The Necessary Angel: Essays on Reality and the Imagination.* New York: Vintage, 1951. Pp. 39–67.

——. *Letters.* Ed. Holly Stevens. New York: Knopf, 1966.

——. *Opus Posthumous.* Ed. Samuel French Morse. New York: Knopf, 1957.

Suzuki, D. T. *Studies in Zen Buddhism.* New York: Dell, 1978.

Sypher, Wylie. *The Loss of the Self in Modern Literature and Art.* New York: Random House, 1962.

Thayer, H. S. *Meaning and Action: A Critical History of Pragmatism.* Indianapolis: Bobbs-Merrill, 1968.

Thompson, Eric. *T. S. Eliot: The Metaphysical Perspective.* Carbondale and Edwardsville: Southern Illinois University Press, 1963.

Tillich, Paul. *The Courage to Be.* New Haven: Yale University Press, 1952.

——. "Religion as a Dimension in Man's Spiritual Life." In *Man's Right to Knowledge.* Ed. Herbert Muschel. New York: Columbia University Press, 1954.

Trosman, Harry, M.D. "T. S. Eliot and *The Waste Land*: Psychopathological Antecedents and Transformations." *Archives of General Psychiatry*, 30 (1974), 709–17.

Wade, Nicholas. "Thomas S. Kuhn: Revolutionary Theorist of Science." *Science*, July 8, 1977, 143–45.

West, Cornel. *The American Evasion of Philosophy: A Genealogy of Pragmatism.* Madison: University of Wisconsin Press, 1989.

Wheelwright, Philip. *Metaphor and Reality.* Bloomington: Indiana University Press, 1967.

Whitaker, Thomas R. *William Carlos Williams.* New York: Twayne, 1968.

Whitehead, Alfred North. *Science and the Modern World.* New York: Macmillan, 1925. Repr. New York: Free Press, 1969.

Wild, John. *The Radical Empiricism of William James.* Garden City, N.Y.: Doubleday, 1969.

Willey, Basil. *The Seventeenth-Century Background: Studies in the Thought of the Age in Relation to Poetry and Religion.* Garden City, N.Y.: Doubleday, 1953.

Williams, William Carlos. *Autobiography.* New York: New Directions, 1967.

——. *The Collected Poems of Wallace Stevens*. New York: Knopt, 1967.

——. *Paterson*. New York: New Directions, 1963.

——. *Selected Essays*. New York: New Directions, 1969.

——. *Selected Letters*. Ed. John C. Thirwall. New York: McDowell, Oblensky, 1957.

Wilshire, Bruce. *William James and Phenomenology*. Bloomington: Indiana University Press, 1968.

Woodman, Leonora. *Stanza My Stone: Wallace Stevens and the Hermetic Tradition*. West Lafayette, Ind.: Purdue University Press, 1983.

Yankelovich, Daniel, and Barrett, William. *Ego and Instinct: The Psychoanalytic View of Human Nature—Revised*. New York: Random House, 1970.

INDEX